UNIDIR
United Nations Institute for Disarmament Research
Geneva

Arms and Technology Transfers: Security and Economic Considerations Among Importing and Exporting States

Edited by

Sverre Lodgaard and *Robert L. Pfaltzgraff, Jr.*

WITHDRAWN

UNITED NATIONS
New York and Geneva, 1995

NOTE

The designations employed and the presentation of the material in this publication do not imply the expression of any opinion whatsoever on the part of the Secretariat of the United Nations concerning the legal status of any country, territory, city or area, or of its authorities, or concerning the delimitation of its frontiers or boundaries.

*
* *

The views expressed in this paper are those of the authors and do not necessarily reflect the views of the United Nations Secretariat.

UNIDIR/95/22

UNITED NATIONS PUBLICATION

Sales No. GV.E.95.0.10

ISBN 92-9045-103-3

UNIDIR

United Nations Institute for Disarmament Research

UNIDIR is an autonomous institution within the framework of the United Nations. It was established in 1980 by the General Assembly for the purpose of undertaking independent research on disarmament and related problems, particularly international security issues.

The work of the Institute aims at:

1. Providing the international community with more diversified and complete data on problems relating to international security, the armaments race, and disarmament in all fields, particularly in the nuclear field, so as to facilitate progress, through negotiations, towards greater security for all States and toward the economic and social development of all peoples;
2. Promoting informed participation by all States in disarmament efforts;
3. Assisting ongoing negotiations on disarmament and continuing efforts to ensure greater international security at a progressively lower level of armaments, particularly nuclear armaments, by means of objective and factual studies and analyses;
4. Carrying out more in-depth, forward-looking, and long-term research on disarmament, so as to provide a general insight into the problems involved, and stimulating new initiatives for new negotiations.

The contents of UNIDIR publications are the responsibility of the authors and not of UNIDIR. Although UNIDIR takes no position on the views and conclusions expressed by the authors of its research reports, it does assume the responsibility for determining whether or not they merit publication.

UNIDIR

Palais des Nations
CH-1211 Geneva 10
Tel. (41.22) 917.42.93/917.42.56
Fax (41.22) 917.01.23

Table of Contents

Page

Preface xi

Opening Address - *Vladimir Petrovsky* xiii

Introduction - *Sverre Lodgaard* and *Robert L. Pfaltzgraff, Jr.* 1

List of Contributors xix

Part I   General Trends in Defense Related Transfers 5

    Chapter 1   Trends in the Proliferation of Weapons
                of Mass Destruction - *Aaron Karp* 7

    Chapter 2   Spread of Conventional Weapons Production
                Technology - *Michael Brzoska* 19

    Chapter 3   Conventional Arms Transfers Patterns -
                Ian Anthony 49

    Chapter 4   Advanced Conventional Weapon Sales Offerings -
                David Markov 61

    Chapter 5   Transparency and Beyond in the Arms Trade 75

        Section I: The UN Register of Conventional Arms -
                  Hendrik Wagenmakers 75

        Section II: Comments 79

v

Chapter 6   Discussion 83

1. *Rakesh Sood*, 2. *Jacques Battistella*, 3. *Suha Umar*, 4. *John Simpson*, 5. *Richard Grimmett*, 6. *Ahmad Kamal*, 7. *Rakesh Sood*, 8. *Winfried Lang*, 9. *Michael Moodie*, 10. *Aharon Klieman*, 11. *Edward Woollen*, 12. *Geoffrey Kemp*, 13. *Aaron Karp*, 14. *Shahram Chubin*, 15. *David Markov*

Part II   Political/Military Factors Associated with the
            Diffusion of Advanced Technology 95

Chapter 7:   Global and Regional Security Concerns 97

Section I: Supplier Motivations 97
             A - *Sten Lundbo* 97
             B - Comments 99

Section II: Post-Cold War Regional Arms Control 104
             A - *Ahmad Kamal* 104
             B - Comments 109

Section III: Regional Contexts and Perceptions -
             Shahram Chubin 114

Chapter 8:   Security Considerations in the Middle East:
             A Regional Perspective 119

Section I: An Iranian Approach - *Javad Zarif* 119

Section II: Responses 124

Chapter 9:	Middle East: Security, Confidence-Building and Arms Control	133
Section I:	Presentation - *Mahmoud Karem*	133
Section II:	Comments	142
Chapter 10:	Impact of the Gulf War on States' Behavior and Attitudes Toward Advanced Technology	145
Section I:	Technology and the Gulf War: Lessons to be Drawn - *Geoffrey Kemp*	145
Section II:	Comments	149

Part III   Economic and Technological Considerations 155

Chapter 11:	Exports and Defense Jobs/Industrial Base in Industrialized States	157
Section I:	A Russian Approach - *Guennadi G. Ianpolsky*	157
Section II:	A US Approach - *Edward B. Woollen*	161
Chapter 12:	The Problems of Defense Industrialization for Developing States - *Luis Bitencourt*	167
Chapter 13:	The Role of Technology Transfers in Economic Development	177
Section I:	Co-operation for Weapon Technology Transfers and Technological/Economic Development - *Kensuke Ebata*	177

Section II: Intellectual Property Rights, Technology Transfers and Economic Development: The Case of Agriculture and Defense - *Amit Bhaduri* 204

Chapter 14   Discussion 209

1. *Ian Anthony*, 2. *Edward Woollen*, 3. *Peggy Mason*, 4. *Edward Woollen*, 5. *John Simpson*, 6. *Guennadi G. Ianpolsky*, 7. *Luis Bitencourt*, 8. *Edward Woollen*, 9. *Richard Grimmett*, 10. *Amit Bhaduri*, 11. *Guennadi G. Ianpolsky*, 12. *Luis Bitencourt*, 13. *Kensuke Ebata*, 14. *Edward Woollen*, 15. *Amit Bhaduri*, 16. *Kensuke Ebata*

Part IV   Facilitation of Economic Growth/Maximizing Regional Security and Stability 223

Chapter 15   The Impact of Technology Control Regimes - *David Hobbs* 225

Chapter 16   NPT, CWC, and BWC: How Effective are they Likely to be? 235

Section I: Evolution of Multilateralism, Definitions and Verification - *Marcos Castrioto de Azambuja* . 235

Section II: Non-Proliferation Versus Eradication - *Sirous Nasseri* 238

Section III: Functioning of the Three Global Multilateral
Regimes - *Richard Starr* 243

Chapter 17 What are the Obstacles to Regional Arms
Limitation Agreements? 249

Section I: Disparities and the Peace Process in the Middle East -
Aharon Klieman 249

Section II: CSCE Confidence-Building Process
and Other Regions - *Rakesh Sood* 253

Chapter 18 Discussion 259

1. *Serguei Batsanov*, 2. *David Markov*, 3. *Rakesh Sood*, 4. *David Hobbs*, 5. *Marcos Castrioto de Azambuja*, 6. *Sirous Nasseri*, 7. *Richard Starr*, 8. *Peggy Mason*, 9. *Rakesh Sood*

Concluding Remarks
Sverre Lodgaard and *Robert L. Pfaltzgraff, Jr.* 267

List of Participants 277

Preface

The issues of technology and armament transfers are increasingly at the forefront of problems of international security and disarmament. Three major reasons could explain this.

First, the disarmament process has been very successful in the last few years, especially in the field of nuclear, as well as chemical and conventional, weapons. For example, the INF (1987), START I (1991) and START II (1993) Agreements come to mind, as do the Chemical Weapons Convention (1993) and the Treaty on Conventional Armed Forces in Europe (1990). Today's imperative is to prevent the return of the arms race, while equally taking into consideration the risks of reviving technological competition which might serve military interests. This preventive dimension necessarily calls for the examination of the transfer of both arms and technology.

Second, the disarmament effort underway concerns primarily the old partners of the East-West confrontation. Hence, it is important to assure that the ongoing reduction of their arsenals be neither counter-acted nor rendered void by multiform proliferation which could develop in other regions and between other countries. The goal of non-proliferation must be equally shared, and to this extent, the transfers of technology plays a fundamental role. The possible organization of these transfers - in order to accommodate economic and scientific development for the beneficiaries with the preservation of security imperatives for everyone - will have to be studied. To enable this delicate reconciliation, any uncontrolled propagation of material and of know-how for military use must be prevented. Such a propagation might allow unnecessary developments that could even be dangerous to international security, be it regional or global.

Lastly, the general context - characterized by the opening and widening of exchanges, the increasingly open and transparent circulation of techniques and material, and the globalization of economic relations - must be taken into account. It is difficult to reduce transfers for security reasons, and at the same time, to open markets for economic reasons. This is even more the case if the technologies concerned are increasingly of a *double use or double capacity* nature. This dilemma obliges the partners to aim at the widest possible agreement on the basis of the objectives defined by the common consent of the parties.

These are the objectives and the constraints examined under various angles by the present Research Report. It follows a conference organized jointly by UNIDIR (United Nations Institute for Disarmament) and by IFPA (Institute for Foreign Policy Analysis), in Geneva, on 14 and 15 February, 1994. The Institute for Foreign Policy Analysis (IFPA), based in Cambridge, Massachusetts and Washington, DC, has sponsored many conferences in the United States as well as in Europe and the Asian-Pacific area as part of an overall research programme which focuses on post-Cold War global and regional security. This was the first meeting with which IFPA has been associated in Geneva.

This Report is comprised of the following subjects: General Trends in Defense Related Transfers (Part I), Political/Military Factors Associated with the Diffusion of Advanced Technology (Part II), Economic and Technological Considerations (Part III), and Facilitation of Economic Growth/Maximization of Regional Security and Stability (Part IV).

This Report was edited by Sverre Lodgaard, Director of UNIDIR, and Robert L. Pfaltzgraff Jr., Director of IFPA. The manuscript was prepared for the publication by Anita Blétry and proof-read by Jerry Williams.

UNIDIR wishes to thank IFPA for its precious contribution, as well as the various contributors. All the efforts brought together have made this Report a work of reference rich in different and competent opinions.

UNIDIR takes no position on the views and conclusions expressed in the Report: they are those of the authors. However, UNIDIR considers that the Report merits publication, and so we recommend it to the attention of our readers.

Serge Sur
Deputy Director

Opening Address

Vladimir Petrovsky

Your Excellencies, Ladies and Gentlemen,

It was with great satisfaction that I accepted the invitation to participate in this conference. The initiative of the United Nations Institute for Disarmament Research to discuss the security and economic considerations of arms and technology transfers among exporting and importing states is most timely. It is particularly satisfying that this issue is addressed in a broad social and economic framework thus stressing the complexity of the problem and the need to find its comprehensive solution. Arms transfers are obviously and directly linked to the security concerns of the states. Any measures in this field will have significant social and economic consequences both for the exporters and the importers of armament. On one hand, large export-oriented military industries are hindering balanced economic development of the donor countries. Arms purchases are draining the resources of the developing countries. On the other hand, military production and sales are providing jobs for tens of thousands of people. From the global point of view, arms and technology transfers seem to become one of the major issues in the controversy between the developed and developing countries.

In recent years the problem of arms and technology transfers has attracted growing attention of the international community and the international organizations. Now almost every inter-governmental organization has arms transfer control on its agenda. Multilateral discussions of arms export regulation have taken place at the United Nations, in the European Community, the CSCE and the G-7 Group as well as within the membership of the Missile Technology Control Regime. The five Permanent Members of the Security Council have also met a number of times to discuss arms transfer and the proliferation of weapons of mass destruction in particular in connection with the situation in the Middle East. This is a most welcome development. Practical measures in the regulation of arms transfers can lead to significant improvement of the international political climate. By the reduction of arms sales we will be able to influence the production of armament, to facilitate the conversion of military industries to civilian production and thus to eliminate one of the major sources of arms race and international instability.

The necessary prerequisite of successful measures in the regulation and limitation of arms transfers is the transparency of such transactions. Before imposing any restrictions in this field we need to have precise and objective information about what is actually going on. In this respect the major recent development was the establishment in 1991 of the UN Register of Conventional Arms. So far more than 82 countries replied for the first reporting year of the Register, including almost all the major arms exporting and importing countries. The Register can effectively help to reduce the occurrence of dangerous misperceptions as well as promote trust and partnership between nations. The analysis of information submitted for the register could eventually become a useful tool of early warning and detection of the potential crisis situations. It can also be used as preliminary basis for consultations and negotiations.

The Register as well as the numerous provisions in the international agreements facilitating transparency of armament provide a good starting point for practical actions aimed at the limitation of arms transfer. However, the Register is not an end in itself. I would like to remind you that in 1920s the League of Nations also tried without much success to slow down the arms race by collecting information about the national armed forces. From this point of view the mechanism of the Register can and should be further developed and refined.

It is obvious that all the UN Member States should submit relevant data to the Register. There is a need to overcome some of its existing limitations. As you are well aware it does not cover, for example, military holdings and stockpiles, and procurement through national production; it is restricted to a limited number of conventional weapons; and it does not cover dual-purpose technology as well as weapons of mass destruction. Hopefully, the work of the group of governmental experts appointed by the UN Secretary-General to consider the expansion of the Register will soon be finalized. This could transform the whole mechanism into an arms acquisition register rather than an arms transfer register, and could establish an unprecedented level of transparency in both the international arms trade and the national production of arms.

If the Register contains information on the national production of armament, the international community will finally be able to approach one of the most complicated issues related to arms transfers. In his report "New Dimensions of Arms Regulation and Disarmament" the UN Secretary-General, Mr. Boutros Boutros-Ghali, specifically recommended to Member States to "take a closer look at international private arms dealers". The fact is that there are now practically no international legal norms regulating this sort of business and experts have only a vague idea of the volume of international arms trade conducted through private channels.

With this in mind I am afraid that the often cited figures of the current decline in world arms sales - presumably by 25% in 1992 in comparison with 1991 - could be misleading. It is quite probable that part of this amount simply became "invisible" being hidden in private channels. Thus, if we really want to restrict arms transfers we can no longer pretend that the "black market" of weapons does not exist or that private arms trade is insignificant.

Another idea of the Secretary-General's report is now particularly applicable to the problem of arms transfers. This is the globalization of disarmament efforts. Globalization means that measures aimed at regulation and reduction of arms transfers could be implemented simultaneously on global as well as regional and subregional levels. On the global level we already have a working mechanism to address this problem which includes the Conference on Disarmament - the only multilateral negotiating body of the international community in this field - and a number of other organs. However, at the regional level, the situation is far less encouraging although these are precisely the regional arrangements which allow for a wide variety of means of the limitation of arms transfers.

For example, the major arms manufacturers can agree not to sell certain destabilizing types of arms to the zones of potential conflicts. It seems that the consultations between the Big Five major arms suppliers which started in 1991 have already initiated such a process. The arms manufacturers can also agree not to exceed certain limits in their arms sales with the aim of gradual reduction of such limits. The countries of the region themselves may undertake the obligation not to acquire destabilizing weapons or to limit their acquisitions to specified quantities. Of course, any regional measures aimed at greater transparency of arms transfers will only facilitate the mutual trust and help reduce tension. As the UN Secretary-General pointed out in his recent address to the Advisory Board on Disarmament Matters, regional registers of conventional arms should be the next step. They have the advantage of allowing the categories of weapons to be registered, to reflect the security concerns felt in the region.

Most of the recent debate on restricting arms transfers, in particular, at the Conference on Disarmament, had been focused on the problem of setting up certain international norms or regulations in this field. I fully share the opinion of those countries which suggested the comparison and harmonization of existing national legislations on this subject and to facilitate the dialogue between the suppliers and recipients of military and dual use technology. Obviously, an international code of conduct perhaps, even an international treaty on arms transfers would be most desirable. However, taking into account the very complicated nature of this problem it seems that the idea of establishing an international control and verification mechanism in this sphere is worth considering. After the conclusion of the Convention on chemical weapons, the international community decided to set up a special organization to monitor the process of elimination of these weapons. In the case of arms transfers, the need for an effective organizational arrangement will be even more imperative.

So far, practical progress in the regulation and reduction of arms and military technology transfers has been rather limited. Most of the changes in national regulations were made in order to implement mandatory decisions reached in United Nations arms embargoes or consensus decisions taken by members in the framework of COCOM and the Missile Technology Control Regime. One of the reasons for the slow progress is that before we can move any further we need to find answers to a number of difficult conceptual questions. I would like to mention a few of them, perhaps, the most controversial:

- some countries expressed justified concern that restrictions on arms transfers and in particular on dual purpose technologies could limit the availability of some material, equipment and scientific and technological information for the developing countries and impede their social and economic progress. Thus, there is a need for criteria and a mechanism to determine in which cases export control will be discriminatory, harmful or counterproductive. Personally, I agree with those who say that it is not technology which is to blame but the people who abuse it. The same chemicals can be used to manufacture explosives and agricultural fertilizers. Computer links can be used to quickly transmit

valuable information or to disseminate destructive viruses. Any technology can be transferred to another country provided there is a reliable verification mechanism allowing for any concerns to be quickly removed by inspection and the exchange of information;
- it is generally agreed that countries should be able to acquire new arms in quantities which do not exceed their legitimate needs, or, using the terminology of General Assembly's resolution 46/36, accumulation of arms should not be "excessive and destabilizing". However, there is no definition or even a common understanding of what precisely the legitimate needs are;
- arms transfers are sometimes divided into defensive and provocative. Again, there is no agreed understanding of the notions "defensive" and "provocative".

Arms transfers are sometimes considered to be a secondary problem in the disarmament field, just a sort of an indicator of military activities. In my opinion this is a false assumption. Reduction and limitation of arms transfers are not just confidence-building measures or an auxiliary tool in disarmament efforts. They go beyond the traditional realm of disarmament. Most vividly this could be seen if we consider the problem in conjunction with the settlement of armed conflicts.

In the report "New Dimensions of Arms Regulation and Disarmament" the Secretary-General stressed that "the integration of the weapons-control features into United Nations-brokered settlements can contribute enormously to peace-building activities in countries long plagued by civil strife." There is a direct correlation between the availability of weapons and the duration and scale of armed conflicts. The experience of many countries shows that excessive acquisition of armaments inevitably triggers a chain reaction of negative social, political and economic consequences such as the expansion of the armed forces, and their disproportionally large role in the political life of the country. The better the country is armed the greater is the temptation to settle problems with neighbours by the use of force. And, obviously, the number of casualties is different if the parties to the conflict are armed with wooden sticks or with heavy artillery.

Concluding my opening remarks I would like again to stress that arms transfers is one of the key issues in the field of disarmament and should be addressed in a comprehensive manner in correlation with social, political and economic factors. I hope that the discussion at our Conference will help to define the agenda of action in this field. However, it should also be kept in mind that today it is important not only to know what to do but to do it as quickly as possible. The contemporary international political environment, despite all its complications, provides a rare opportunity for a real breakthrough in disarmament efforts. If we do not move fast this chance might be lost.

Thank you for your attention.

List of Contributors

Ian ANTHONY, Stockholm International Peace Research Institute (SIPRI), Stockholm, Sweden
Marcos Castrioto DE AZAMBUJA, Ambassador of Brazil to the Republic of Argentina, Buenos Aires, Argentina
Daryal BATIBAY, Senior Advisor to the Prime Minister of Turkey, Ankara, Turkey
Serguei BATSANOV, Director, External Relations Division, Provisional Technical Secretariat, Preparatory Commission for the Organisation for the Prohibition of Chemical Weapons, The Hague, Netherlands
Jacques BATTISTELLA, Directeur délégué pour la politique industriels et les affaires stratégiques, Aerospatiale, Paris, France
Amit BHADURI, Professor, Nehru University New Delhi, India, and visiting Professor University of Bremen, Germany
Luis BITENCOURT, Director, Strategic Studies Center, Brasília DF, Brasil
Pascal BONIFACE, Directeur, Institut des relations internationales et stratégiques (IRIS), Paris, France
Michael BRZOSKA, Unit for Study of Wars, Armaments and Development, University of Hamburg, Hamburg, Germany
Shahram CHUBIN, Middle East specialist, The Graduate Institute of International Studies (IUHEI), Geneva, Switzerland
Martin DAHINDEN, Nuclear and Disarmament Section, Political Division III, Federal Department of Foreign Affairs, Bern, Switzerland
Kensuke EBATA, Military Technology Specialist, Tokyo, Japan
Peter J. ENGSTROM, Chief, National Security Negotiations, US Air Force, The Pentagon, Washington DC, USA
Gérard ERRERA, Ambassador, Representative of France to the Conference on Disarmament, Geneva, Switzerland
Mary Margaret EVANS, Director, Conventional Arms Control and Compliance, Office of the US Secretary of Defense, Pentagon, Washington DC, USA
Curt GASTEYGER, Director, Programme of Strategic Studies and International Security, The Graduate Institute of International Studies (IUHEI), Geneva, Switzerland

Richard F. GRIMMETT, National Defense Specialist, US Congressional Research Service (CRS), Washington DC, USA

Alain GUILLAUME, Ambassador, Permanent Representative of Belgium to the Conference on Disarmament, Geneva, Switzerland

David HOBBS, North Atlantic Assembly, Brussels, Belgium

Wolfgang HOFFMANN, Ambassador, Representative of the Federal Republic of Germany to the Conference on Disarmament, Geneva, Switzerland

HOU Zhitong, Ambassador, Delegation of the People's Republic of China to the Conference on Disarmament, Geneva, Switzerland

Gennady G. IANPOLSKY, Deputy Chairman, Russian State Committee on Defense Matters, Moscow, Russian Federation

Ahmad KAMAL, Ambassador, Permanent Mission of the Islamic Republic of Pakistan to the United Nations Office, Geneva, Switzerland

Mahmoud KAREM, Director, Dept. of Disarmament Affairs, Ministry of Foreign Affairs, Cairo, Egypt

Aaron KARP, Adjunct Professor, Old Dominion University, Norfolk, Virginia, USA

Geoffrey KEMP, Senior Associate, Carnegie Endowment for International Peace, Washington DC, USA

Aharon KLIEMAN, Professor of International Relations, Dept. of Political Science, & Senior Research Associate, The Jaffee Center for Strategic Studies, Tel Aviv University, Tel Aviv, Israel

Brian KNAPP, Designated Representative of the US Assistant Secretary of Defense for Counter Proliferation, Office of the Secretary of Defense, The Pentagon, Washington DC, USA

Marie-Hélène LABBÉ, Chargée de Mission, Fondation pour les études de défense (FED), Paris, France

Winfried LANG, Ambassador, Permanent Mission of Austria to the United Nations Office, Geneva, Switzerland

Stephen J. LEDOGAR, Ambassador, Representative of the United States of America to the Conference on Disarmament, Geneva, Switzerland

Itzhak LIOR, Ambassador, Permanent Mission of Israel to the United Nations Office, Geneva, Switzerland

Sten LUNDBO, Deputy Director General, Ministry of Foreign Affairs, Oslo, Norway

Miguel MARIN-BOSCH, Ambassador, Permanent Mission of Mexico to the United Nations, Geneva, Switzerland

David MARKOV, Institute for Defense Analysis, Washington DC, USA
Peggy MASON, Ambassador for Disarmament (IDX), Dept. of Foreign Affairs & International Trade Canada, Ottawa, Canada
Sirous NASSERI, Ambassador, Permanent Mission of the Islamic Republic of Iran to the United Nations Office, Geneva, Switzerland
Merle OPELZ, Head of the International Atomic Energy Agency (IAEA) Office in Geneva, Switzerland
Paul O'SULLIVAN, Ambassador, Permanent Representative of Australia to the United Nations for Disarmament Matters, Geneva, Switzerland
Vladimir PETROVSKY, Director-General, United Nations, and Secretary-General of the Conference on Disarmament, Geneva, Switzerland
Serhiy PIROSHKOV, Director, The National Institute for Strategic Studies, Kiev, Ukraine
Jean DE RUYT, Permanent Representative of Belgium to the Western European Union (WEU), Ministry of Foreign Affairs, Brussels, Belgium
Juan Carlos SANCHEZ ARNAU, Ambassador, Permanent Mission of the Republic of Argentina to the United Nations Office, Geneva, Switzerland
Gerald SHANNON, Ambassador, Permament Representative of Canada to the Conference on Disarmament, Geneva, Switzerland
John SIMPSON, Director, Mountbatten Centre for International Studies, Highfield University of Southampton, Southampton, United Kingdom
Rakesh SOOD, Director, Disarmament Office, Ministry of Foreign Affairs, New Delhi, India
Richard STARR, Assistant Secretary, Arms Control Branch, Department of Foreign Affairs and Trade, Canberra, Australia
Diane STEINBERGER, Chief, Conventional Arms Control and Compliance, Defense Nuclear Agency, Alexandria, Virginia, USA
Yoshimoto TANAKA, Ambassador, Delegation of Japan to the Conference on Disarmament, Geneva, Switzerland
Suha UMAR, Minister Plenipotentiary, Deputy Director General for Mutual Security and Disarmament Affairs Ministry of Foreign Affairs, Ankara, Turkey
Hendrik WAGENMAKERS, Ambassador, Representative of the Kingdom of the Netherlands to the Conference on Disarmament, Geneva, Switzerland
Edward B. WOOLLEN, Vice President for Corporate Marketing, Raytheon Corporation, Lexington, Massachusetts, USA

Mounir ZAHRAN, Ambassador, Permament Mission of the Arab Republic of
Egypt to the United Nations Office, Geneva, Switzerland

Javad ZARIF, Deputy Foreign Minister for International Affairs, Ministry of
Foreign Affairs, Teheran, The Islamic Republic of Iran

Valeri N. ZEMSKOV, Deputy Permanent Representative, Permanent Mission
of the Russian Federation to the Conference on Disarmament, Geneva,
Switzerland

UNIDIR

Sverre LODGAARD, Director
Serge SUR, Deputy Director
Chantal DE JONGE OUDRAAT, Senior Research Associate
Péricles GASPARINI ALVES, Research Associate
Sophie DANIEL, Officer-in-charge of Conference

IFPA

Robert L. PFALTZGRAFF, JR., President
Michael L. MOODIE, Senior Fellow
David R. TANKS, Senior Staff Member

Introduction

1. *Sverre Lodgaard*

The politics of arms and technology transfers are at the heart of contemporary international affairs. First, because transfers of weapons and weapon-related technologies may create or alleviate security concerns - depending on the context in which they are introduced. Few technologies, if any, are inherently offensive or defensive, malign or benign. Second, because in large measure, the development and dissemination of advanced technologies shape modern societies and determine the distribution of resources between them. Hence, the main policy objective of this conference is to explore ways and means of reaching agreement on a set of rules for technology transfers that better meets the twin objectives of development and security. The salience and sensitivity of the issues can hardly be overestimated: control of technology is an increasingly powerful means of political influence - in effect, a matter of high politics.

The arms and technologies we are going to talk about are weapons of mass destruction, missiles and air-breathing delivery systems for such weapons, conventional arms, weapon components, production tools, and dual-use technologies. The first trigger list published by the so-called London Club - later the Nuclear Suppliers Group - defined technology as technical data "in physical form" including, on the soft side, scientific and technical explanations on paper. May be, technical assistance should also be included. This is where we are drawing the line at this conference. We are not going to address transfers of scientists, engineers and technicians, however important their movements may now be for weapons proliferation. At UNIDIR, we have another project devoted to the human dimension of such problems.

The case of Iraq highlighted that today, the motors of WMD proliferation are largely running on dual-use technologies. These technologies are at the core of the development/security predicament. Long supplier lists of dual-use items may impact adversely on bona fide patterns of trade - unless some way can be found to focus the controls more accurately on real security problems. In this connection, there are those who claim - in a much simplified but pointed fashion - that there are no sensitive technologies, only sensitive countries. It is hard, however, to lay down clear criteria for the determination of national credentials. On the other hand, holding a great many countries in the South - which may have as good or better non-proliferation credentials than many countries in the North - vulnerable to the weapons-related activities of a few, is no tenable position either. Unfortunately, there are no easy solutions.

Exports controls for security purposes feed into larger arms control endeavours. Arms control, in turn, is more or less integral to broader security equations. In the aftermath of the Cold War, security considerations changed fundamentally. The changes meant a veritable boost for arms control and disarmament. They also meant a number of new challenges, i.a. in the field of export controls. As COCOM disappears, a new multilateral arrangement to supplement existing non-proliferation regimes is on its way in, and the non-proliferation regimes are being revised - do we need a complete overhaul of export regulations? Would a more modest approach of incremental changes be better? Should we not try to develop a broader consensus between suppliers and recipients on the rules to govern international transactions in armaments and related technologies?

We shall start with a review of general trends in defence-related matters. It will be followed by an examination of factors that drive defence manufacturing and arms and technology transfers. Then we shall wind up discussing how to facilitate economic development while maximizing regional security and stability. To guide us in this complex terrain, we are pleased to have such a broad range of expertise at the table - from politics, diplomacy, international organizations, industry and academic life. In a period of great international transition, the politics of technology transfers acquire special import. At the same time, the problems are complex in theory and even more intricate in practice. There are devils in a great many details. All your expertise will therefore be needed.

2. Robert L. Pfaltzgraff, Jr.

This conference has been designed to provide a forum for consideration of a series of intertwined issues that are of central importance in the post-Cold War security setting. At the core is the question of how can we make the most effective use of technology in order to achieve our respective goals of economic modernization and growth, while at the same time providing for our own security and minimizing political-military instability. We are in the midst of the development of a global economy within a system that is linked as never before by technology. Without access to advanced technologies no society can meet its development goals. At the same time we are in an era of political fragmentation and the break-up of existing states - a kind of shifting of the earth's political tectonic plates, resulting in, or the result of, political conflicts.

For political and military, as well as economic reasons, technologies of many types are being transferred. Because in this economic and security setting such phenomena as arms control, economic growth and modernization, and technology transfers bear a close relationship to each other, we have organized this conference around these themes. Our goal is to provide a forum for candid discussion focused on the economic and security dimensions of arms and technology transfers from a variety of perspectives. Our focus includes exporting as well as importing states. Our interest encompasses government and industry, as well as the international and domestic dimensions of arms and technology transfers, together with the military and civilian applications within the meaning of the term "dual-use" technology.

In this conference we will endeavour to consider how the needs of regional and global political-military security and stability can be reconciled with our respective national and international economic concerns. We will examine major trends and forces shaping arms and technology transfers in the recent past and we will attempt to project into the future as well.

For this purpose we have brought together a distinguished group of participants from many parts of the world, with diverse perspectives and professional interests, and drawn from exporting and importing states.

First will have a focus on defense-related transfers, including political-military factors with an emphasis on conventional systems and weapons of mass destruction. Then we will address economic and technological considerations that are driving defense manufacturing and exports/imports as well as the role of technology transfers in economic development and ending with a discussion of regional security and stability and arms control issues and possibilities.

Part I

General Trends in Defense Related Transfers

Chapter 1
Trends in the Proliferation of Weapons of Mass Destruction

Aaron Karp

I - Introduction

A broad array of individual concerns have transformed the international agenda. But the general implications of those changes are only slowly becoming apparent. Are our perspectives and tools, all designed to manage Cold War priorities, adequate to the challenges of a new world order?

It is important to remind ourselves of the environment within which all of us gained our education in peace and security. It was world in which peace and security debates were dominated, sometimes overwhelmed by two subjects; Super-Power nuclear weapons, and to a lesser degree, the world's conventional forces. We spent over 40 years of the Cold War becoming intimately familiar with those issues and learning to deal with them in a routine way.

What we confront now is the beginning of an effort to make two different issues equally familiar and routine. Neither is new or unknown, but previously they were secondary issues, rarely the stuff of high-level summits or international conferences. In a curious reversal, what was of primary importance now feels very distant, and what was secondary has become dominant. One of the two leading issues, obviously, is ethnic conflict and all of the diplomatic and the military problems relating to national self-determination. The other is weapons proliferation.

Personally, I find proliferation to be the easier of the two to address both intellectually and diplomatically; the essential elements of proliferation politics are clearer and more amenable to outside intervention than even the most straight-forward ethnic conflict. Despite these advantages, proliferation has perplexed us for decades and doubtlessly will continue to for a very long time to come. Although it is essentially about physical technology, proliferation is dominated by the politics of uncertainty. By uncertainty I mean that we often do not have a clear apprehension of the threats and even in those cases where the dangers are unambiguous, there is often a great deal of obscurity.

Non-proliferation politics increasingly are about the management of ambiguity. Exactly what weapons do suspect countries have? What are they capable of doing with them? What do they intend to do? How can they best be dissuaded? All of these, to a greater or lesser degree, are unanswerable questions and all measures to deal with the problem ultimately must rely on some element of guess-work. In this uncertain environment, the key to successful non-proliferation policy-making may be constructing mechanisms that reduce the risks of miscalculation to manageable proportions.

II - The Nature of Proliferation

In refining our outlook, it is probably important to remind ourselves that the problem is not as severe as we can sometimes imagine it to be. Indeed, at no point in my lifetime has the list of countries who considered major proliferation threats been so short. Which is not to say threats today are minor, but they certainly are much less severe than we previously imagined they could be.

The threats may be smaller in an absolute sense but the fears they arouse probably never have been greater.[1] Not only is weapons proliferation concentrated in unstable regions or in countries that appear unstable themselves, but there is a certain sense of tragic frustration at having escaped one nuclear confrontation only to find ourselves stuck many others. We have a variety of regimes and policies to try and cope with proliferation threats. Many are strong. Yet even the strongest ones contain elements of fragility, which must always be of great concern.

The basic problem arises from the ineluctable aging of technology. The weapons of mass destruction that dominate proliferation debates are themselves. Although there are exceptions such as especially frightening

---

[1] Recent assessments from both Russia and the United States give similar impressions. *Proliferation Issues: Russian Federation Intelligence Services Report: A New Challenge After the Cold War: Proliferation of Weapons of Mass Destruction*, JPRS-TND-93-007, 5 March 1993; and R. James Woolsey, "Threats to the US and its interests abroad," Opening statement, US Senate, Select Committee on Intelligence, 25 January 1994.

developments in biological agents in recent years, most of the weapons of greatest concern today are based on concepts from the 1930s and hardware from the 1940s. Old, however, does not mean that they are easy. It is very important to remind ourselves that even a technological virtuoso like Nazi Germany faced its greatest technological failure in its inability to acquire nuclear weapons. Other countries today seem to be facing equal problems with their major weapons programs. And it is indeed heartening to see many countries either choosing deliberately to slow the pace of their advance weapons programmes or deciding to abandon them altogether. The great lesson of the past five years is that proliferation remains a terrible threat, but not an inevitable one. Proliferation battles perhaps can never be won in any absolute sense but they need never be lost in a permanent sense either.

III - Nuclear Proliferation

It is especially useful to review the situation in nuclear proliferation and ballistic missile proliferation, and then deal with some of the proposals and the efforts underway to try and deal with those proliferation threats. There are, of course innumerable forms of the proliferation problem. The United Nations has seen its greatest accomplishment in the creation of the 1993 Chemical Weapons Convention.[2] Just to list those other areas where formal regimes or regular international consultations already exist one would have to add biological weapons, aerial refueling, diesel submarines, dual-use manufacturing technologies, super computers and the migration of engineers. More questionably, some would add conventional arms transfers to the list of existing control regimes as well.

Nuclear and missile proliferation are neither unique nor necessarily the most imposing proliferation challenges. But they probably are the most visible and mature aspects of the problem. In nuclear proliferation, the news

---

[2] This endeavor is thoroughly described in Thomas Bernauer, *The Projected Chemical Weapons Convention: A Guide to the Negotiations in the Conference on Disarmament* (New York: United Nations, 1990); and more formally in Bernauer, *The Chemistry of Regime Formation: Explaining International Cooperation for a Comprehensive Ban on Chemical Weapons* (Aldershot: Dartmouth Publishing and the United Nations Institute for Disarmament Research, 1993).

is very ambivalent. We do not face those long lists that we once feared of 20 nuclear powers, 30, 40, nuclear powers, however many. Today we face somewhere between 7 and 9 countries with nuclear weapons: the 5 acknowledged nuclear weapons powers, Israel, the Ukraine, as well as the uncertain status of North Korea and Pakistan. Many other countries undoubtedly are capable of going nuclear, but for a variety of reasons choose not to.

Equally impressive are a growing number of countries that have given up their nuclear programs. Most spectacularly Argentina, Brazil, and South Africa have abandoned decades of determined rhetoric and huge investments in nuclear weapons development. More recently Kazakhstan has signed the NPT and Belarus seems certain to follow. The basic principle of the unacceptability of nuclear weapons has never had wider support.

The problem list is a short one now. Although the list of problem states is shorter than ever, we are left with a handful of very hard cases. The problem list is more concentrated around countries that refuse to participate in orthodox diplomatic dialogues. Some make no effort to conceal their hostility toward the nuclear non-proliferation regime. The problem of Ukraine is being dealt with in a trilateral dialogue with Russia and the United States, a process largely outside the usual proliferation debate, but its significance for the proliferation process cannot be under estimated. What is left of the Iraqi nuclear programme is under very tight restrictions and will stay that way under Security Council resolution 715. But the Iraqi problem will remain troubling for years to come. Iran's nuclear programme shows great ambitions if not great capabilities at the moment. Libya certainly has not abandoned its ambitions although again, its capabilities are weak. And, finally, there is the overwhelming problem of North Korea.

The kind of threats that we are trying to deal with in nuclear proliferation have evolved considerably over time as well. From the time that the NPT was completed in 1968 through the early 1980's, nuclear non-proliferation was understood to be a business of dealing with the spread of reactor technology. The technology lists composed by the Zanger Committee and the original Nuclear Suppliers Group were set up to try and control the trade in major nuclear installations: nuclear reactors, enrichment and reprocessing facilities. In those cases where questionable facilities were transferred, the regime sought to implement safeguards and verification procedures inhibit military work. For over a decade, though, the reactor trade, has been all but dead. In its place now we have a very lively trade in dual use equipment, which has risen to the center of current proliferation debates. In addition to dual use equipment there is the ever looming threat of the trade of nuclear warheads - instant proliferation. This has been made especially lively as a result of the disintegration of the Soviet Union.

In dealing with these problems the primary tool we have is a nuclear regime, a regime that is very strong but also very fragile. It is based upon a norm, the principal of nuclear non-proliferation and the unacceptability of nuclear weapons, to which all States subscribe. Even those countries that would tell you that they are unhappily burdened with nuclear weapons accept that norm. And, indeed, the extraordinary number parties to the NPT testifies to the strength of that norm. Countries who we do not really believe are sincere in their adherence to the NPT - such as Iran, Iraq, Libya and North Korea - publicly will tell you that they believe in the principle.

At the same time that the regime is so strong, it is a very fragile. Should one signatory of the NPT acquire a nuclear weapon, the utility of the entire regime is thrown into serious doubt. While it takes thousands of conventional weapons to alter regional power balances, just one or two nuclear weapons are sufficient to change everything. The nuclear non-proliferation system carries a tremendous responsibility; it has to be fully effective stopping proliferation among its parties or it looses all credibility. I can think of very few other international agreements that are as fragile.

Since the Iraqi invasion of Kuwait and the events of the following war, the international community has been well mobilized to deal with the nuclear proliferation threat. We have had a variety of very important reforms.[3] First the system of Full Scope Safeguards has now extended to included all major suppliers, making virtually all nuclear exports dependent on acceptance of IAEA safeguarding. Full Scope Safeguards, previously a perverse demand of the few, are now the accepted principal of all major nuclear exporters. The Nuclear Suppliers Group has seen its membership double and it has greatly extended the number of technologies that it controls, particularly by adding a lengthy control list specifically on dual use technology.

---

[3] These are summarized in Harald Mueller and Lewis A. Dunn, *Nuclear Export Controls and Supply Side Restraints: Options for Reform*, PPNN study No. 4 (Southampton: Mountbatten Centre for International Studies, October 1993).

Even as it reaches new levels of strength, the non-proliferation regime is plagued by three major problems, all of which casts somber shadows over the regime's greatest successes. The oldest is the unresolved question of how to handle countries that refuse to join the regime. Today that means in particular Cuba, India, Israel, Pakistan. Developing policies to deal with those countries has always been an extreme headache for non-proliferation specialists. Although one always can hope, there is little reason to think that these countries can be reached through the non-proliferation regime. Like Ukraine, their nuclear potential probably must be addressed through regional conflict resolution, if at all. Second, we face the problem of North Korea, inheritor to the disruptive mantle previously worn by Iraq. North Korea raises all kind of difficult issues for the NPT and IAEA. The most pertinent one for this meeting is the question of whether or not a country who is a signatory of the NPT can violate its terms with utter impunity. Indeed, in many respects Pyongyang has used the threat of defecting from the NPT for outright benefit, gaining an unprecedented series of concessions from the IAEA, Seoul and Washington.

Unfortunately there is no international forum where these issues are receiving the attention they deserve. Rather than being permitted to complicate the already tricky NPT debates, they are deliberately suppressed, left off formal agendas and consigned to backroom murmurings of unhappiness. More likely than not, these issues will be all but overlooked at the 1995 NPT Extension Conference.[4] There the deliberations will be preoccupied by a third and more fundamental challenge, the question of how to prolong life of the NPT. While all parties are agreed that the treaty should survive, there is vigorous dispute between those governments who view the NPT as a non-proliferation treaty and those who perceive it as a nuclear disarmament treaty. If this gap cannot be overcome, the NPT could find itself renewed for a brief period that would bring its permanence into doubt.[5]

---

[4] Jim Wurst, "Countdown to the NPT continues", *BASIC Reports*, 3 February 1994, pp.1-3.

[5] David Fischer, *Towards 1995: the Prospects for Ending the Proliferation of Nuclear Weapons* (Aldershot: Dartmouth Publishers and the United Nations Institute for Disarmament Research, 1993) esp. ch. 13.

IV - Ballistic Missile Proliferation

Missile proliferation presents a very different situation. The process of proliferation is more advanced and the instruments to control the spread are more rudimentary. We know that there are a large number of countries that have some kind of missile technology or are interested. At least 30 countries are trying to acquire missiles of some sort. Many countries have a little technology and roughly 20 have Scud-B missiles or the equivalent. Despite the many highly publicized efforts to establish independent missile programmes, however, only 4 emerging powers at this point have self-sustaining ballistic missile programs: Israel, India, North Korea and Ukraine.[6]

The reason why so few would-be missile proliferators have encountered much success lies in the great demands of the technology itself. Unlike nuclear weapons this is not laboratory scale technology, it involves the total mobilization of national resources. The Indian experience is especially illustrative. India has started a large number of space launch and ballistic missile programmes, including the 2500 km range Agni and the even larger PSLV space rocket projects. Yet India's only success after 20 years of work has been with the very smallest project, the 150 km range Prithvi missile. Other programs have encountered a great number of difficulties, amongst other reasons because even a country with all the resources of India cannot afford a full scale test programme.[7] And if India cannot successfully develop a large rocket, it is very questionable exactly who can.

The regime that we constructed to deal with the threat, based on the 1987 Missile Technology Control Regime, is an ambivalent one. It is a leaky regime. A lot of technology already was in the hands of potential proliferators before the MTCR became effective. Since coming into effect, though, the MTCR has tripled its membership and become very strong at the

---

[6] William C. Potter and Harlan W. Jencks (eds), *The International Missile Bazaar: the New Suppliers' Network* (Boulder, Colorado: Westview, 1994). This impressive review of emerging missile supplies in marred only by the lack of a chapter on Ukraine.

[7] Indian officials have a much different outlook. For example, see interview of A.P.J. Abdul Kalam, "It will take four years," *Sunday* (Calcutta), 12 September 1993. Some Indian analysts acknowledge the slow pace of Indian rocketry, but put the blame on Washington for denying technology. See Brahma Chellaney, *Nuclear Proliferation: the US-Indian Conflict* (London: Sangam Books, 1993, Ch. 8.

job of controlling the exports of potential suppliers. The greatest challenges that it faces today are familiar; primarily China and North Korea. They are the only two countries that are still exporting ballistic missile technology in any large scale. North Korea especially is worrisome. It is easy to imagine other suppliers emerging. Russian arms firms regularly publicize their wares including some ballistic missiles. They do not seem to have Moscow's approval to resume actual missile exports, but this easily could change. Thus the importance of finding ways to strengthen the ballistic missile regime.

The real battle on ballistic missiles fortunately though is not over large intercontinental systems. Although advocates in the West of large defensive systems claim that simple technology can be used to create very large rockets, no regional power appears to believe this sufficiently to try. Because it is so demanding, the technology for very large ballistic missiles is the easiest to control, just as the technology for very short range systems is hardest to restrain. At the moment the most serious control efforts are concentrating on Scud-B type technology, suitable for missiles with ranges of roughly 150-1,000 kilometers. It is at this technical level that the real battle of missile proliferation is being fought.

V - Responding to the Challenge

How then to deal with proliferation problems in the future? There are any number of proposals, only the most important of which can be mentioned here. What is essential as we try to assemble a balanced approach to the new world order, is that we approach the widest range of policy options openly and frankly. The ideological and political assumptions that channeled the debates of the Cold War may be completely irrelevant today. Just as the nature of the proliferation debate has changed, so must our attitudes toward policy responses.

First, and perhaps the easiest to implement is a universal registration system for all military and dual use technology. The United Nations has taken a first step towards in creating the arms register. Many countries already have a comprehensive licensing system to regulate their own exports. The technology is there to create such a system on a global scale. The burdens would not be very great. Several governments, led by Japan, clearly favor of such a system.

A second thing that we should deal with is the possibility of going beyond registration to a single export control regime. We have elements of it in all of the other major regimes, the MTCR, the NSG, the Australian group and the half-dozen or so smaller arrangements. All of these diverse systems, rather than becoming part of a coherent solution now are becoming part of the problem. The most coherent mechanism, CoCoM, will close shop on 31 March 1994 and the planned replacement will narrower and much less powerful. The duplication of regimes has become part of the problem, with the same people are going to all of these meetings, the human burden has simply become intolerable. The lack of a secretariat to keep the process working sensibly is another problem. And, moreover, by distributing the non-proliferation job among so many regimes we tend to dilute the impact that we could potentially have through an integrated system.

The strongest argument against a single integrated regime has long been that of recipients who fear that it will interfere with their civilian economic development. This is an important allegation. I think the most important response is that no longer are these regimes being seen in terms of geographic battles: east versus west, north versus south. It is now exporters trying to maintain control over their own products in the hands of potential proliferators. The key to insuring balance is of course to minimalize dual use lists and the way to do that, ultimately, is through safeguarding key technologies. We have the long standing example of the IAEA and an important lesson in Chemical Weapons Convention. No one wants to see anything that huge dealing with a full range of dual technologies. But the approach has great merit for extension.

How to deal specifically though with those countries refusing to join any regulatory scheme? The obvious response is toleration; do nothing. That is approach to which the international community through sheer inertia is most inclined. It is also obviously the least satisfactory. Some have proposed compensation as a way of dealing with countries that are clearly going in the direction of weapons acquisition. Trade technologies, give them something else. If you do not pursue nuclear weapons we will give you civilian reactors, as per Article IV. Instead of ballistic missiles, we will give you better access to civilian launch services, etc., etc. The great flaw in this method is that recipients do not seem very interested. If a country is going after a nuclear weapons they are not going to take sugar as an alternative. Governments make serious decisions when procuring anything that significant--and they are very difficult to sway from that path.

An obvious alternative is a punitive one; sanctions of rising severity, leading ultimately perhaps to the use of force. This is not something anyone likes to talk about. But it needs discussing very clearly. Only one country that I am familiar with has ever suffered for its nuclear weapons program, and that is Pakistan. And, even Pakistan has not suffered very much.[8] Israel certainly has not felt any penalty. India's unverified programmes have cost India virtually nothing. And, at the moment North Korea seems to be benefitting from its nuclear weapons project. It is increasingly evident that proliferators must be made to suffer for their decision to evade international norms. One also needs an explicit dialogue on what kinds of sanctions are appropriate and when. At the far extreme, Israel's attack on Iraq's Ossiraq/Tammuz reactor facility in 1981 looked pretty stupid to most international observers in 1981. It looked pretty brilliant by 1990. There may be times in the future when the use of force must be considered, but on what basis and to what extent?

Ultimately, defences become a very real option. The main problems with defences is their expense and their potentially provocative nature. In the past year a series of reports has come out of Europe on these question, two reports out of NATO, one from the Western European Union considering the possibility of a defensive scheme for Europe.[9] The general conclusion is that a system of missile defences for Europe (on the Patriot level) would cost about $5 billion. To defend against missiles with ranges of 1,000 to 2,000 kilometers would cost between $30 and $40 billion, much of that for early-warning satellites. There are important issues, especially regarding the ABM treaty, to be dealt with before defences can be pursued much more seriously. Moscow and Washington are discussing re-interpretation of the ABM Treaty in the Standing Consultative Commission, but it is a matter to be pursued with great care.

---

[8] *Interpreting the Pressler Amendment: Commercial Military Sales to Pakistan*, Hearing, US Senate, Committee on Foreign Relations, 30 July 1992 (Washington: US Government Printing Office, 1992).

[9] *Anti-Missile Defence for Europe* (Paris: Assembly of the Western European Union, 1993).

The final and perhaps most ambitious way of dealing with proliferation threats are outright weapons bans. We just had the example of the completion of the CWC in 1993. The next obvious step is a comprehensive nuclear test ban. And, here the dramatic change in the American position is especially intriguing. The big problem with total weapons bans is that of course they do not appeal to the smaller nuclear powers highly dependent on missile forces like Britain, China and France or emerging missile powers. There also are problems of effectiveness. A comprehensive nuclear test ban has a tremendous problem of being a very good mechanism for stopping modernization, but a very poor way for stopping a first time nuclear power with their first bomb. Similarly, a ballistic missile ban will always face the problem that civilian space launchers can be converted to ballistic missions.

Ultimately, and in conclusion, let me say that there is no such a thing as a non-proliferation panacea. We will never solve the proliferation problem. Amongst other things, because even if you can deal with all the proliferation problems that we are use to discussing, countries will come up with new ones. Proliferation is the result of an interactive process. So long as the basic motives are there, countries will find new weapons to try and deal with their basic security problems. The solution ultimately is conflict resolution and collective security action.

It is very intriguing to return to the examples of conflict resolution and actual disarmament. The precedents of Start-1 and -2, the CFE Treaty, South Africa's unilateral de-nuclearization have only been examined superficially. What do they tell us about the possibilities for reversing proliferation else where? Of most obvious relevance to regional non-proliferation is the extraordinary progress between Argentina and Brazil.[10] Starting in the 1970s two long-time antagonists reached an unprecedented modius vivendi, allowing them to abandon their military nuclear programmes, their ballistic missile projects, and to cut back military expenditures. Regional spokesmen elsewhere, trying to avoid the obvious onus, have been quick to assert the uniqueness of this and every other reconciliation. But the lessons are unavoidable: if you can solve the problem politically, finding the military solutions is very easy. One is left with the conclusion that conflict resolution is the ultimate solution of proliferation battles.

---

[10] John R. Redick, *Argentina-Brazil Nuclear Non-Proliferation Initiatives*, PPNN Issue Review No. 3 (Southampton: Mountbatten Centre for International Studies, January 1994).

# Chapter 2
Spread of Conventional Weapons Production Technology

Michael Brzoska

I - Introduction

The production of conventional weapons is a fairly widespread phenomenon, even in less industrialized countries (LICs). A current count is that there is some form or other of arms production going on in 36 countries in Latin America, Africa and Asia, not counting the special cases of China and Japan (see Map 1).[1]

Why study the spread of conventional arms production technology? I suggest that there are two major clusters of issues involved that make it worthwhile to take a closer look at arms production in States that do not have a modern tradition of such production. One is the cluster related to the diffusion of power, to the independence of less industrialized States in the acquisition of power or, looked at from the other end, to the capabilities of the major arms-producing States to manipulate the behaviour of lesser States through the flow of arms technology.

The availability of weapons and the means to maintain them is a precondition for military policy, and thus closely linked to the exercise of power and the conduct of war. A State without the means to produce the weapons deemed necessary to hold, and dependent on the importation of military goods, is in danger of not being able to conduct the kind of military policy it wants to pursue. Looked at from the other side, a government dependent on the demand of weapons can be manipulated by the supplying side. But manipulation has become more difficult with the increase in the number of suppliers, a number that was already growing before the end of the Cold War. What is the history of import substitution through indigenous

---

[1] China is excluded in this discussion since it has a very large arms industry that puts it into a different category from the other cases discussed here.

arms production? Is substitution of arms transfers still a desired strategy? How important is arms import dependence in the post-Cold War era? And for whom?

Behind these issues lurk the larger questions of war and peace and world order: Does the spread of conventional weapons production capabilities increase the likelihood of wars? Does it make efforts to build a more peaceful and just world more difficult?

The other cluster of issues stems from the fact that arms production is an economic industrial activity. It substitutes imports and can save foreign exchange costs, if expenditures for parts, technology and foreign experts do not outrun costs of imports. But it also binds capital and talent that might be used for civilian purposes. Even as an industrial activity, arms production is closely linked to the activities of the respective State. Arms production is at the junction of military strategic considerations and industrial economics. There are few examples of arms production in developing countries where it is not heavily regulated and subsidized by the respective State. There is also little arms production in countries without a considerable industrial base. What is the economic balance of arms production in developing countries? Has that balance changed in the post-Cold War era?

There is an important link between these two clusters of issues, connected to the spread of arms production capabilities. That link is technology.

Conventional arms production covers a wide spectrum of industrial activities on very different levels of technology. Unlike the production of missiles or nuclear weapons, conventional arms production of a wide range of goods does not require the mastery of complicated production technologies. But there is an in-built tendency in military thinking that demands the most advanced military technology. That thinking has roots in history and recent experience: The importance of advanced technology in military strategy was demonstrated by the victory of the US-led Coalition forces during the Second Gulf War. But it is also partly a myth and, given the limited means to produce and field advanced military technology, often not realistic. The more advanced the technology, the more costly is development and production, especially in countries lacking a diversified industrial infrastructure. Costs can be reduced to some extent through imports of components and foreign experts, but that implies less independence in arms production. In addition, it is especially the latest advances in technology that major arms exporters try to protect through export control regimes.

There is, in general, a tradeoff between the level of technological aspiration, independence of production and costs. Aspirations often have to be adapted to capabilities, if arms are to be produced domestically. What is the technological level of arms production in developing countries? What has changed over time?

These are some of the issues and questions that make the study of the spread of arms production capabilities an interesting subject. It is impossible to cover them in sufficient detail in this paper,[2] but luckily some of them are dealt with in other papers in this volume. I will concentrate here on an overview of the development of domestic arms production capabilities in LICs, in the past, present and near future, and try to just hint at links with the larger issues.

II - The Past

Conventional arms production in LICs grew rapidly during the 1960s, the 1970s and the early 1980s (see Figure 1). From the late 1980s, growth came to a halt, and the available evidence[3] points in the direction of a steady or slightly declining level of arms production since then. Production under license, usually from some industrialized States, grew steadily, albeit at a slow pace, while indigenous production, that is weapons designed in LIC's, had high growth rates into the 1980s.

The halt in growth in the late 1980s can be contrasted with the decrease in direct imports of arms. During the 1960s and until the early 1980s arms production grew at a slightly faster pace than even the trade in weapons (see Figure 2). Conventional weapons production slowed, but it did not decline

---

[2] The security, economic and technological implications of the spread of conventional weapons production are discussed in works which include; Wulf 1980; Eide/Kaldor 1980; Miller 1980; Neuman 1984; Brzoska/Ohlson 1986; Katz 1984, 1986; Brzoska 1989; Kwang-in Baek et. al. 1989; Sanders 1990; Ross 1991; OTA 1991; Krause 1992.

[3] There is not much quantitative data to work with in this field of research. The pioneering works were SIPRI 1971 and Lock/Wulf 1977. This was followed up in Brzoska/Ohlson, 1986 and Anthony, 1993. Much of this data is based upon tedious accumulation of information from reference handbooks, such as the Jane's yearbook series, and arms trade journals.

in any way as dramatically as the import of major weapons did. The result is an increase in the ratio between domestic production and direct imports of complete major weapons systems (see Figure 2). That ratio grew during the 1960s, the 1970s, and into the 1980s, but most markedly in the late 1980s. We do not as yet have sufficient data to document whether this trend has continued or not in the early 1990s.

An impressive number of conventional weapons were developed across the board, from supersonic fighter aircraft to rifles. In Table 1, indigenous production projects are counted in various categories of modern conventional weaponry. Some of the technologies required to produce weaponry such as guided missiles are of rather recent origin, so it is no surprise that the number of projects increased over time. But if the growing list of countries where such demanding indigenous production occurs is also taken into account, it becomes clear that there has been a fast pace of growth in modern weapons systems projects. That growth peaked in the late 1970s and early 1980s, as can be seen from the increases in the number of projects. It has since fallen off. The number of countries where modern arms production occurs has increased steadily over time, but has remained much smaller than the total list of countries with conventional arms production.

That list has not grown very much since the 1970s. In fact, if one simply asks whether conventional weapons production is occurring or not, there is not much change in the last decade or so (compare Map 1 to Map 2). The obvious conclusion is that - to put it into arms control "slang" - there has been limited horizontal proliferation of conventional arms production capability in the last two decades, but a high degree of vertical proliferation in a few countries. Much of this can be explained by looking at the complexity of the process of making weapons.

Not too long ago, a government interested in building up a domestic arms industry, could follow a fairly simple plan, the "five steps of successful arms production": First, assemble weapon parts sent from another country in your own country. Second, begin to build some of the parts in your own country. Third, acquire a license to build a weapon designed in another country, using some parts built abroad and some at home. Fourth, build up a research and development capability and design your own weapons. Fifth, build weapons of your own with only very few parts imported from abroad.

Some of these steps obviously depend on the availability of industries from which to buy components and on the training of qualified personnel, including scientists and engineers. This indicates the close relation between civilian and military production. The data in Table 2 demonstrates the correlation between the size of the domestic manufacturing sector and the size of the domestic arms production sector. This has also been found in a number of quantitative studies (Wulf 1980, Neuman 1984, Lock 1986). There are some States, Mexico, for instance, with an unexpectedly small arms industry, and Israel with an unexpectedly large arms industry, but in general the fit is good.

With sufficient determination to bear the costs of investments, including necessary inputs such as trained labour and "dual-use" production machinery, a government in the past could hope to catch up with the technological frontier within a couple of years, or a decade at most. One such example was the Brazilian aircraft industry in the 1960s and 1970s. In the 1960s, aircraft including US-designed F-5s were assembled and produced under license. In 1978, design of the EMB-312 Tucano began, a trainer aircraft that was so successful it was sold to the British Royal Air Force. But not everything went as well as the Tucano project. Things turned out to be more complicated than the "five steps" strategy suggests.

First, a civilian domestic industry that could build components was lacking in a large number of countries. This was sometimes a question of no industry at all, and sometimes a question of no industry capable of producing components of the required quality. Efforts to deliberately build up such supporting industries in Argentina, for instance, proved costly. The integration of qualitatively problematic components led to problematic weapons. More successful, at least in some sectors of arms production, was the strategy to try to enlist multinational companies as suppliers of components for dual-use goods, destined for both the military and civilian markets.

Second, at least some States had difficulties finding scientists, engineers and technicians in sufficient numbers. That was, on the one hand, a problem of education, but also one of keeping qualified personnel in the country. From time to time, developing countries' arms-producing entities have been showered with foreign expertise, for example immediately after the Second World War with German engineers, in the 1960s with British engineers, and in the early 1970s with US experts. While such foreign advice has been crucial, for instance, in the early phases of the Argentine or South African aircraft programmes, they have not always been beneficial. Sometimes programmes faltered when the foreign experts left; sometimes they brought designs that were beyond domestic means. More important has been the foreign advice coming from foreign companies. Some of the more advanced designs now in development or in production in developing countries, such as the South Korean Rockit MBT (Main Battle Tank, see Table 3), or the Indian LCA (Light Combat Aircraft), have benefitted greatly from close collaboration with foreign companies. The most privileged producer in this respect has undoubtedly been Israel, with its close collaboration with US educational institutions and arms-producing companies.

Third, a number of arms producers discovered that arms technology was growing faster than their capacity to catch up. The research and development budgets of the West European arms producers and the USA are so much larger that whenever a developing country had mastered a new technology, it was already outdated. This has been a problem, for instance, in India's arms industry. It has been successful in turning out domestic designs of aircraft, tanks and ships, but few reached the production stage, since the armed forces preferred to import foreign-designed weapons and have them produced under license in India. The share of domestically produced weapons in Indian acquisitions of major weapons has grown steadily, but India is still far from self-sufficiency (see Figure 3).

New strategies of arms production were developed as alternatives to the "5 easy steps". One was to add-up components available in civilian areas and integrate them into complete weapon systems. These weapon systems, while not as advanced as dedicated military systems, were reliable, easy to operate and to service. That was the secret of the success of the Brazilian armoured car sales in the 1970s and 1980; it was also an element in the build-up of the South African arms industry in the 1970s and 1980s. Another strategy was to take successful, though somewhat outdated designs from industrialized countries, and improve them bit by bit. Masters of such add-on engineering can be found among successful arms producers in a number of countries, including Israel and South Africa.

A common element of these strategies is that the technological aspiration is limited. The focus is on workable weapons. It is no surprise that approaches in arms production strategies, stressing the immediate use value and less so technological aspirations, were most predominant in countries in isolation or with military difficulties, such as South Africa or Chile. This strategy was also chosen by commercial producers in Brazil and Chile, whose interest was limited to making a profit.

III - The Present

The difficulties experienced by individual arms producers have led to a very diversified picture of conventional arms production in the developing world, both between and within countries. I will review some of the elements that characterize arms production presently.

One indicator that growth in conventional arms production in LICs has come to a halt, or even decreased in the 1990s, is the decline of arms exports from these countries (see Figure 4). Many producers benefitted from the Iraq-Iran war, so statistics about arms sales in the early to mid-1980s are somewhat misleading. Still, there is a notable decrease in the LICs' share of arms sales to the third world in the early 1990s. Another indicator is that among some of the larger producers, activity is reduced, such as in South Africa, but also Latin America. This followed from the collapse of several of the ambitious arms production projects in Argentina after the fall of the military government in 1983, and the rapid decline of the export-oriented sectors of arms production in Brazil.

On the other hand, there are cases where arms production is growing, especially in South East Asian States. Two ASEAN States with growing civilian industries, South Korea and Taiwan, were among the more successful arms producers of the late 1980s and early 1990s.

Governments have become more concerned about the costs of domestic arms production. In a number of countries, including Argentina, subsidies were cut. In others, such as India, concerns about the management of arms production in state-owned arsenals have resulted in changes in the structure of arms production. The model now seems to be a profit-centred enterprise, managed by civilians and privately or state-owned rather than the old-style, military-run State arsenal.

Exports of indigenous weapons from developing countries decreased after the mid-1980s. The major factor here was the end of the Iraq-Iran war, which had attracted a large number of suppliers, and even helped in the establishment of some arms production projects in the developing world, such as in Chile and Egypt. While producers especially from Latin America experienced a drastic decline in exports, exports from some East Asian countries and South Africa have grown. Not all of this is covered in available arms transfer statistics, where exports of small arms and ammunition are a difficult area to verify.

Some third world producers are very active in the market for retrofits of weapons and of components, most notably from Israel. This is a growing section of the arms market that is also not adequately covered by available arms transfer statistics.

There is a wide spectrum of military production in developing countries. With respect to the level of technology, four groups may be distinguished.

First, at the high end, some attempts to produce weapons indigenously at the technological level of the industrialized world have succeeded. This is true for many of the weapons manufactured in Israel; some of the systems produced in Brazil, such as the Astros MLRS; in South Africa, such as G-4 howitzers; in South Korea, such as the Ulsan Class frigates; in Taiwan, such as the IDF fighter; in Singapore, such as the SAR-80 range of rifles; or India, such as the Arjun MBT. The investments to achieve these successes have generally been very great. Numbers produced are small, with some exports to other developing countries. There is an almost equally long number of failed projects, or projects that continue to absorb large funds without being produced. Examples range from the Laví in Israel, to the Osorio and Bernardini MBTs in Brazil, the LCA in India and the indigenous air defence system in Taiwan. The number of countries capable and willing to develop and produce such weapons is small. Foreign support is large in the form of components, foreign experts, and outright co-operation with companies from industrialized countries.

Second, on the low end, production has generally been growing. There is a long list of producers of landing ships, patrol boats, vehicles armoured with sheet metal, rifles, mortars and ammunition. Still, since the early 1980s it has been growing only slowly. In many countries there is a high degree of self-sufficiency in these categories. Components are imported, but they are often also used for civilian products that are not subject to export controls by supplying States. The degree of independence is therefore high. Little data is available on the cost aspect of production at the low end of technology. It seems that costs are a function of the efficiency of management and investment in modern machinery.

Third, the practice of license production has remained widespread. It has turned out not to be a phase in the development of a domestic arms industry, but to be an enduring compromise between outright import and indigenous production. The production of a modern weapon system, such as a submarine, is a comparatively cheap way to close the technological gap between industrialized and developing countries. Since the level of complexity of weapon systems produced under license is now generally rather high, economic linkage effects with domestic economies are limited. Available cost data for the production of Italian frigates in Peru, or the US M-1 tank in Egypt, indicate that production under license increases costs compared to direct imports of products because of high learning costs.

The fourth is a mixed bag of intermediate technology, including not only add-up and add-on engineering mentioned above, but also the continued production of outdated weaponry. The latter is continuing in a number of countries, such as in Egypt's Military Production Industries sector, in Pakistan, and in some sectors of the Indian arms industry, but without much enthusiasm on the part of the respective armed forces and governments. Again, there is little cost information and what information we have points to the importance of management styles. Self-sufficiency in intermediate technology products seems to be high, and imports consist mostly of machinery and components also in civilian use. While in the abstract this category of arms production may seem to be the most promising, it has received strong support neither from armed forces nor from governments, probably because of the prevalent orientation towards modern technology.

IV - The Future of Arms Production in Developing Countries

There are a number of factors that shape the spread of conventional arms production technology in the post-Cold War world, including the advance of military technology, the availability of weapons imports and the use of arms technology transfers as a great power policy instrument.

First, it is probable that arms production will continue to become more difficult because of the increasing complexity of modern weapon systems. There are only a few arms production activities left where the technological frontier is easy to reach, such as small arms, ammunition, small ships and other weapon platforms, neither made out of materials difficult to shape or complicated to integrate or containing customized electronics.

It is very probable that the technology gap between industrialized and developing countries, in general, will increase - mostly because of spending patterns on military research and development. Exceptions, at least in some sectors, will be Israel, with its close ties to the US and possibly South East and East Asian States.

Second, with the end of the Cold War and reduction of procurement in most industrialized States, the arms market is very much a buyer's market, although outright military aid is limited to very few recipients. This affects producers across the spectrum of technology, but producers of intermediate technology may come under the greatest pressure. There is much of such technology on offer from former socialist countries at very low prices. At the same time, as outlined, it has been difficult to justify subsidies to intermediate technology in the past. At the high end of technology, there is also a general increase in the availability of products at lower prices, but here the arguments in favour of domestic production can be expected to carry more weight with domestic decision-makers. Probably least affected will be established production at the low end. Supply, especially from former socialist countries, has increased but savings from imports do not seem to be large compared to the investments already made in self-sufficiency.

Third, even with the current buyer's market, recent experience makes decision-makers in developing countries cautious with respect to independence from industrialized suppliers. In fact, with the number of embargoes, both at the international level and by individual countries growing in the post-Cold War world, the incentive to seek self-sufficiency may well have increased.

This can be inferred from looking at the matter of embargoes from the other end, that of the industrialized suppliers. The chances to agree on embargoes against governments deemed to destabilize the current order, or to be violating the rules of the game, have increased with the end of the Cold War. There is now, in the aftermath of the Second Gulf War, also an increased realization on the part of many industrialized countries' governments that the transfer of components, machinery and dual-use goods has to be watched closely. Embargoes are now more likely than before the Second Gulf War to encompass transfers of technology necessary for indigenous arms production.

V - Summary

The spread of conventional arms production capabilities has slowed considerably. The number of producers and the volume of production has stagnated since the early to mid-1980s. Producers have run into difficulties, especially at the high-end of technology. Recently, some of the most advanced projects were cancelled or cut down in favour of cheaper imports. Production at the low end of technology seems destined to increase, though with lower growth rates than before the mid-1980s. Indigenous production has decreased less than military expenditures and arms imports, so that the share in domestic procurement seems to have increased on average.

The level of independence from the possible interference of suppliers is greatest with respect to weapons that are simple to produce. At the higher end of technology, efforts to reduce dependence on industrialized producers have largely failed, though dependence has shifted to a certain extent, from the supply of complete designs to the supply of components and technical advice.

Thus, predictions about the future of arms production in LICs differ between countries and sectors of arms production. One important element will be the question of cost consciousness of arms producers in the developing world. Subsidies to arms production will be under greater scrutiny, and there will be an increased emphasis on privatization. At least in some cases, reviews of arms production programmes may be instigated by the International Monetary Fund and the World Bank, in the framework of structural adjustment lending programmes. But domestic production will not be cut to the levels justifiable by economic criteria alone - strategic arguments will continue to play an important role in many States.

Arguing from the perspective of power diffusion, this differentiation in the level of arms production with respect to technology points in two directions. Considering the balance of force between industrialized and developing countries, the contribution of domestic arms production to change is rather small. Considering the level of weaponry available to fight World War I-type wars and guerila wars, the general increase in the means for violence in the developing world is fuelled to a great extent from domestic sources.

Map 1

Central and South America:
Arms Production in Less Industrialized Countries
Early 1990s

- Mexico — G N
- Dominican Republic — G
- Venezuela — G N
- Columbia — G N
- Peru — G M N
- Brazil — G M N
- Bolivia — G
- Chile — G M N
- Argentina — G M N

G Ground Equipment
M Aircarft & Missiles
N Naval Equipment

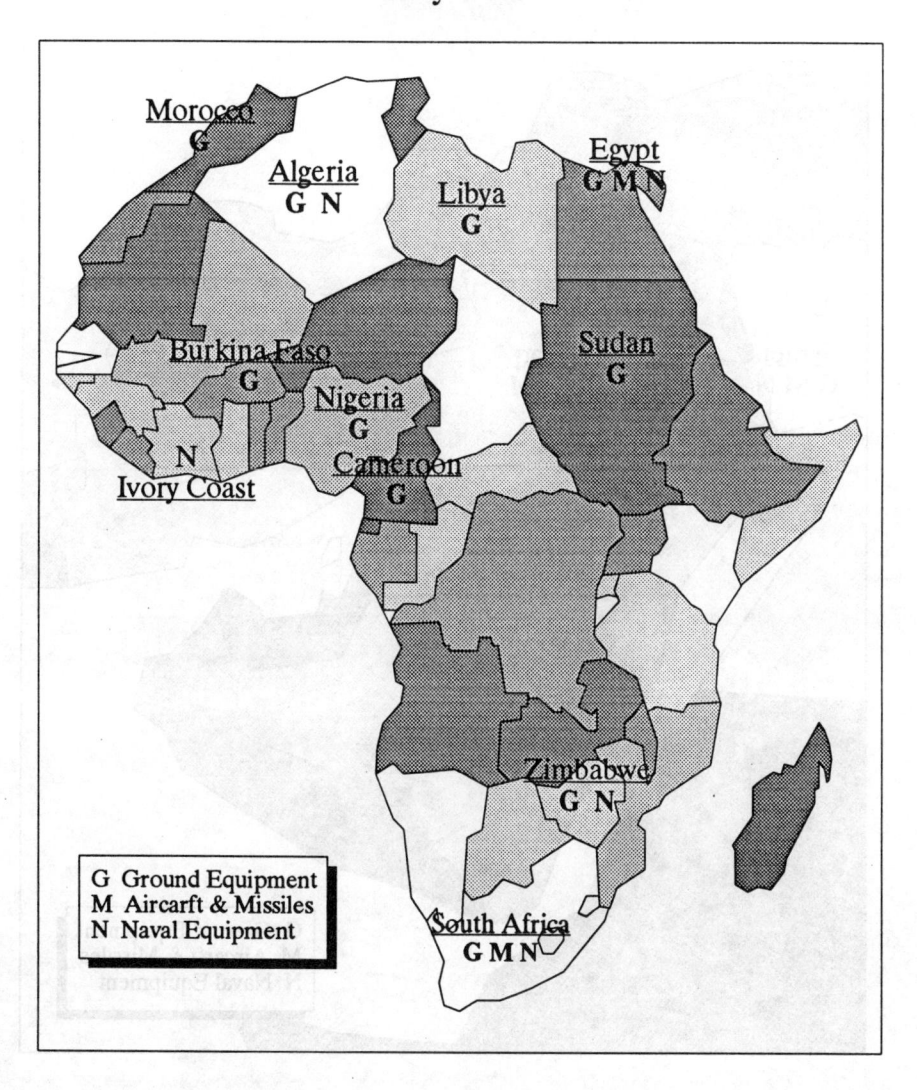

Map 1 (continued)

Africa:
Arms Production in Less Industrialized Countries
Early 1990s

Morocco G
Algeria G N
Egypt G M N
Libya G
Burkina Faso G
Sudan G
Nigeria G
N
Ivory Coast
Cameroon G
Zimbabwe G N
South Africa G M N

G Ground Equipment
M Aircarft & Missiles
N Naval Equipment

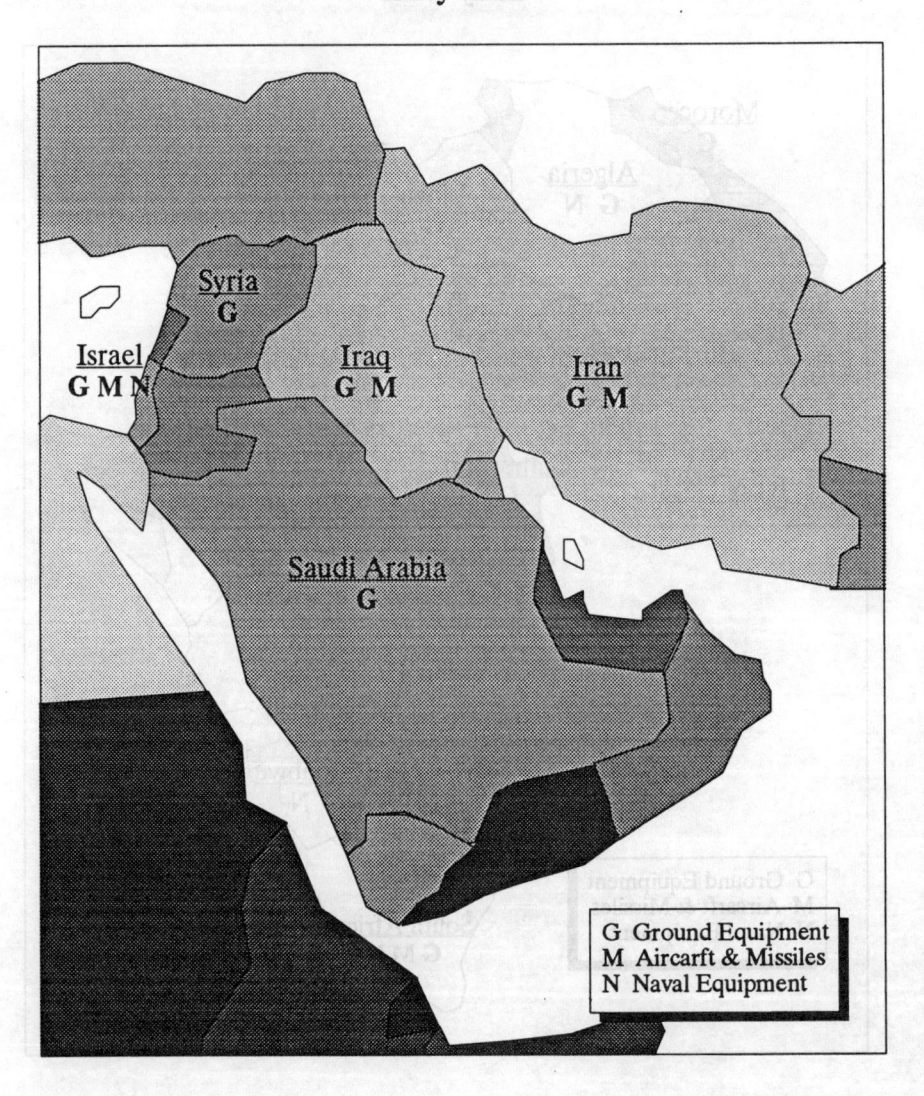

Map 1 (continued)

The Middle East:
Arms Production in Less Industrialized Countries
Early 1990s

Syria
G

Israel
G M N

Iraq
G M

Iran
G M

Saudi Arabia
G

G Ground Equipment
M Aircarft & Missiles
N Naval Equipment

Map 1 (continued)

Asia:
Arms Production in Less Industrialized Countries
Early 1990s

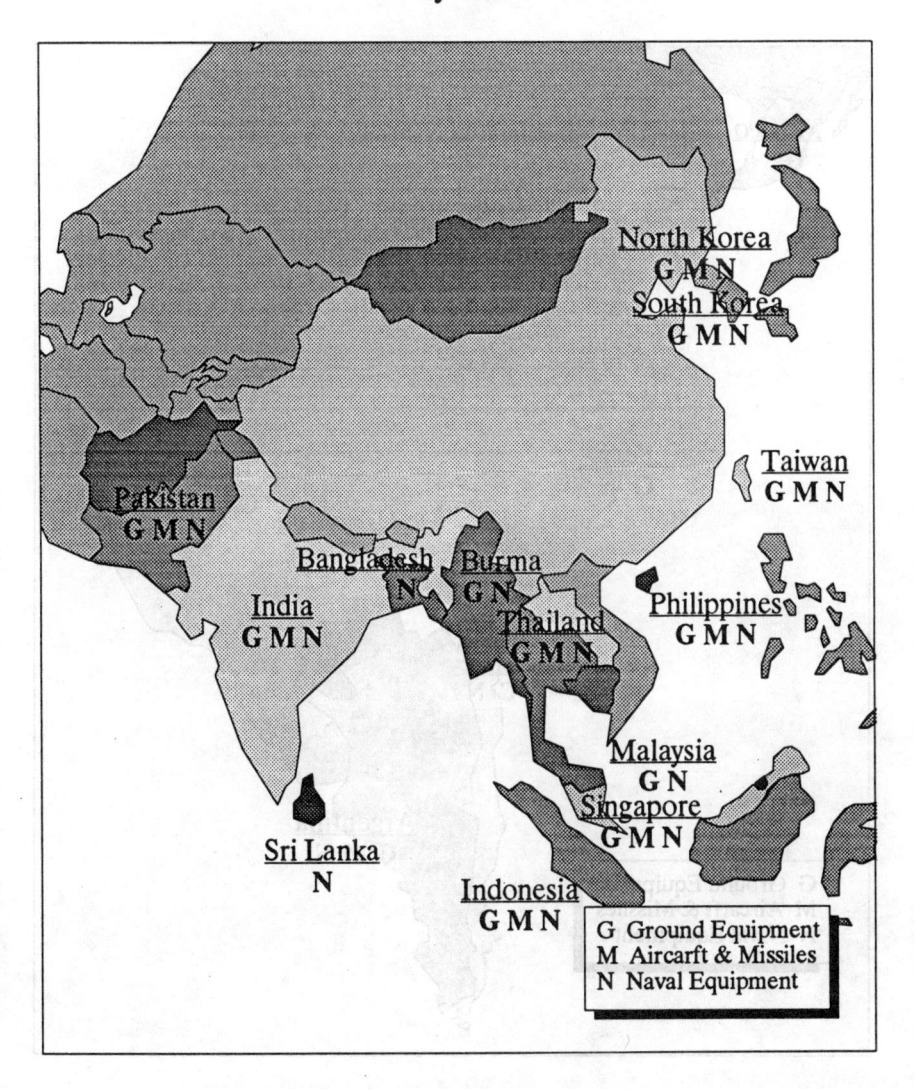

North Korea
G M N
South Korea
G M N

Taiwan
G M N

Pakistan
G M N

Bangladesh
N

Burma
G N

India
G M N

Thailand
G M N

Philippines
G M N

Malaysia
G N

Singapore
G M N

Sri Lanka
N

Indonesia
G M N

G Ground Equipment
M Aircraft & Missiles
N Naval Equipment

Map 2

**Central and South America:
Arms Production in Less Industrialized Countries
Mid 1970s**

- Mexico: G N
- Dominican Republic: G
- Venezuela: G N
- Columbia: N
- Peru: G N
- Brazil: G M N
- Chile: G N
- Argentina: G M N

G Ground Equipment
M Aircarft & Missiles
N Naval Equipment

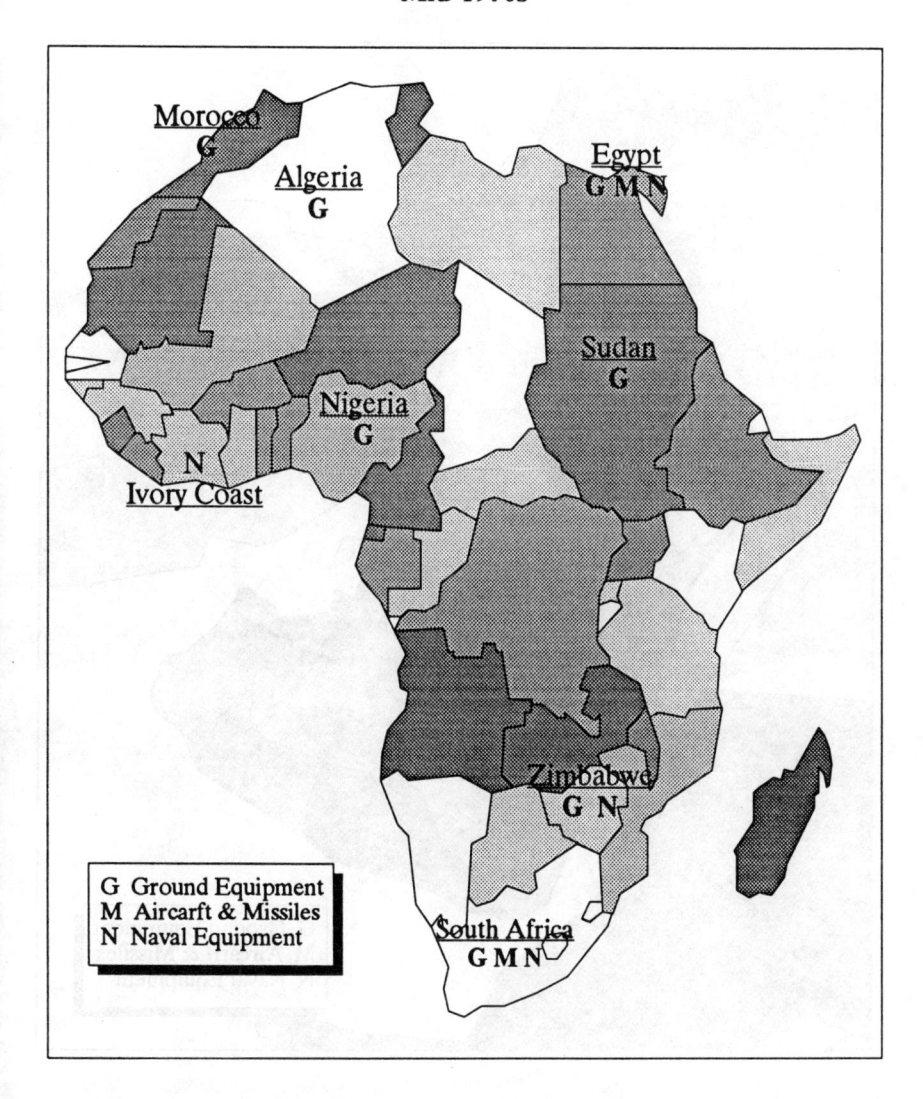

Spread of Conventional Weapons Production Technology 35

Map 2 (continued)

Africa:
Arms Production in Less Industrialized Countries
Mid 1970s

Morocco
G

Algeria
G

Egypt
G M N

Sudan
G

Nigeria
G

N
Ivory Coast

Zimbabwe
G N

G Ground Equipment
M Aircarft & Missiles
N Naval Equipment

South Africa
G M N

Arms and Technology Transfers

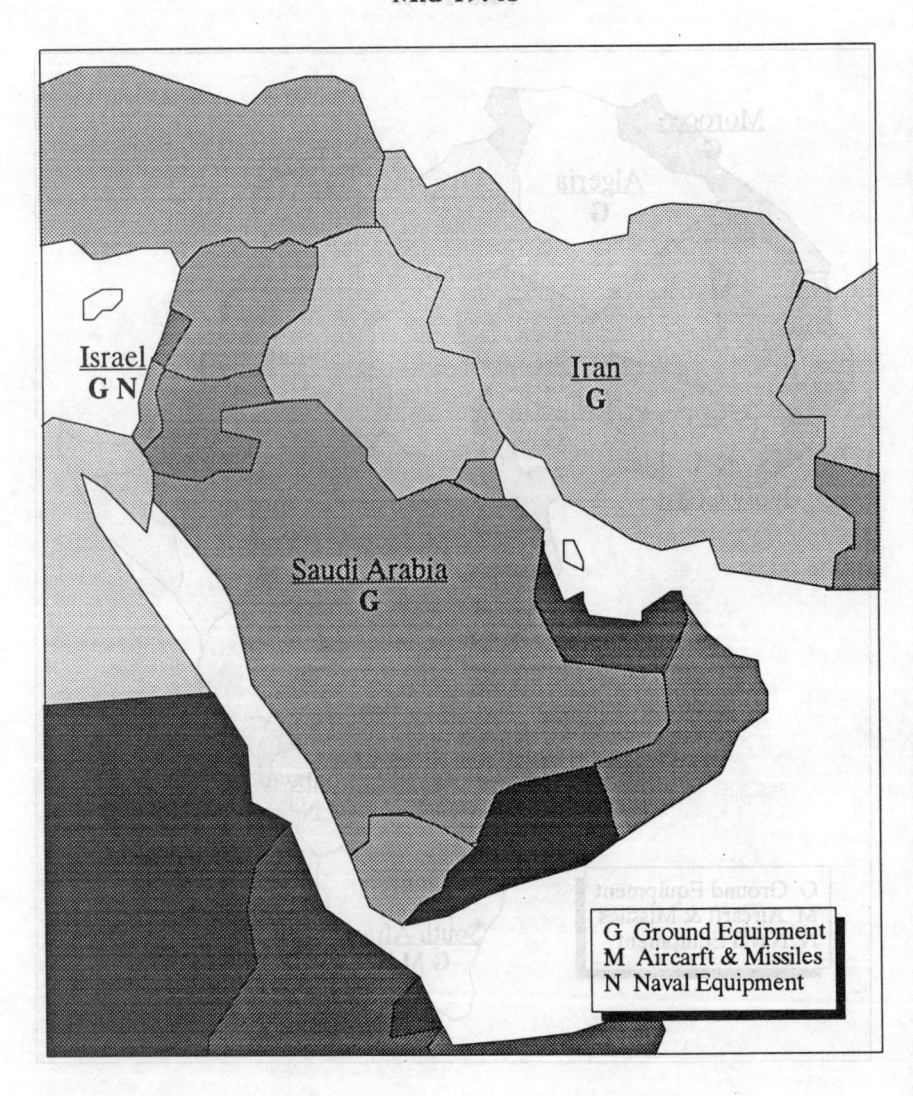

Map 2 (continued)

**The Middle East:
Arms Production in Less Industrialized Countries
Mid 1970s**

Israel
G N

Iran
G

Saudi Arabia
G

G Ground Equipment
M Aircarft & Missiles
N Naval Equipment

Spread of Conventional Weapons Production Technology 37

Map 2 (continued)

**Asia:
Arms Production in Less Industrialized Countries
Mid 1970s**

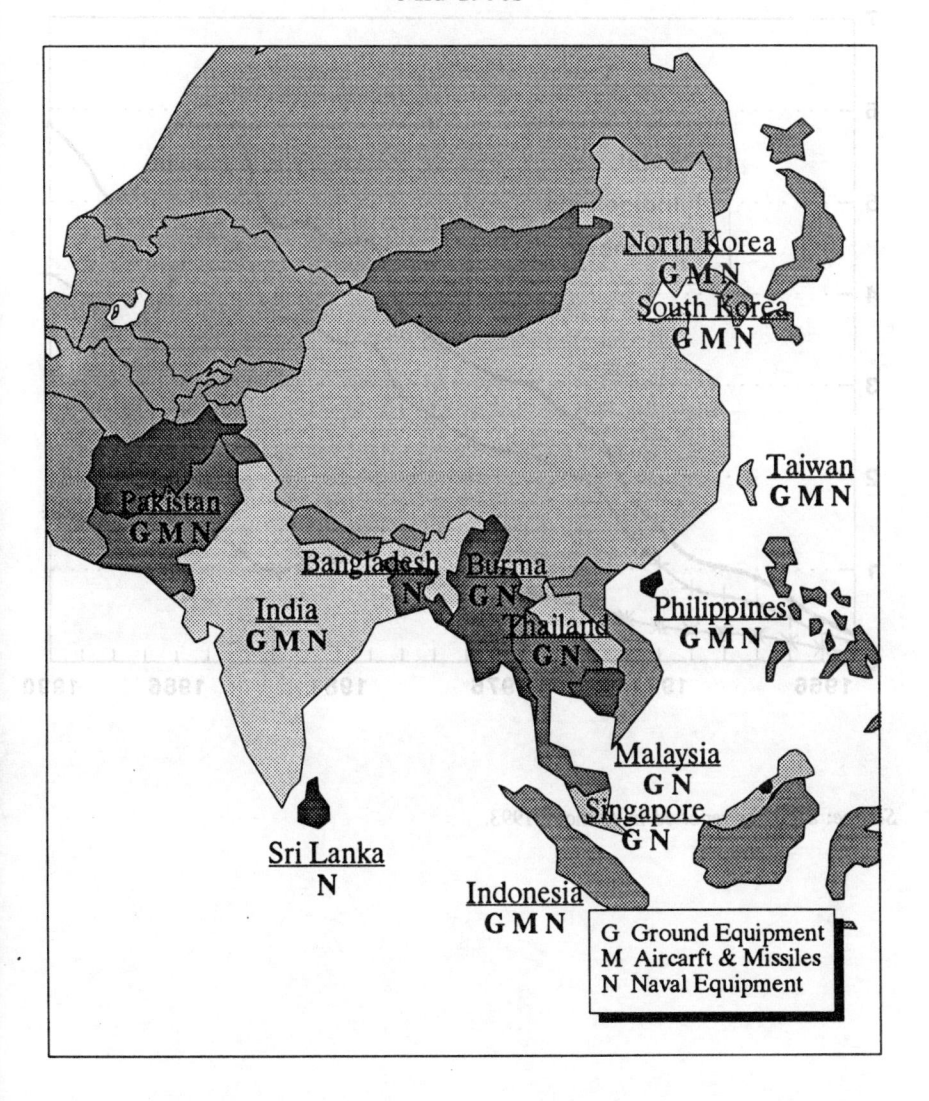

North Korea
G M N

South Korea
G M N

Taiwan
G M N

Pakistan
G M N

Bangladesh
N

Burma
G N

India
G M N

Thailand
G N

Philippines
G M N

Malaysia
G N

Singapore
G N

Sri Lanka
N

Indonesia
G M N

G Ground Equipment
M Aircarft & Missiles
N Naval Equipment

Figure 1: Production of Major Weapons in LICs
SIPRI trend estimate in constant $ of 1990, 3-year-moving average

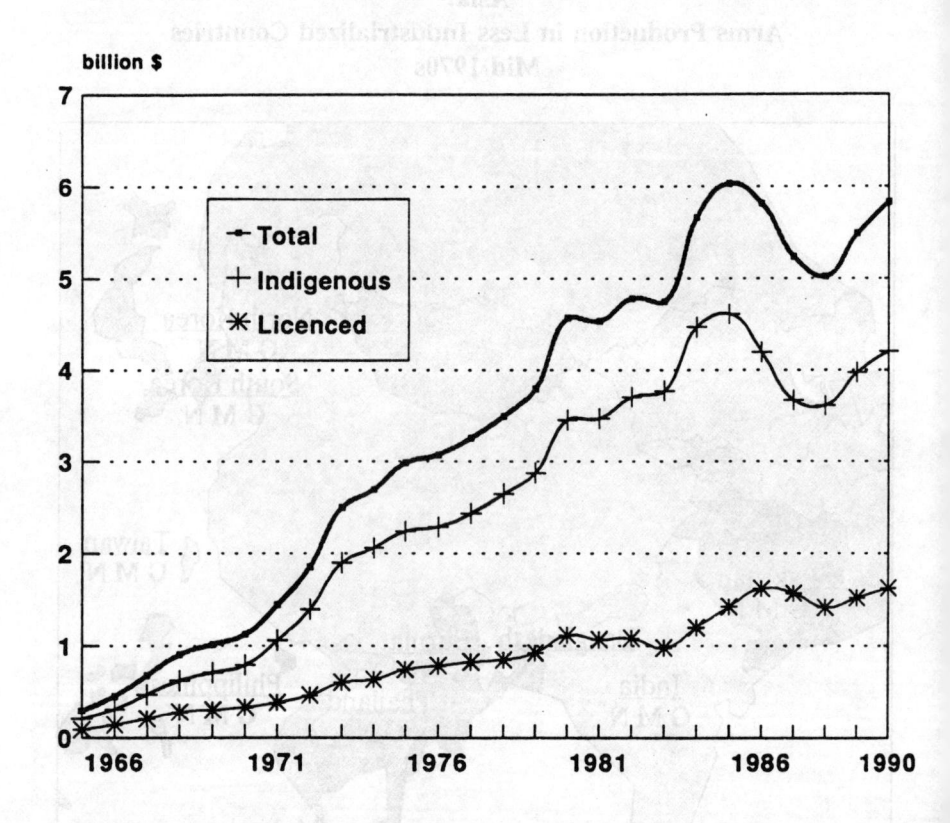

Source: SIPRI as reported in Anthony 1993.

Spread of Conventional Weapons Production Technology

Figure 2: Major Weapons in the Developing World
SIPRI trend estimates of imports and production, index 1985=100

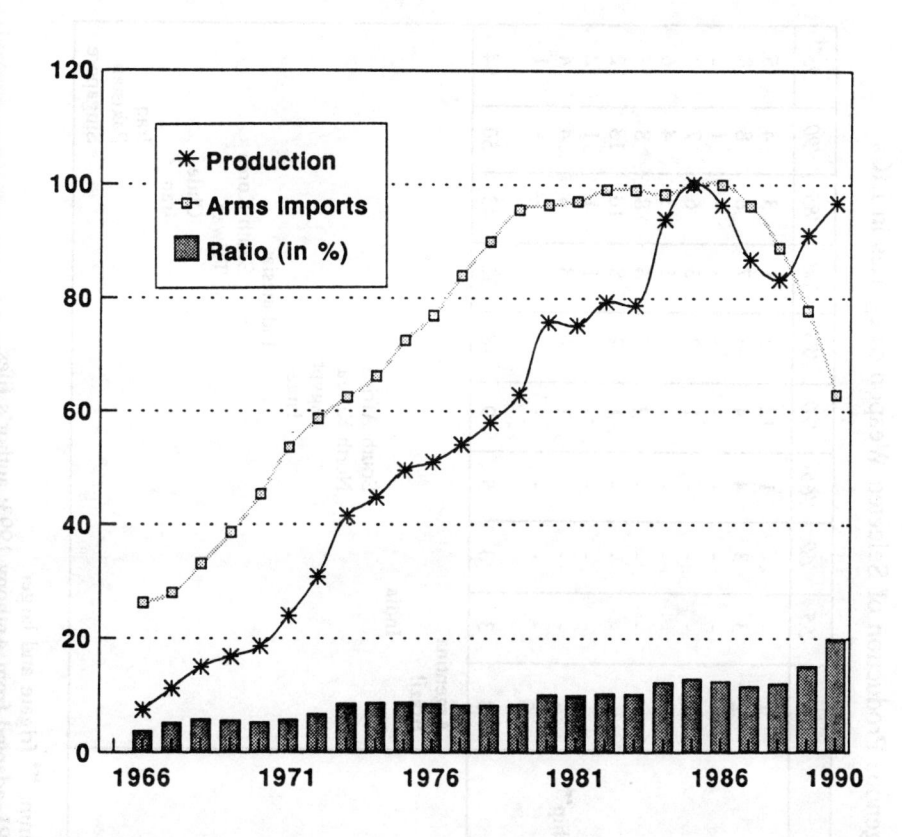

Source: SIPRI.

Table 1: Indigenous Production of Selected Weapon categories in LICs

	1950	'55	'60	'65	'70	'75	'80	'85	'90	'95*
Jet aircraft	1	-	-	1	12	2	1	3	4	5
Propellor aircraft	2	3	3	4	4	6	7	8	8	8
Helicopters	-	-	-	-	-	-	-	-	1	2
Guided Missiles	-	-	-	-	1	2	5	6	7	8
Main battle tanks	-	-	-	-	-	-	1	3	4	6
Armored vehicles	-	-	-	-	2	5	6	8	8	7
Large-calibre artillery**	-	-	-	-	1	2	8	10	13	12
Stand-alone radar	-	-	-	-	-	-	1	1	1	2
Large modern surface warship***	-	-	-	-	1	1	3	4	4	4
Submarines	-	-	-	-	-	-	-	-	-	1
Number of projects	3	3	3	5	9	18	32	43	50	54
Countries involved	Argentina Brazil	India			South Africa North Korea Egypt Israel		Indonesia	South Korea Taiwan Chile Iran		Iraq Pakistan Singapore

* planned; ** over 100mm; *** frigate and larger
Source: Based on SIPRI, adapted from Anthony 1993; author's files.

Table 2: Industrial Manufacturing and Arms Production in LICs, early 1990s

in manufacturing	\multicolumn{7}{c}{*Employment (in thousands) in arms production*}						
	100 and more	50-100	25-50	10-25	5-10	2.5-5	below 2.5
5,000 and more	India						
2,500-5,000		North Korea*	Brazil South Korea Taiwan				
1,000-2,500		South Africa Egypt	Indonesia	Argentina	Thailand		Mexico
500-1,000			Iran Pakistan		Philippines Malaysia		

Table 2 (continued)

Employment (in thousands)

in manufacturing	in arms production					
	100 and more	50-100	25-50	10-25	5-10	2.5-5	below 2.5
250-500		Israel				Algeria	Bangladesh Colombia Venezuela Sri Lanka Nigeria
				Singapore	Peru		
below 250**				Chile	Iraq	Syria Saudi Arabia	Cameroon

* rough estimate; ** reporting in table limited to countries with limited arms production.
Source: based on SIPRI, adapted from Wulf 1993, 14-15; UNIDO, Industry and Development, 1992; author's files.

Table 3: Selected Components of the Korean Type 88 Main Battle Tank

Design of the tank	General Dynamics, USA
Composite armour	General Dynamics, USA
Commander's sight	SFIM, France, now manufactured by Samsung in Korea
Auxiliary sight	Kollmorgen, USA
Laser rangefinder	Hughes Aircraft, USA
Gunner's sight	Hughes Aircraft/Texas Instruments, USA, component production by Hyundai in Korea
Ballistics computer	Control Data, Canada, now manufactured in Korea
Tank gun	US-designed M68A1, German designed 120mm smoothbore on trial
Machine guns	Browning, USA
Smoke discharger	British Aerospace, UK
Transmission	ZF, Germany, now manufactured in Korea
Engine	MTU, Germany, now manufactured in Korea

Source: *Jane's Armour and Artillery.*

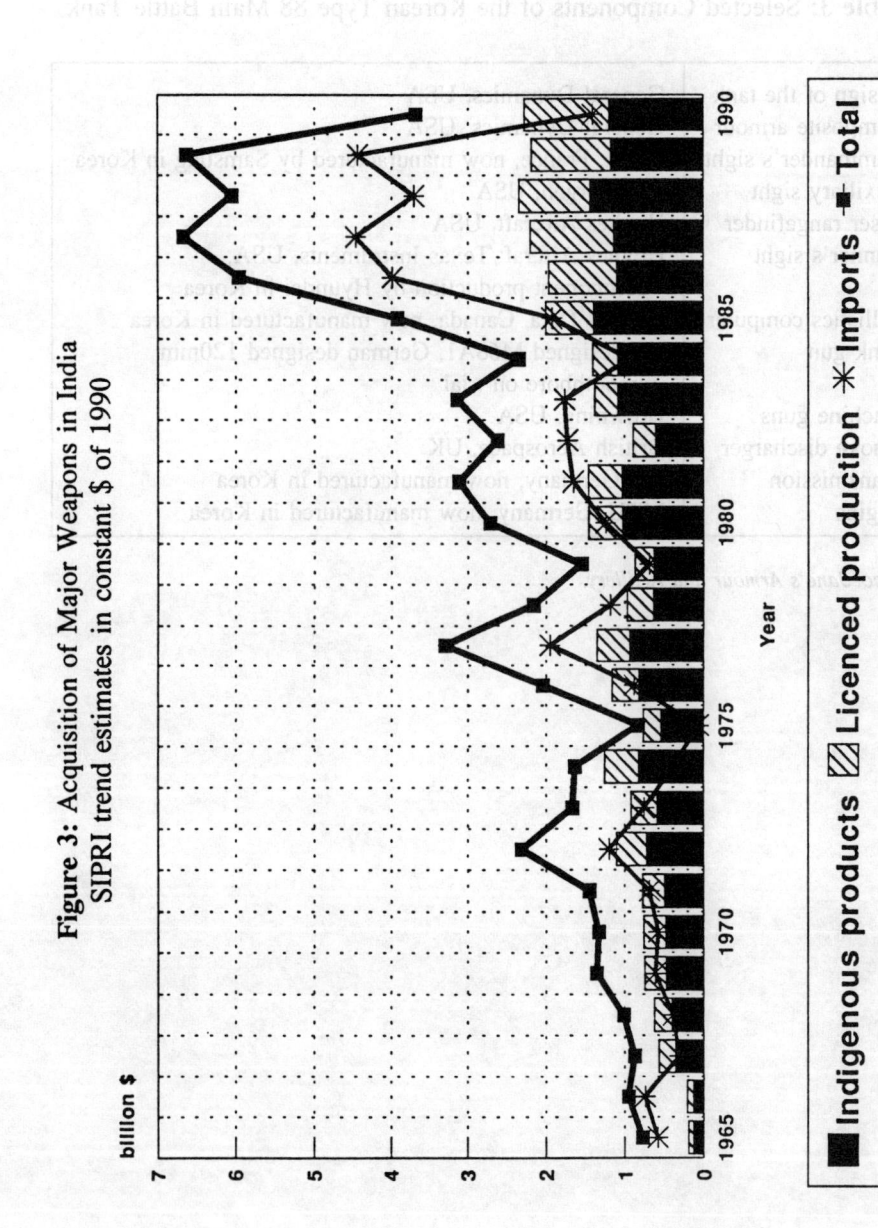

Figure 3: Acquisition of Major Weapons in India
SIPRI trend estimates in constant $ of 1990

■ Indigenous products ▨ Licenced production ✳ Imports ■- Total

Source: SIPRI.

Figure 4: Arms Sales by LICs
US government estimate in constant 1992 $

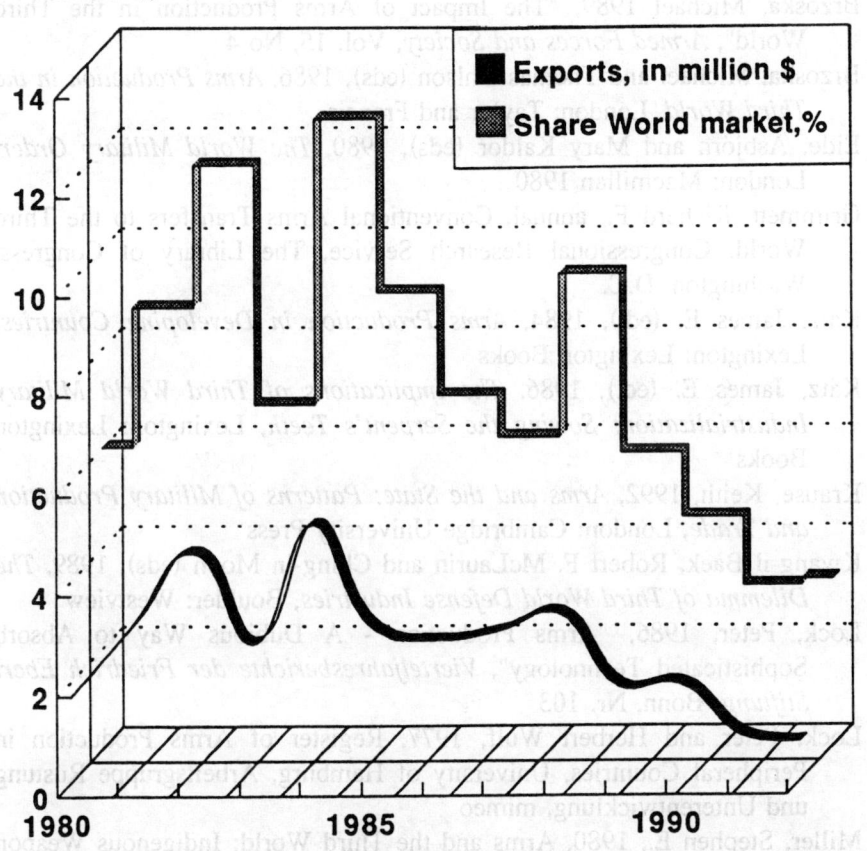

Source: US government as reported in Grimmett 1986, 1993.

Bibliography

Anthony, Ian 1993, "The 'Third Tier' Countries: Production of Major Weapons", in: *Wulf* 1993
Brzoska, Michael 1989, "The Impact of Arms Production in the Third World", *Armed Forces and Society*, Vol. 15, No 4
Brzoska, Michael and Thomas Ohlson (eds), 1986, *Arms Production in the Third World*, London: Taylor and Francis
Eide, Asbjörn and Mary Kaldor (eds), 1980, *The World Military Order*, London: Macmillan 1980
Grimmett, Richard F., annual, Conventional Arms Transfers to the Third World. Congressional Research Service, The Library of Congress, Washington, D.C.
Katz, James E. (ed.), 1984, *Arms Production in Developing Countries*, Lexington: Lexington Books
Katz, James E. (ed.), 1986, *The Implications of Third World Military Industrialization: Sowing the Serpent's Teeth*, Lexington: Lexington Books
Krause, Keith, 1992, *Arms and the State: Patterns of Military Production and Trade*, London: Cambridge University Press
Kwang-il Baek, Robert F. McLaurin and Ching-in Moon (eds), 1989, *The Dilemma of Third World Defense Industries*, Boulder: Westview
Lock, Peter, 1986, "Arms Production - A Dubious Way to Absorb Sophisticated Technology", *Vierteljahresberichte der Friedrich Ebert Stiftung*, Bonn, Nr. 103
Lock, Peter and Herbert Wulf, 1977, Register of Arms Production in Peripheral Countries, University of Hamburg, Arbeitsgruppe Rüstung und Unterentwicklung, mimeo
Miller, Stephen E., 1980, Arms and the Third World: Indigenous Weapon Production, Graduate Institute of International Studies, PSIS Occasional Paper 3, Geneva
Neuman, Stephanie, 1984, "International Stratification and Third World Military Industries", *International Organisation*, Vol. 38, No 1
Office of Technology Assessment (OTA), United States Congress, 1991, *Global Arms Trade*, Washington, D.C.: US Government Printing Office
Ross, Andrew L. (ed.), 1991, *The Political Economy of Defense: Issues and Perspectives*, New York: Greenwood Press

Sanders, Ralph, 1990, *Arms Industries: New Suppliers and Regional Security*, Washington, D.C.: National Defense University Press

SIPRI (Stockholm International Peace Research Institute), 1971, *The Arms Trade with the Third World* Stockholm: Almqvist and Wicksell

SIPRI (Stockholm International Peace Research Institute), annually, *SIPRI Yearbook. World Armaments and Disarmament*, London: Oxford University Press

UNIDO (United Nations Industrial Development Organization), annual, Industry and Development, Vienna: UNIDO

Wulf, Herbert, 1980, *Rüstungsimport als Technologietransfer*, München: Weltforum

Wulf, Herbert (ed.), 1993, *Arms Industry Limited*, London: Oxford University Press

Chapter 3
Conventional Arms Transfers Patterns

Ian Anthony

It is useful to begin by sketching what these major conventional weapons consist of. There is now a confusing proliferation of different types of discussion within the overall debate, and a proliferation of statistics also. What I am talking about are international transfers of major platforms, things which are unambiguously military like fighter aircraft, main battled tanks, warships, and these kinds of systems.

This Chapter is essentially devoted to three points: to sketch the current pattern of the international transfers of major conventional weapon systems, to try to take a slightly more forward-looking picture of how things might develop over the medium term in the market, and thirdly to try and look at the implications of what seems to be the growing domination of the United States within the market for major conventional platforms.

I - Current Pattern

From the late 1940's to the current 1990's, the global arms trade was dominated by two Super-Powers, who used arms transfers to support their foreign security policies in the framework of the Cold War. One of the key determinants now in looking at the structure of the market is who can pay. That is a recent development. If you look at the period of the Cold War, the level of wealth that a country had was not a particular determinant of their place in the international arms trade system. Some of the most important bilateral arms transfer relationships were with countries that were clearly poor: Cuba, Afghanistan etc...

With the collapse of first the Warsaw Treaty organization, and then the dissolution of the Soviet Union, this political ideological element of the trade has been taken out of the international arm trade system. The consequence of this has been that the volume of transfer has shrunk dramatically. There has been a reduction in many cases of termination of transfers between the four members of the Warsaw Treaty Organisation. Many of the bi-lateral relationships which were extremely important during the Cold War period are now over, though it is true to say that we are seeing the opening of some new bi-lateral relationships which in the period of the Cold War were impossible for ideological or political reasons. The most important of those is the relationship between Russia and China, but there are other examples; sales from Russia to Turkey, for example; co-operation between the Czech Republic and Israel on military aircraft programmes. All of these are things which five or six years ago would have been unimaginable. While the global arms market is becoming increasingly complex, some of its features are agreed by the various people who look at these things.

What are the "robust" findings, of the people who survey the market? The first is that among the exporters the United States has now become predominant largely because of the extraction from the system of the former USSR. This is not an indication in itself that US exports have grown dramatically. In fact if you disregard the estimated data and you look at the official data from the United States the overall volume of transfers has actually been remarkably stable over the last few years: that is if you measure deliveries. There has not been a dramatic rise in the volume or value of US deliveries of major conventional weapons. If you look at the first of the Figures that was circulated, the most interesting finding is the percentage share of the overall share of the market for major conventional weapons. The most interesting feature is the bottleneck which occurs around 1991, something which is created by this growth of the US share of the market. But if you look at the period 1991 to 1993, what you find is a stabilisation in that part of the chart which is accounted for by Russia.

It is reasonable to conclude that although it is a much less important player than it was during the period of the Cold War, Russia is nevertheless going to continue to be an important factor in the international arms market. It is less important but it has not gone away. Another interesting finding is that the share of the trade accounted for by the West European countries, the most important of them being France, Germany and the UK, is reasonably stable, but if you turn to Figure 2 and take a look, what you find there is that in the period after 1990 there is an important shift in the proportion of sales from Western Europe with the traditionally most important producer, France, having a shrinking share of the overall volume of deliveries, and Germany having a significantly increased share in the West European sales. Another interesting subtext to the Figure is the top level which is the other EU producers, just to indicate that there are other West European manufacturers who do have a significant defence industrial capacity. Of those the most important are the Netherlands, Spain and Italy. This question of the pattern of transfers from Western Europe is one that will be discussed later on.

If you look at the major importers, what you find is that there is a similar concentration in the global market, whereas it is true to say that a small number of exporters dominate. Equally there are only around 25 to 30 countries which constitute the market for major conventional weapons. Of the 182 States in the world what we are really talking about when we talk about the arms trade is the activities of around 25 to 30 countries. If you turn to Figure 3, it suggests that the regional distribution of these importers has also changed in a significant way. If you look at the period after 1987 to 1988 you see a significant reduction in the volume of deliveries to the Middle East. You see a significant increase in the importance of Asian and a slightly less significant increase in the importance of European customers for major conventional platforms. It is not a particularly mysterious development; it coincides with the end of the Iran-Iraq war.

In 1984 there were no CSCE countries among the ten largest recipients of major conventional weapons. By 1993, three CSCE countries, Greece, Turkey and Hungary together accounted for 15% of total aggregate deliveries. So the South-Eastern part of the CSCE, the area which is including the Balkans and the southern area adjacent to the new republics which have emerged of the former USSR, has become a significant market for major conventional weapons.

II - Medium Term Prospects

Another question is to take a slightly more forward-looking view of the market and suggest ways it might change over the medium term. The medium term means the next five years because in this context that is reasonably predictable. Once you get beyond that then we are becoming more speculative.

The recent past has been characterised by sudden and dramatic shifts in the international system as we noted in the above. The arms trade has felt the full impact of this change in the international system. So to what extent has this dramatic shift and the turbulence that it has created begun to stabilise? Some of the factors which are transient are beginning to come to an end. The demilitarisation of Germany, for example, is a process that is likely to be over in the next two or three years. As a result those transfers which were associated with the implementation of the CFE Treaty and those transfers which are associated with the withdrawal of US forces from Europe and the disposal of surplus equipment will also come to an end in the next two years. It is predictable that this is going to lead to a further reduction in the overall volume of the trade.

The war fought in 1991 between Iraq and an international coalition of States not only removed Iraq from the global market for major conventional weapons, but it also stimulated a significant number of transfers of major weapons into Israel, Kuwait, Saudi Arabia and to a lesser extent, the smaller Gulf States. Had it not been for that the reduction in the overall trade would have been even more significant. Again most transfers which were associated directly with the conflict are nearly over. It is another factor which is likely to lead to a further downward pressure on deliveries of major conventional systems.

Another development is tending to exert a downward pressure on the volume of trade in major platforms is a shift in secondary centres of arms production away from Europe to Asia. But these are the countries which have both the financial resources and the technical capacities in their civilian industries to produce these weapons successfully. Outside this area in East Asia it is a very open question whether other countries have those kinds of financial resources and technical capacity. But these are the countries which are over the next ten to fifteen years expected to represent a significant proportion of global aggregate demand.

If we put together these two things, the shift in secondary centres of arms production and the fact that more and more countries are going to be relying on those systems already in their inventory to make up the largest part of their armed forces, then it is predictable that two things are going to happen. First of all there is going to be a stimulation of the already observable trend towards retrofits and modernisation instead of sales of major platforms. Countries are going to be introducing new technologies to old platforms to try and upgrade the combat power of platforms without paying the full costs of a new system. This is something that has been discussed over the last five or six years and this is a trend which is robust and clear. Another clear trend is likely to be the transfers of production technologies and recipient countries insisting that as a condition of entering into bi-lateral arms transfer relationships they receive the capabilities to produce the major systems themselves. We are here talking about East Asia.

If we look at a slightly less certain but more long-term trend the question is whether countries in East Asia which have relatively limited domestic demand for major weapons systems can establish these production capacities and maintain them over the longer term without being subject to very significant commercial pressures to look for export markets. It seems unlikely that the countries of East Asia are ever going to occupy a position in the global arms market comparable to the position which they already occupy in the global market for civilian durables. But it is clear that they are going to occupy a more important place in the market for major conventional weapons than they do now.

What are some other factors which might be predicted to lead to uncertainties in the future demand for major conventional weapons? In other words, most of the things mentioned herewith tend to depress demand for major platforms. Are there things which are likely to increase demand? Probably yes. One is that the arms trade is currently characterised by a lack of purchasing power. That does not necessarily correlate to a lack of demand. There are countries, many in central Europe, others in the Middle East who have their inventories built around Soviet weapons, and who would very much like to shift the nature of their inventories to at least a more diverse structure, and preferably move away from dominance of Soviet systems altogether. If they are going to do that it is going to depend upon large-scale imports. So the question is, if countries like Poland, the Czech Republic, Hungary or some other Middle Eastern countries experience significant and sustained growth, will that transfer into increased orders for major weapons platforms? A very good case can be made that it will. If you look at the position of a country like Hungary, for example, at the first opportunity they had in their bi-lateral relationship with Russia, the thing that they were interested to acquire was the Mig-29.

Finally there is a need to come back to a question which is whether this category of conventional major conventional weapon platforms is losing its utility as a barometer of the international arms trade. It is a question you have to think about quite a lot. Is there any utility in expanding the definitions of major conventional weapons even if you have the technical possibilities to do it? The systems which are currently defined as major conventional weapons resemble in many ways the categories which were employed in the CFE Treaty. They go slightly beyond that, but in many ways they resemble those categories. Now you can have a very long and interesting academic debate about whether or not those categories are sufficient for the tasks that they were set, which was to restrict the capacity of countries to launch major cross-border offensive operations. But the fact is that there is the group of systems around which we have a political consensus. So that is the group of systems on which people who are interested in making decisions about control are almost obliged to focus, because if they go beyond that they are committing themselves to an open-ended discussion over what constitutes offensive/defensive military capabilities. And that is an open-ended discussion which could lead to a long and unproductive set of discussions, but could also lead to an unravelling of the whole idea of multilateral conventional arms control.

So while from an academic point of view it is an exciting new era to discuss different arms control possibilities, one should not lose sight of the fact that the historical approach to conventional arms control in Europe worked. It led to a treaty which is now being implemented. However, there is a case to be made for considering whether or not the categories can be supplemented by looking at some of the systems which do appear to make a key contribution to offensive operations. There is now the possibility of a secondary market developing for things which in the past have never been traded. Military satellites, for example, are not currently traded, but you do see rumours and possibilities based on government to government negotiations of sales of US military reconnaissance satellites to countries like the United Arab Emirates, South Korea and Spain. You also see a secondary market even for images taken from commercial satellites. It is a very open question whether this is something that can reasonably be included in control discussions, but in terms of monitoring the changing nature of the trade, that is something worth looking at.

III - Implications of the US Domination of the Market

Finally the issue of the implications of the increased US dominance of the international trade in major conventional weapons. The first point to be made is that the US dominates some specific sectors in the international trade: fixed-wing aircraft, especially combat aircraft over the size of jet trainers: helicopters and a broad category of air defence systems. Those are really the areas where the US dominates. Those are in many ways the areas which many people argue are crucial to operational success in these large-scale military operations which have been the focus of conventional arms control. Other sectors like naval systems really cross the board, although the fact that the US navy is decommissioning such a large number of major warships and is prepared to lease or give them to friendly States may change that, but at least naval systems and land systems are areas where there is a much more diverse set of suppliers and the US does not really dominate the market.

What are the political implications of this? It seems that most major US transfers are linked to security relationships. These can be, and often are, formal relationships such as treaty-based alliances. In other cases they are politically binding bi-lateral arrangements. To the extent that these relationships are sustained, the arms transfer relationships are going to be sustained. It seems unimaginable that the US would have formal alliance with a country like Japan or South Korea or any or any of its European allies, and say, well we are allies but we are sorry, you cannot have any major conventional systems. But it is worth the US administration in its review of arms export policy, which we are told is at the early stages, considering whether the fact that they have commitments to allies means that they are obliged to give allies everything and anything that they demand. One may have some concerns about that. If you look at some of the countries which everybody now focuses on as the potential areas which will lead to problems: the Korean peninsula, south-eastern Europe, essentially those countries that border on Turkey, there are some questions about whether the US has responsibilities not only to its allies, but also to some of the other countries in the region. An unfortunate development which is being taken up with some gusto by the US administration in the formulation of a new follow-on to COCOM is the division of the world into two sets of States, us and them, and them is a very small number of States consisting of probably five or six. The criteria for their selection is not exactly clear, but I am sure we all know who they are: North Korea, Libya, Syria, Iran and Iraq.

The question which is worth addressing is whether it is sensible to continue meeting the demands of allies which border on those problem States without taking into consideration the fact that the small States which are now identified as the problem share several characteristics; they are poor; they have been cut off from their major supplier of conventional weapons and they are clearly being targeted as the major problems in international security. If you were a decision-maker in one of those countries, and you could see your neighbours accelerating away from you in economic development, in their integration into the global economy. If you felt surrounded and you could see your neighbours being armed with these sorts of major conventional weapons; what would you do? It is not difficult to understand what the motivations for the acquisition of weapons of mass destruction are. And it would be useful if the US administration, in looking at its conventional arms transfer policy, consider the implications for these broader questions of the linkage of conventional and unconventional military capabilities.

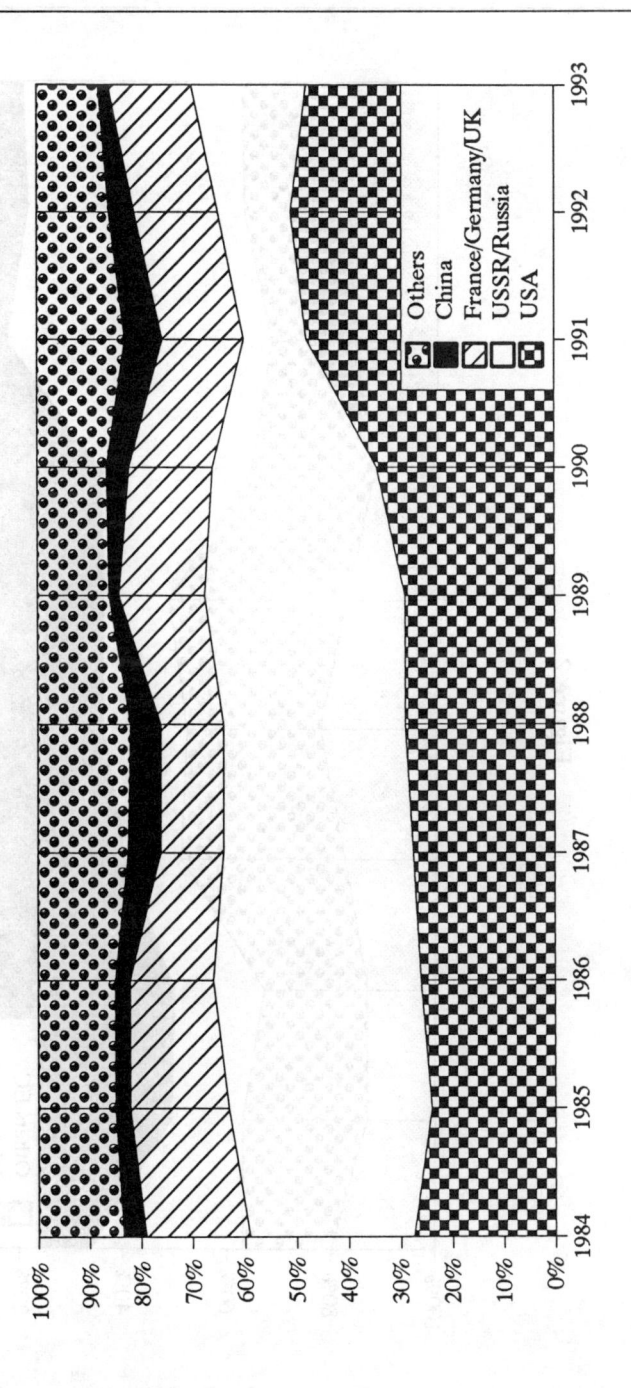

Conventional Arms Transfers Patterns

Figure 1

Figure 2

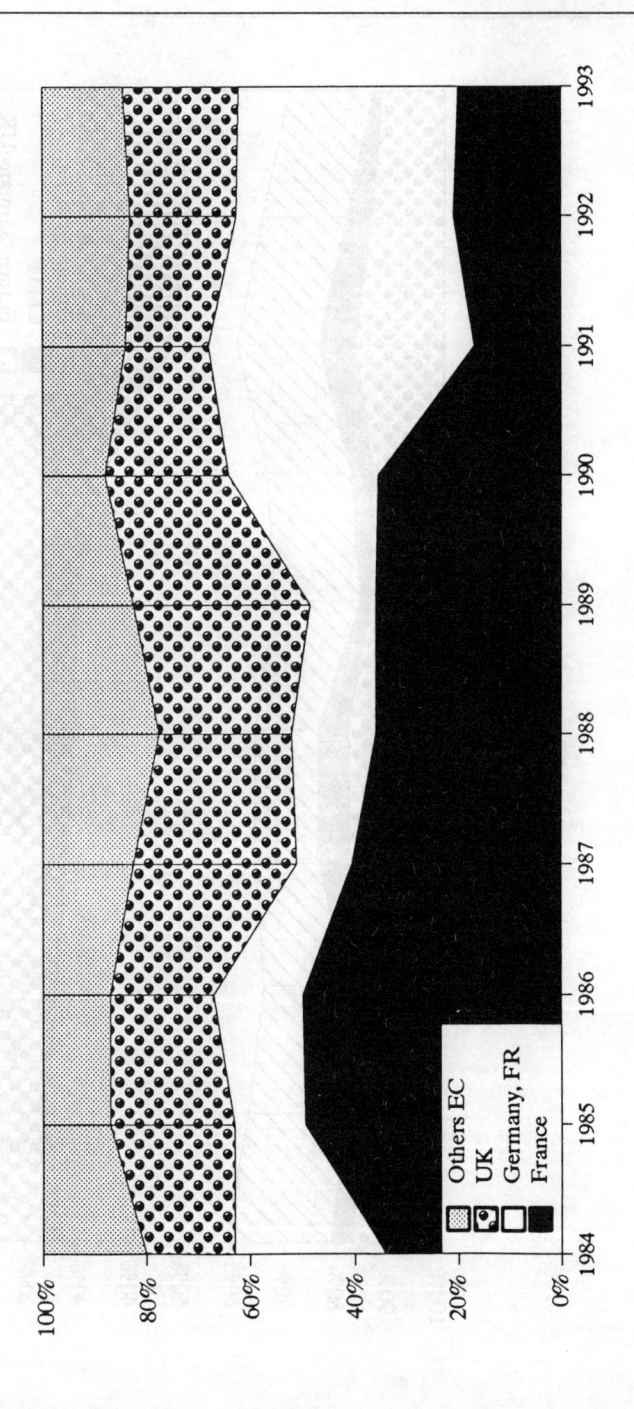

Figure 3

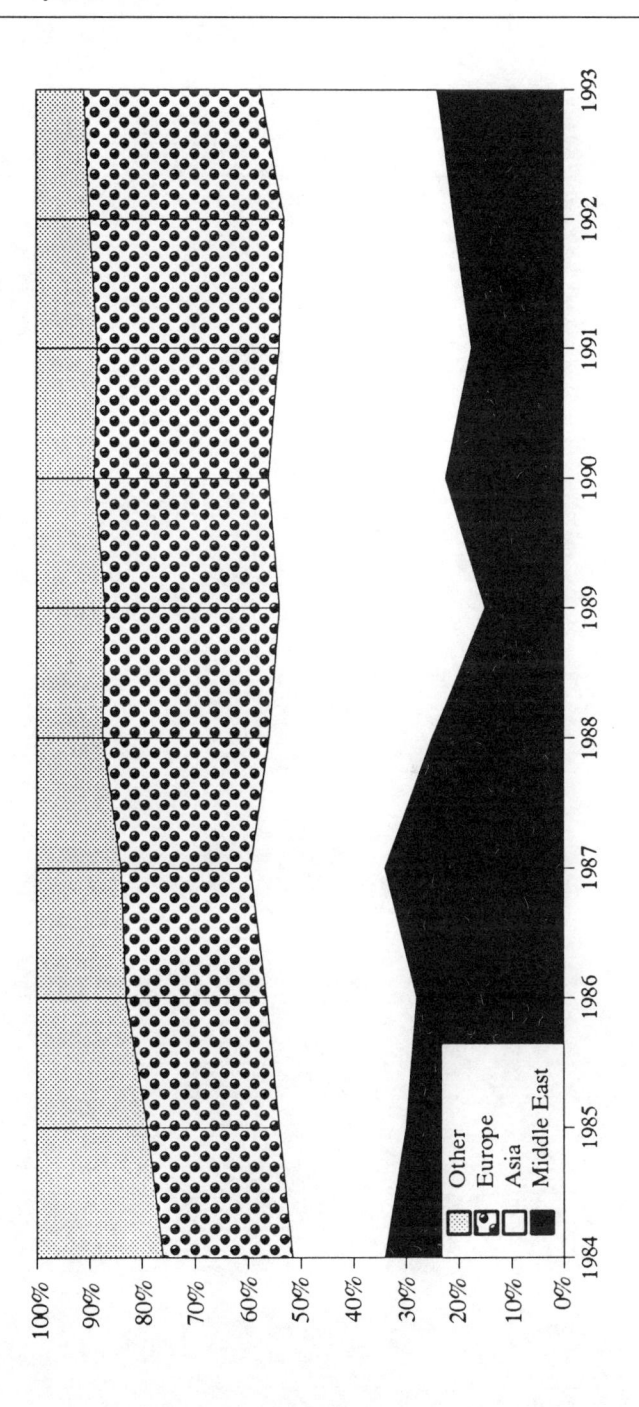

Chapter 4
Advanced Conventional Weapon Sales Offerings

David Markov

The previous presenters did an excellent job presenting the United States and Western Europeans as major exporters of weaponry. This Chapter will deal with the other major exporters of weaponry: the Chinese, the Israelis and, particularly, the Russians. This presentation is not based on a formal study or finished analysis but represents opportunities to speak with several of the world's premier aerospace representatives about their problems and their future hopes in the international arms market. In addition, this is not just a reflection of a few international defence industries. It is a wide coverage of a number of arms exporting countries as seen at three major arms shows held in Paris, France; Moscow, Russia; and Dubai, United Arab Emirates. These arms shows were highlighted by flight demonstrations, numerous static air/space displays, and a large number of trade show pavilions that displayed an unprecedented array of models and literature on sophisticated space platforms, fighters, advanced conventional munitions, surface-to-air missiles (SAMs), and armored vehicles. The results of these and previous interchanges form the heart of this presentation. With that in mind, this presentation will look at three questions which must be raised when looking at the recent flurry of activity in the international arms market in advanced conventional munitions: What has changed in the world to make advanced conventional weapons more accessible? What weapons are being offered on the world market as displayed at world arms shows? And finally, what are the implications of these weapons for the world market, particularly for the UN and its coalition forces in a future conflict?

I - What Has Changed in the International Arms Market?

There has been a fundamental transformation in the international arms market characterized by a number of emerging trends. The relationship between arms exporters and the demand for arms has changed dramatically between the 1980s to the 1990s. Do these current patterns represent a durable change in the nature of the market, or are they a temporary anomaly which will again shift as regional conflicts continue to erupt? Although the dominant market position of the United States will probably continue for the foreseeable future, several countries are taking measures to remain viable competitors and to erode the US market share.

Demand

The demand in conventional arms has steadily declined since 1987, falling by 50 percent within the last five years alone. Fundamental changes in the international arms market, especially in the 1980s and continuing through the 1990s, have allowed this to happen. Trends observed in the 1980s and 1990s and forecast for the year 2000, are illustrated below:

- 1980s: Cold War military spending a high priority punctuated by several significant wars (e.g., Iraq, Iran, Afghanistan, and Angola).
- 1990s: Reduced defence spending due to post-Cold War downsizing with regional conflicts (e.g., Bosnia and Somalia) smaller in scale than 1980s conflicts
- 2000: Regional pressure will continue to increase and may manifest itself in larger regional arms purchases.

Unlike the 1980s, which saw many large-scale regional wars, the 1990s have so far seen a reduction in demand for arms due, in part, to the lack of such conflicts. Whereas the 1980s could be characterized as the "arms acquisition" decade, typified by high technology weapons systems being the primary investment priority for many nations rather than domestic infrastructure requirements, the 1990s has been characterized by spending declines stemming from post-Cold War downsizing around the world. The United States and several of its European partners are reducing forces to comply with limits established by the Conventional Armed Forces in Europe (CFE) Treaty. There is also a reduction of demand for new equipment as a number of countries have been eliminating or selling surplus capability.

In contrast, a number of countries perceived some benefits that could be gained by building their own armaments. First, it would be harder for them to be cut off by an embargo if they had an indigenous production capability. Secondly, there was profit to be made. The Iran-Iraq war demonstrated that money could be made by selling arms to either one or both of the two conflicting parties. As a result, a number of countries began to export their indigenous production (*i.e.*, China, North Korea, Israel, and Brazil to name a few). Finally, because of this proliferation of suppliers, customers are now demanding more from each sale than they had in the past. This is amply illustrated by the growing demand of potential customers for co-production rights, trainers, simulators, and extensive warranties to close recent deals. This trend will likely continue and will greatly strain the ability of many arms suppliers to comply.

The turn of the century will probably see regional pressures increasing, and these pressures may manifest themselves in larger regional arms acquisitions. This trend will be reinforced by a couple of lessons learned during the current period. First, the Bosnia crisis has illustrated to countries around the world that the UN cannot provide security guarantees or protection. Secondly, it has been demonstrated that it takes some period of time for the UN to establish a consensus in order to finally take action. A number of countries have observed this pattern and are seriously considering arms purchases and security arrangements which guarantee short-term regional stability based on an ability to defend one's interest. On the other hand, UN coalition response to the Iraqi invasion of Kuwait created an unprecedented international consensus around the idea that the accumulation of advanced weapon systems can be a major factor in the outbreak, conduct, and termination of armed conflict. Whether this conflict was a clear example of such accumulation being destabilizing and leading to negative consequences even for the major powers is unclear at this point.

Suppliers

In the early 1980s there were fewer suppliers of arms and weapons technologies than in the 1990s. Another feature of the 1980s was the ability of the suppliers to dictate the kinds of technology sold and the terms of the sale. However, many regional players such as China, Israel, Brazil, and Turkey, which developed large-scale defence production capacities during the 1980s, became mature industries and began to focus attention on large-scale exports by the 1990s. Hence, there has been an increase in the supply of armaments on the world market. This situation means that customers in the 1990s dictate the terms of the sale.

Two trends greatly effecting the United States, Western Europe, and Russia are the Conventional Armed Forces in Europe (CFE) Treaty reductions and post-Cold War downsizing. The effects of these trends is to increase the pressure to export. For example, Secretary of Commerce Ronald Brown noted that the United States needs to sell weaponry overseas in order to convert our defence industrial complex to civilian uses. Similarly, Russian President Boris Yeltsin and other individuals such as the Russian First Deputy Defence Minister, Andre Kokoshin, have also stated that Russia needs to sell weapons overseas to convert. Thus, pressures developed that have resulted in the current trend toward selling the best weaponry at the lowest prices. This trend likely will continue for at least the next five to ten years.

Countries around the world are trying to convert their excess defence industrial capacity and hope to use the revenue from arms sales, in some cases, to fund their own defence conversion efforts. Countries such as Israel, Russia, China, and many Western Europeans are taking extraordinary measures to make sales and to maintain a viable defence industrial base while converting excess capacity. This is a core objective for many indigenous producers and their governments.

What is happening today is that customers are starting to dictate, in a way they did not five years ago, what will be sold, what the terms of the sale will be, and what co-production agreements will be required. This situation will likely continue to develop and to expand in future arms deals. If you have a client base which is demanding certain kinds of weapons, and that is the only kind of weapons that they are willing to buy, it is a real challenge to the sellers to offer the kinds of technology that nations want to buy.

We are out of the mode of having a large-scale arms trade based on the transfer of thousands of heavily armored vehicles. We are more into the mode of selling or upgrading a small number of sophisticated technologies and weaponry. Weapons like anti-tactical ballistic missiles systems and long-range anti-radiation missiles are being offered for sale rather than of large numbers of "antiquated technologies" like older Russian T-55 and T-54 main battle tanks.

The collapse of the Former Soviet Union (FSU) has greatly exacerbated many of the trends already noted and will continue to fuel their progress. The Russian central government and defence industries are desperate for the hard currency that could be obtained through arms sales, but they have had lackluster results thus far. Russia may, however, enjoy some success in the international arms market in the short term because it has:

- Lower weapons prices due to lower labor, energy, and material costs;
- Ability to accept barter, loan/debt forgiveness, or other unconventional financing arrangements instead of cash;
- Large existing stockpile of arms or upgraded old weapons;
- Unique technologies and weapons not available anywhere else;
- Lower maintenance and education requirements to operate Russian military equipment.

On the other hand, Russia could continue its poor performance in the international arms market as seen from 1991 to 1993, causing it to:

- Lose scientists, engineers, and factory workers and their "know-how" en masse;
- Offer better levels of technology for sale;
- Sell or transfer intellectual property rights;
- Engage in sales and support of "turn-key" production facilities;
- Dump arms at bargain basement prices to capture a larger market share;
- Form a Russian import-export bank to finance arms sales to small countries.

Russia is interested in forming a safe, stable system of international relations which would be an objective basis for co-operation and development of partnership projects. However, only the Russians believe that it is important not to allow actions from outside to undermine strategic stability and the defence potential of Russia as well as its position in the world armament markets.

The main form of military-technical co-operation for the future will be the export of armaments and military technologies and the performance of corresponding works and services within the framework of interstate agreements. At the same time, in order to increase the market effectiveness and encourage industrial conformance with world standards of quality, the Russians are establishing a system of direct export of production and military services by the defence enterprises themselves, provided that a strong, competent State control and regulation system can be implemented. In short, the introduction of a supplier, like Russia, who must sell its most sophisticated arms at attractive prices to survive could rapidly shift radically change a region's military capabilities and, hence, its stability.

The Influence of Russia on the Cause and Effect Relationships of the New World Order's Arms Market
Cheap, yet technologically sophisticated, weapons become available "for sale." Russia is selling weapons/systems below the international market price. Distortions in Russia's factors of production (labor materials) allow it to do so for some period of time (*i.e.*, Russian industry currently pays 2 cents a kilowatt hour for electricity and $700 a man-year (fully-loaded) for a scientist and/or engineer). ↓ Joint ventures with European, Israeli and US firms provide an infusion of advanced Western technologies into Russia's defence industries. Resulting changes to Russia's arms production make hybrid systems easier and cheaper to obtain/produce and, hence, more difficult to identify and counter. Russia increases its "after-sale" support including logistics and system upgrades. ↓ Some enterprises are more viable and, hence, survive and thrive (*i.e.*, anti-shipping missiles like SS-N-22 *Sunburn* there is no Western equal to this system). Global arms market becomes customer oriented (a real change from the 1980s supply market driven by the wars in Afghanistan, Iran-Iraq, and Angola). More advanced weapons will be placed in the hands of Third World countries; introduction could destabilize regions. (Even the introduction of weapons in small numbers may, in fact, have no real impact on US forces, but could draw the US into a conflict by the perception of threat to the regional players. This action could promote regional arms races, like the introduction of Su-27 *Flanker* into China which has resulted in Taiwan and Malaysia buying new combat aircraft or the introduction of 3 Iranian *Kilo* submarines on the Persian Gulf States drove new requirements for ASW equipment.)

Advanced Conventional Weapon Sales Offerings

> Global arms markets are becoming more competitive than in the 1980s when the introduction of Russian "hedge" technologies into the marketplace drove the suppliers to offer higher levels of technology to stay competitive.
>
> ↓
>
> US influence on the market will likely decline (*i.e.*, Missile Technology Control Regime [MCTR], etc.).
>
> International agreements will have less impact on international arms control.
>
> US will have to develop new/different systems to counter hybrid aircraft, munitions, electronic warfare systems, armored vehicles, and sensor equipment.

II - What Weapons are Being Offered?

In discussing the kind and scope of weapons currently being offered by Russia and other suppliers to prospective clients at international arms shows, there are two very broad arms categories: new weapons systems and upgraded or modified weapons. Both new and older weapon systems range in kind from sophisticated front-line combat aircraft all the way to simple infantry-based small arms. It is also interesting to note that there is a trend toward assembling hybrid systems which mix sturdy eastern weapon frames with western electronics or avionics.

Several examples of the kind and scope of arms currently on the market will now be discussed. What is for sale? Basically, everything is for sale. From aircraft to SAMs to *Scuds*, there is a provider of that kind of technology trying to sell it. In addition, arms exporting countries are no longer selling the stripped-down export versions of weaponry. Arms exporting countries are now selling the best, first line equipment that they have to offer. In some cases, they are even offering identification friend and foe (IFF) technology and electronic warfare equipment which in the past was usually restricted for overseas sales. An additional point is that countries are now not only selling the first line of air frames, but they are also selling technologies that they have only begun to introduce into their own service. An example of this trend is the Russian *Zhuk* radar (similar to the US F/A-18 and F-16 radar) which is designed for use in the MiG-29M *Fulcrum* multi-role fighter. It is a brand new development program which the Russian Mikoyan Design Bureau is now offering to retrofit to existing MiG-29s worldwide. Again, countries are not only selling sophisticated air-delivered munitions, they are also selling excellent radars needed to employ them. The clear trend is that better, more precise conventional munitions will be used on older aircraft platforms already in the inventories of importing nations.

Ballistic missiles that are under the limits specified by the MTCR are also being offered for sale. For example, the Russian SS-21 *Scarab*, a short-range ballistic missile priced at $1.3 million, was fired at the February 1993 Dubai Air Show to show clients that this system, in fact, can hit targets and has significant military capabilities.

Both the Russian central government and their defence industries are using arms sales as a way to convert their industries into other product lines. The Russians are doing whatever it takes to make arms sales a trend that will continue in the near future. It is amazing that a number of articles in *Jane's Defense Weekly* and *International Defense Review* continue to report that prices on MiG-29s and other similar aircraft product lines continue to fall. For example, the Russian MiG-29S (an uprated multi-role fighter aircraft) is being offered at $12 million a copy. Reported prices have been cited in such articles as low as $9 million per aircraft.

In the case of Russia, the Su-35 *Flanker*, a large air-superiority aircraft, is being marketed vigorously in the Middle East market. In fact, the Russians are said to be looking for foreign partners to finish the development of its weapons systems that were started under the former Soviet Union, not only to raise hard currency, but also to reestablish their failing arms trade and to bring in desperately needed western currency and technology.

It is just not Russia. It is also countries like Sweden who have recently signed a deal with British Aerospace to market the JaS-39 *Gripen* fighter aircraft along with the British *Tornado* deep interdiction aircraft and the European Fighter Aircraft (EFA) when it comes along in the late 1990s. China has also been a very aggressive marketer of combat aircraft. The Chinese F-7 fighter aircraft (a MiG-21 copy) is purported to have been sold to the Iranians. Pakistan has also expressed an interest in this aircraft with western avionics, according to western publications.

Also of note is the A-50 *Mainstay*. This aircraft is the Russian equivalent of the US E-3 Boeing *Sentry* AWACS. This is an aircraft that can be used to command and control an air battle and to vector aircraft against an incoming air threat. Again, this aircraft was displayed at the Moscow Air Show which was held in 1992 and then again in September 1993. Also displayed was the MiG-31 *Foxhound* which is an advanced air defence fighter roughly equivalent to the US F-14 *Tomcat* in its ability to fire long-range missiles against cruise missiles and bomber targets.

An aircraft which has generated an immense amount of speculation regarding its sale is the TU-22M3 *Backfire*, a medium-range bomber. Rumors abound regarding its sale to Iran and China. Publicly, the Russians have denied that this aircraft is being offered, yet the Russians have said at other times that they, in fact, are offering this aircraft on the world market. As a further complication, the Ukrainians are making a real effort to sell their TU-22M3 *Backfire* inventory; it is not clear whether or not this will cause other countries like the Russians, who have *Backfire* inventories, to offer their supersonic bomber aircraft inventory on the world market as well. Apparently, the primary motive of the Ukraine is to eliminate surplus aircraft capacity in order to raise much needed revenues and to comply with the CFE aircraft limitations.

Regarding aircraft modernization efforts, two primary platforms are being targeted by a number of countries' aircraft defence industries: the Russian MiG-21 *Fishbed* and the US F-5 *Freedom Fighter*, both are short-range multi-role aircraft. The India aircraft company Hindustan Aeronautics, Israeli Aircraft Industries (IAI), and the Russian Mikoyan Design Bureau all have expressed interest in upgrading the MiG-21.

To date, the Israeli Aircraft Industries have the most robust MiG-21 upgrade program called MiG-21 "2000". They are currently substantially upgrading 100 MiG-21s for the Romanian air defence forces in consortium with a Romanian company called Aerostar with prices that vary between 1 to 4 million dollars for either the MiG-21 or F-5. The IAI upgrade provides the MiG-21 with the ability to fire radar missiles beyond visual range. This is a substantial increase in capability for the MiG-21, thus creating great interest in the MiG-21 upgrade potential by many Eastern European countries who must construct an independent air defence capability in the wake of the vacuum left by the Russian withdrawal from their region. They have few resources to devote to this task.

Not to be outdone by Israeli Aircraft Industries, the Russian aircraft design bureau Mikoyan has also produced their own MiG-21 improvement program, in consortium with Thompson-CSF, called MiG-21 (I-Improved). Thompson-

CSF is a French firm that will provide the signal processing and data processing computer systems to the radar that will be used on this upgrade as well as some other avionics systems to be named later. Thompson's contribution on the MiG-21's upgraded *Kopyo* radar is similar to the US MIL-STD 1533 data processing and signal processing unit designed to improve the radar's total performance.

Countries are not only selling the best platforms, but they are now also selling the best munitions. One example being offered for sale is the Russian air-to-air missile version of the US *AMRAAM* called R-77, or AA-12 in the West. In addition, the Russians are looking for foreign partners to finish development of the next generation of Russian AMRAAM, which utilizes a RAM-jet intake version of the Russian R-77 *AMRAAM*. They are also aggressively seeking foreign partners like Great Britain, Sweden, France or Israel to help co-develop/produce these missile systems.

Likewise, Russia brought to the market unique technologies that no other country is offering for sale. A classic example is the super long-range air-to-air missile, the KS-172. This missile is advertised as having a 400-kilometer range to attack AWACS, airborne refueling aircraft, and JSTARS. Once produced, this missile would be the largest deployed air-to-air missile currently available to any air force in the world. Again, the Russians are advertising for partners to finish development or to, in fact, purchase finished systems.

After the illustrated during the Gulf War, many Third World countries are looking to purchase, if not co-develop or produce themselves, precise guided munitions. Such systems have not been exported overseas by the United States, but the Russians, the French, and the Israelis have been very aggressive in trying to market their own particular smart munitions systems overseas. In addition, many nations are offering cruise missiles like the Russian AS-15 *Kent* (called the Kh-65S by the Russians). This particular missile has an anti-ship warhead designed to go after very large ships at great range.

One particular anti-ship cruise missile system is the SS-N-22 *Sunburn*. Again, there have been numerous reports in publications like *Jane's Defense Weekly* and *Aviation Week and Space Technology* and others that have cited the purported Ukrainian transfer of eight coastal launch versions of these systems to Iran. The SS-N-22 is a large anti-ship missile and currently has the capability that no other system in the world has. This missile is capable of traveling at Mach 3 and has a 705 pound warhead.

The Russians are offering their version of the US *Harpoon* anti-ship cruise missile, called the Kh-35 by the Russians, or SS-N-25 in the West. Again, it can be fired off a number of different platforms. The Chinese are offering an air-launched *Silkworm*, the C-601, while the French have been very aggressive in the marketing of the *Exocet* MM-39 and a new version of the *Exocet* MM-40 anti-ship cruise missiles. Another important trend to note is that it does not take thousands of these precise missile systems to make a difference within a regional conflict. An inventory of 10, 15, or 100 of these missiles can have a devastating impact on a naval engagement, as illustrated by the Falklands War.

At the lower end of conventional weapons are surface-to-air missiles (SAMs) and conventional armor and infantry weapons. The Chinese have been very aggressive in marketing a new main tank called the T-92. The T-92 essentially incorporates Chinese technology but was also done in consortium with a number of American, French, and Western European companies to improve the capabilities of this system and also to make it more affordable to a lot of Third World countries.

On the surface-to-air missile side, again the Russians are exploiting the lesson of *Desert Storm* regarding the need for anti-tactical ballistic missile systems; the Russians are marketing tactical missile defence systems, specifically the SA-10 and the SA-12 (known in Russia as the S-300PMUI and S-300V). The Russians produced a brochure comparing the capabilities of the SA-12 (S-300V) system to engaged ballistic missile systems like *Scud*, picturing debris from a recent *Scud* engagement. Again, the Chinese are also offering their version of the Russian SA-2 called the HQ-2B for sales overseas.

Another interesting trend to note is the offerings of integrated air defence systems that network eastern and western SAMs in one vehicle. Third World countries have learned how difficult it is to integrate diverse weapons systems of both eastern and western origin. The Russian *Bakal* is a vehicle designed to overcome this difficulty. It integrates every currently fielded Russian surface-to-air missile system; moreover, two additional empty channels are provided to integrate within one vehicle C^2 of either the western-based *Patriot*, I-*Hawk*, or *Roland* with all currently fielded eastern SAMs.

One of the arms categories that is experiencing ever smaller transfers is heavy armored vehicles. However, a number of countries are still trying to sell their latest main battle tanks (MBT) overseas. The Russian T-80-U MBT was shown and aggressively marketed at the Dubai Arms Show in February 1993. The Russians are also working to cater these systems to specific regional customers. The T-80U, for example, has a dust recuperator on the back of the turbine engine designed to allow the vehicle to operate within a desert environment.

The Russians are also trying to sell the BMP-3, the world's most heavily armed armored infantry fighting vehicle. The BMP-3 has been sold to the United Arab Emirates and is being offered in several different versions. One of the things which is interesting to note on the UAE's BMP-3s is the Forward Looking Infra Red (FLIR) device attached to the side of the vehicle's turret. This device was designed and installed by a French company called France SEC and was put on the side of a BMP-3 to allow the vehicle to have nightfighting capability. It is purported that the FLIR costs $800,000, and the BMP-3 itself costs $800,000. At $1.6 million this vehicle still represents one of the cheapest, most heavily armed combat vehicles of its type in the world. The Chinese are offering a brand new Type-90 armored vehicle in a number of different configurations for sale around the world.

Another lesson of *Desert Storm* was that the Iraqis learned to fear multiple launch rocket systems (MLRS) which they called "steel rain." A lot of countries are interested in procuring multiple launch rocket systems, the Russians are offering their BM-21 and BM-22 systems, along with other countries, like Brazil with its *Astros II* MLRS system.

A huge variety of specialized small arms are now beginning to be modernized and improved, e.g., Rocket Propelled Grenades (RPGs) and Anti-Tank Guided Weapons (ATGWs). The Russian RPG-7 is currently being fitted with a new tandem-shaped charge designed to defeat reactive armor on new combat vehicles being offered around the world. In addition, several models of Russian ATGWs are being fitted with tandem-shaped charges such as the AT-3, AT-4, AT-5, and AT-7. Also of note is the Russian RPO, a rocket projectile which is essentially a portable fuel-air explosive that was used in Afghanistan against people in caves or in enclosed buildings. In addition, things like Russian Cosmonaut self-defence pistols and Russian AK-47s designed to fire under water for special purpose forces are being offered for sale. Several types of Russian night fighting equipment, flak vests and grenade launchers, which were not available on the world market five years ago, are now being offered publicly at arms shows not only across Russia but also at arms shows in Turkey, United Arab Emirates, Greece, Singapore, Malaysia, Chile, United Kingdom, and France. Again, the Russians are unique in their ability to offer this kind of technology across the board.

III - Implications for the United Nations and Its Members

Finally, what do these changes mean for the United Nations and its members? What are the implications of this technology for today? The first issue is that, clearly, advanced and increasingly sophisticated weapons technologies are being offered for sale and will continue to be offered through the end of this decade. There is a demand for these arms, a demand which is further reinforced by the clear combat effectiveness of these new weapons as vividly demonstrated in the Persian Gulf War. Many countries are looking to buy a limited number of highly capable systems to improve significantly their capabilities in a regional context.

Significant increases in combat effectiveness of old delivery platforms can now be achieved through upgrades or modification programs as illustrated in the MiG-21 aircraft program. The import of these developments is that an even smaller number of these new or upgraded weapons systems could change perceptions within regions where they are acquired. Past history has shown that the United Nations and coalition forces have used these sophisticated weapons against regional powers to great effect. Future regional powers could acquire and use these weapons to similar effect to deter or inflict unacceptable levels of losses against UN or coalition forces. The UN and other forces have been accustomed to having the high technology frontier when imposing peace in the past. In the future we are likely to see the UN being opposed by countries or factions who may be armed with sophisticated technologies and weapons.

The second point is that the low prices of advanced conventional munitions and the modest cost of upgrading or modernization could result in significant improvements in combat capability and in the proliferation of these systems into new regions of the world at modest cost. Although one must never underestimate the ability of training and other factors in determining combat capability, the introduction of new technologies will certainly be an important factor in calculating the combat capability equation in a region. A combination of eastern and western weapons technology hybrids could make sophisticated weapons more affordable to a greater number of nations who operate a mixture of eastern and western weapons.

Potentially, this outcome could mean the introduction of more capable weapons systems into a region where previously no such capability existed. One example of that is an airborne early warning aircraft which was recently sold by Israel to Chile called the *Phalcon* aircraft (a 707 airliner converted to carry a non-steerable phased-array radar). That is the first introduction of a strategic airborne early warning aircraft into Latin America. This trend will continue as countries who thought technology was beyond their grasp begin to look at them seriously as the price of these systems continues to drop and as their effectiveness increases.

Finally, the mechanisms for transferring sophisticated weapons technology are, and will continue to be, more difficult to monitor than were the large arms deals of the 1980s, primarily because of the explosion of small sales worldwide to non-traditional clients. It is becoming increasingly difficult to monitor the flow of sophisticated weapons transfers, and it will be very difficult, if not impossible, to control or restrict such arms transfers in the future.

Chapter 5
Transparency and Beyond in the Arms Trade

Section I: The UN Register of Conventional Arms

Hendrik Wagenmakers

My point of entry is my involvement since 1991 in the Transparency drive of the International Community. Transparency in Armaments (TIA) fell into my lap by chance; the Netherlands assumed the Presidency of the Twelve during the second semester of 1991, when the Twelve introduced a draft for a UNGA-resolution that would provide for the establishment of a UN Register of Transfers of Conventional Arms. The negotiations between the Twelve plus Japan, on the one hand, and the Non-Aligned, on the other, about the text of the enabling GA-Resolution 46/36 L, were complex and tenacious. The resulting resolution certainly does not qualify for a prize in a beauty contest. The main contribution from the Non-Aligned to the original concept of the Twelve and Japan was the widening of the Transparency concept to cover not only transfers, but in due course, holdings and procurement through national production as well. This is so, for the obvious reason that a transfer, as such, does not reveal the aggregate military strength of a particular State which may give concern to its neighbour.

1. The establishment of the UN Register of Conventional Arms, a universal and non-discriminatory instrument, is one of the best things the UN has done these last years. Here, the UN is not just launching verbal attempts at preventing unnecessary and destabilizing accumulations of arms. One of the strong points of the Register is the relative simplicity which pertains to its procedures and definitions, notably its one sheet Standardized Reporting Form.

Government-supplied data concerning imports and exports of seven categories of major conventional weapons platforms, suitable for cross-border offensive actions, can henceforth be the object of bilateral, regional, or even international consultations. Dangerous misperceptions which fuel fear and mistrust can thus be rectified, thanks to Transparency. Nations may feel enabled to exercise restraint and plan their security requirements on the basis of better knowledge.

These remarks are a reflection of an arms control practitioner, it is not a report from a study room. The documentation contains an evaluation of the first year of reporting to the UN Register of Conventional Arms, from Prof. Laurance (Monterey) and Dr Wulf (Duisburg University). The analysis done on the same subject by Prof. Chalmers and Dr Greene of Bradford University also stands out in terms of quality.

In 1992 a Panel of Governmental Technical Experts produced a consensus report on the technical procedures and adjustments to the Annex of Resolution 46/36 L, necessary for the effective operation of the Register. Since that time Transparency and the Register have become objects of consensus in New York.

2. The first time the Register came into action was last year. In fact, the returns from Member States on transfers having taken place during the calendar year 1992 have become available in the consolidated report of the UNSG, of October 1993. In early 1994, a Governmental Experts Group was set up by the UN Secretary-General to review the operation of the UN Register of Conventional Arms and to examine its further development. The Group just held its first session in New York last week. Two more Group sessions will follow later on this year.

The first Group session went relatively well. We were able to avoid procedural wrangling.

In the execution of its mandate concerning the *operation* of the Register, the Group had a first go at an analysis of the returns from Member States on transfers that had taken place during the calendar year 1992. The Group deferred any final judgement on this analysis until the reports for 1993 become available. The main points of this discussion can be summarized as follows:

- The maintenance of simplicity. The Government branches that fill out the forms should be enabled to perform a clear administrative job. The data must be easily accessible. In particular, some simple procedural fixes might help to make the Standardized Reporting Form even more operational. Some adjustments to existing categories might be helpful,

for instance lowering ship tonnage or the inclusion of ground-to-air missiles.
- The importance of wider participation, also in the form of so-called nil returns, since the Register is a political instrument. Nil reports indicate willingness to participate in the Transparency drive.
- The inaccuracies and inconsistencies in the 1992 reporting, noting that:
  - Governments are still on a learning curve; it is early days.
  - Information on the operation of the Register must be widely disseminated.
  - Minor technical changes might help. Mathematical accuracy is subordinate to the purport of the Register as a political instrument.
- Regional differences and concerns, and in its connection:
  - Scope of the Register, including reference to how weapons of mass destruction are being dealt with.
  - Links with regional organizations, also with a view to using the Register for bilateral, regional or international consultations to address issues of concern.
- Background information: Noting the views on military holdings and procurement from national production.
- Voluntary additional information: whether and how this might be encouraged.
- Future reviews of the Register.

3. Given the youth of the Register - sometimes referred to as a baby which cannot yet take big steps - there seems to be little movement to add new equipment categories to the Register.

On the other hand, the signs for further *development* of the Register seem to be encouraging. The Group might well end up finding consensus on expansion of the scope of the Register, to include data on military holding and procurement through national production. In this respect an interesting evolution has come to the fore, *i.e.* Western reticence is disappearing.

The UN Secretary-General's Group of Governmental Experts is well aware that they are required to take account of the work of the Conference on Disarmament (CD), based here in Geneva. The CD was requested, in operative paragraphs 12 to 15 of Resolution 46/36 L, to elaborate universal and non-discriminatory practical means to increase openness and transparency related to military holdings and procurement through national production, as well as to the transfer of high technology with military applications, and to weapons of mass destruction, in accordance with existing legal instruments.

What the CD could do is to develop all sorts of CBMs pertaining to the issues just mentioned. First, in the nuclear domain, Nuclear Weapon States might voluntarily supply more information on their nuclear arms holdings. The same could be done in relation to plutonium stocks. Recommendations for prenotification of major military manoeuvres involving nuclear arms might be agreed upon.

Secondly, quite a few practical proposals related to transparency and openness in the conventional field have been tabled in the CD, as well. There is a British proposal on the size and organization of armed forces; an Italian proposal on the declaration of closure or conversion of military production facilities; there are Japanese ideas on regional transparency. It seems the AHC/TIA might expect to be approached with an Indian CBM proposal soon.

The CD may well develop adequate recommendations for parallel measures. The Register can only fare well if it is solidly enshrined in what I like to call: "a family of efforts" which are intended to encourage responsibility and self-restraint. The overall objective is co-operative security. An important effect is the avenue opened for reallocation of socio-economic resources.

4. While absorbing the data and information exchanged here, revealing as they do some rather troubling trends in our post-Cold War world, at times one is tempted to feel some nostalgia for the "good old Cold War" with its clear, bipolar, quasi-Manichean divide. This thought is, of course, a fallacy, with all due respect to Rakesh Sood.

In relation to the Register one could ask about the possible applicability to the Register of this remark that Generals sometimes prepare themselves to fight the last war again, although technological and military developments have gone way beyond. Indeed the Register does more than alleviate concerns about last wars' weapons.

Let's express the hope that in due course the scope of the Register might be brought to bear also on what Dr Kemp so aptly calls, and I quote: "the concept of cyberwar, which targets the centrality of information systems in the modern war-machine. This novel approach to future warfare advocates conducting, and preparing to conduct, military operations according to information-related principles. Its techniques include destroying enemy information and communications systems, and winning the "balance of information and knowledge", especially when the enemy has numerical superiority. Thus, it prevents the enemy from "knowing itself": who it is, where it is, what can it do when, why it is fighting, which threats to counter first, etc. The Apache helicopter strike against Iraqi air defence controls at the outset of the Gulf War, and the deception practiced by a relatively small number of Marines to lead astray the Iraqi army, embodies some principles of the above approach, of warfare could radically alter the nature of future conflicts". End of quotation.

Section II: Comments

Edward Woollen

One point on the Register as it relates to air defence missile systems. A 21-inch diameter canister (such as can be put on almost any ship), that is about 20 feet long, can overfly 500 kilometers easily. If one wanted to put submunitions in that same device, it could also attack targets on the ground. I would assume 500 kilometers range with the ability to do ground attack from a surface-to-air missile system probably would qualify for the UN Register.

Curt Gasteyger

I hesitate to throw some cold water on Mr Wagenmaker's excellent and also optimistic presentation, as far as the UN Register is concerned. It is difficult to consider the arms register as a mechanism that creates the impression of growing transparency in the arms trade. We all know that this does not adequately reflect reality. While I welcome arms registration, I also think we have to be extremely cautious when publicizing it and making people believe that we can introduce, or enhance, transparency in the arms market when we all know there are considerable limitations to transparency. This for at least two reasons.

The first is the black market. We know that it is beyond our control and is flourishing almost world wide. The second phenomenon is a new one, and should worry all of us. It is the fact that States (governments) have less and less control over all kind of groups which have access to arms and are ready to use them at their own volition and for their own purposes. We have merely to look at what is happening in ex-Yugoslavia where we see that there are groups which are beyond or below State control. Another example is Somalia. Here a number of weapons were introduced from the outside in connection with the tribal conflicts. Now many of these arms are being transferred to Kenya and become a major concern for that country. How do we control this kind of "uncontrollable" arms transfers? They are certainly not on the Register, but are probably as important as those which find their way into the UN Register.

Geoffrey Kemp

I would like to mention a couple of issues that came up during the Gulf War.

There were extraordinarily detailed inventories presented for analysis throughout the world during that period of time. A great many very good analysts made idiots of themselves predicting what was going to happen on the battlefield. Part of the problem is that there is an increasing disconnect between what is listed in weapons inventories, such as the *Military Balance* published by the *International Institute for Strategic Studies*, and what the actual force capabilities are at the time of battle.

One of the methodological issues that clearly needs more work is to take into account how the force multipliers actually work and whether or not some methodological way can be found to crank them into the equation. If you look at the IISS *Military Balance* today, which is perhaps the most comprehensive register we have in the non-official sector, it does not tell us very much about capabilities.

Part of the weakness in measuring military capabilities has to do with the trends where the things that really count militarily are to be found in software and electronics and simply are not capable of being measured in any way that we are aware of at this time. This is an area that needs a lot more work. It is potentially a very profitable one, and what has been done so far is extremely useful.

Peggy Mason

I am referring to the UN Disarmament Commission and the whole question of small arms and illicit arms transfers and the destabilizing effects of small arms and illicit arms transfers. That issue, too, after a debate of about three years, has been put into the Disarmament Commission - the first year for consideration will be the 1994 session. I take heart from all of those who have said this is an important issue. We really urge you to support consideration of this issue in your own countries and in your own governments. The basic Western position was that there are about three Western countries that were even mildly enthusiastic about going forward with this issue in the UN Disarmament Commission.

Hendrik Wagenmakers

To respond briefly: we all know, especially in Western Europe, that in modern urban road traffic, red lights are more and more ignored. But would you like to do away with red and green traffic lights at road junctions? We need them.

I do not claim that we can bring transparency to this whole difficult area of weapons trade. First, the exercise is voluntary. Secondly, the data is government supplied. It is not IISS, it is not SIPRI data, which are no more than estimations. The data for the Register are government supplied. One government can go to another government and say, "Hey, what are you doing? We want to know! Why is this!"

Regarding the illicit arms trade, of course the impact of a certain weapon system depends very much on the particular features of the region in which it is located. One could say, with some exaggeration, that in certain areas an AK-47 equals an armored command vehicle functioning in another region. That is what our friends from Africa tells us: "You guys, you are busy with a registry which does not relate to the kind of weapons that cause security or insecurity in Africa." But I hope that in due course we can try to do more. It is a complex family of efforts. It is a transparency drive.

Chapter 6
Discussion

1. *Rakesh Sood*

1. There is nothing new about "dual use". We may think that we discovered the concept of "dual use", but the fact is that "dual use" has existed from time immemorial. In fact, restraints on access to dual use technology is also something which is very old. But, it has never worked. It can increase the political cost, and it can increase the delays, but it cannot stop "proliferation". Even the gods could not deny Prometheus fire, and that was the first example of dual use. We need to accept this clearly. Therefore, what is new today about dual use technology? What is new today is that we are talking about weapons of mass destruction which have a global reach. Therefore, if we want to tackle dual use technologies with a global reach, then we need to look at these things from a global imperative.

2. Secondly, the Non-Proliferation Treaty has been described as very strong and, at the same time, very fragile. If we look back on it, it has 160-odd States Parties. There has been one case of violation, namely that of Iraq. There has been another case of withdrawal which was suspended, namely that of North Korea. And yet, 1995, which for the NPT community should be an occasion for mutual reassurance, is becoming an occasion for a lot of soul-searching and anxiety. I frankly cannot understand the reason why. The anxiety is not coming from the three significant countries that are outside the NPT, namely Israel, India and Pakistan. The anxiety is coming from within the NPT community.

3. The third point concerns the MTCR (Missile Technology Control Programme). I think here once again the controversy on the transfer of cryogenic engine technology from Glavkosmos, a Russian Company, to ISRO in India and the sanctions on the two companies reflect basically the inherent drawbacks of the MTCR. Namely, it does not make a distinction between civilian and non-civilian applications. The other aspect of it is that, given the manner in which MTCR has evolved, it is an opaque regime; it is not

transparent. Until these two aspects are taken care of within the context of MTCR, it is not going to achieve its objectives.

4. And lastly, the Chemical Weapons Convention and the Comprehensive Test Ban Negotiations. It has been said that it may be good for stopping modernisation, but it does not prevent development of a crude bomb. But that is why we should look at going beyond the test ban. It is here that the CWC offers a model that reflects the strengthened norm against chemical weapons.

2. Jacques Battistella

Just a fast and quick comment about the issue of dual use or no dual use. What is new today, compared to the past, is that we have a situation where civilian and commercial technology are in better shape than military technology. If you look at a launcher or a missile, for example, you need more accuracy to launch a satellite into geosynchronous orbit than that needed to launch a nuclear warhead to 2,000 kilometers. The same thing is true of processing capability today. Any of the computers on your desk has more processing power than that installed in the nuclear ballistic missiles which are now in the forces. This is what is new. This is what is making dual use and MTCR so difficult to handle. The commercial technology is probably ten or fifteen years in advance of comparable military technology in terms of performance.

3. Suha Umar

For instance, unless you are ready to deal with ethnic and other conflicts you will hardly have any opportunity or ability to solve the problems before us.

1. With the proliferation of nuclear and other weapons of mass destruction and advanced conventional weapons and technologies (*i.e.*, all the combinations of weapons and technology), the issue is how to make a distinction between two important aspects of the subject matter. One aspect is how to deal with those countries who feel insecure and thus need to obtain armaments - not just conventional weapons, but also missiles and missile technology. The second aspect that must be dealt with are those countries that

try to obtain armaments with an objective of becoming able to impose their will on others. The distinction is not very easy to make - at least not at all times.

A second point concerns the need to develop a national armaments industry as a means of protecting one's self against an embargo. This is a major point indeed. All these point toward the reality that unless we are able to tackle the causes of future conflicts, unless we are ready to go into the deep roots of the conflicts and make the road more secure than it is now, it will be nearly impossible for us to stop the proliferation of weapons of mass destruction, the associated technology, or contain the proliferation of conventional armaments and technology to prevent the excessive accumulation of conventional armaments.

With this in mind, we might try to find solutions to the proliferation problem, but we believe that solutions will not come easily and they will take time. The solutions are more in the general areas of conflict prevention and making the world more secure than in trying to convince people not to arm themselves or in trying to punish people in these countries in those cases where they do the contrary.

2. It is becoming more and more difficult to determine who is doing what, with whom, and for what purpose in the field of arms sales and technology transfers. Of course, we have to accept that there are no ethics at work in the field of the arms trade. There are only political and economic considerations, either of which might from time to time have an effect on the decisions of the arms exporters, which in turn has its effect on the decisions of those countries who are in need of armaments for their defences. This is an important security issue. No country is willing to leave its security and defence capability to the mercy of another.

One is whether there is a difference between an ideological approach to arms sales or arms imports, or it is a matter of urgency and need. For example, my country (Turkey) was mentioned for having bought armaments from the Russian Federation. Yes, this is true. There was a pressing need for this purchase. The purchase included only a couple of helicopters, ACV's and some small caliber armaments. These were an urgent necessity. If we tried to obtain these through traditional channels, that is to say from our Allies, it would take more than a couple of years due to the political and other reasoning involved in the decision.

Also, my country was mentioned as one of the three or four countries who made up 15 percent of the recent arms imports. There must be a distinction, a clear cut distinction between "cascading", or "harmonization" as it is called, within the context of the CFE (Conventional Forces in Europe) Treaty, and simply arms imports. Cascading is a very special mechanism. Every single tank obtained through cascading requires the destruction of an existing tank currently in the receiving country's inventory. Cascading can result in a qualitative increase in a country's armaments inventory, but not a quantitative rise. So, cascading should be put aside. It should not be confused with other arms transfer issues. Cascading is a very special mechanism. If you sell and buy arms outside of the CFE Treaty, it is not cascading!

4. *John Simpson*

1. What is the proliferation threat, and why is one concerned about it? If you ask that question, rather than just accepting the threat as a given, you actually find yourself addressing two different sorts of threats. One is a threat from weapons of mass destruction. We can engage in a discussion as to whether weapons of mass of destruction are different from other weapons, but to my mind, they are. In the case of weapons of mass destruction, the issue is one of banning them. In the case of other weapons, you are talking about controlling them. You are talking about issues such as stability or reducing the number of most threatening weapons. This is the old language of arms control.

One of the interesting aspects of this is that the MTCR teeters on the edge between the two issues. Is it addressing weapons that ought to be banned, or is it addressing weapons that ought to be controlled? If you are going to talk about proliferation, you have to ask yourself, why do we want to prevent proliferation? That, in turn, leads you into a discussion of whether you want to ban weapons, or control them. I think one of the problems of controlling proliferation is what criteria you are going to use to determine how much is enough.

2. A second point at issue raised about the non-proliferation regime: if one signatory acquires nuclear weapons, is the whole regime thrown into doubt? Yet it seems that this is not really the issue in 1995. The issue in 1995 is that the further duration of the NPT is in doubt. The issue of a State

acquiring nuclear weapons, a signatory acquiring nuclear weapons, is actually much broader than it appears. What we are actually addressing is a break-out from the regime. Given the issues which are inherent in the discussions on the nuclear non-proliferation regime, is it an anti-proliferation regime or is it a total nuclear disarmament regime? Yet if you are trying to persuade States to move to total nuclear disarmament, it is very important that you should demonstrate an ability to deal with break-out. That is why the North Korean case goes beyond just being concerned with nuclear non-proliferation.

3. Very briefly, the third point. As far as the arms trade is concerned we are having increasing difficulties in actually grappling with what it is. The more we look at all of the statistics that have been produced the more confused we become. It seems to me that one of our difficulties is to know what arms now are. I would look for further elucidation of this point as the discussions proceed.

5. Richard Grimmett

There is a key correlation between national wealth of an arms purchasing State and the size and nature of its conventional weapons acquisition program. This is the case for a direct purchase and for a co-production program aimed at developing an indigenous arms manufacturing capability. If you examine the weapons purchasing trends of the last 15 or 20 years and their size, nature and scope, this factor stands out most prominently. It is those nations with the greatest wealth that have the greatest prospect of obtaining the most sophisticated items for their conventional weapons programs.

The most obvious example of such a wealthy country is Saudi Arabia. A Latin American country, like Argentina, would illustrate those nations on the lower end of the continuum. The Condor missile development program in Argentina faltered in part because international pressure was brought to bear to halt it, but a lack of independent funding to support it played an important role as well.

By contrast, a nation with a higher degree of national wealth could purchase missile production technology independently and engage in production activities with others prepared to assist it, despite the opposition of major powers in the West. A country with oil wealth like Iran could readily purchase weapons or military technology from nations like China or North Korea because the latter States have the requisite weapons and/or knowledge and are willing to sell both. Iran has the resources to purchase both. The common link is a buyer with the wealth to make the purchase and a supplier that has the item desired and is willing and interested in making the sale and transfer for money.

6. Ahmad Kamal

This statement about the correlation between wealth and arms transfers is impressing but obvious. Even more attractive is the correlation between having membership in the Security Council and being a seller of arms. But what does that prove? It is self-defeating to try and put the spotlight just on these core correlations. The membership of the Security Council accounts for 90% of arms sales. Does that mean that if you expand the Security Council membership, the new countries will also be arms sellers? This remains doubtful.

The real point is *why* - the *why* of arms sales, not the fact that you need money to buy them. It is obvious that you need money to buy arms. It is a very lucrative thing. But should we not go a bit deeper into why certain countries have the incentive to export arms and why other countries have the incentive to import arms?

7. Rakesh Sood

The scientific community, immediately after 1945, had the right ideas in terms of tackling the nuclear issue. They realized that the traditional approach of dual use control would not work because the nuclear technology was the first dual use technology with a global dimension. We seem to forget this today. But it was the first, and when we look at the Baruch Plan and similar initiatives, we find that these were designed to address the nuclear technology issues in that global context.

Subsequently, somewhere along the line, we started moving on a different track, namely, the conventional approach of technology denial, which is why the question of a test ban is today under consideration. What will be achieved by a Comprehensive Test Ban Treaty today?

Recently, the French Defence Minister, the French Ambassador to the Conference on Disarmament, plus the US Ambassador to the Conference on Disarmament have all made statements that a comprehensive test ban would not affect the quality of their deterrent. That means that these countries would like a CTBT to be in place and yet allow them to continue to be able to refine or do whatever is necessary to maintain their deterrent. In the fifties, a test ban was seen as a move towards nuclear disarmament. We must therefore ask the question as to whether a comprehensive test ban can do today what it could have done when it was first suggested in the early 1950s?

8. *Winfried Lang*

There has been some reference to the motivations for arms sales and for arms exports. One consideration which should be discussed is the argument that certain countries (especially medium and smaller countries) use to justify their involvement in arms exports. Essentially, the argument is that arms export earnings are necessary to maintain local production which is necessary in order to reduce domestic dependency on arms deliveries from abroad. This might be a circular argument, but it is used by certain countries and should not be neglected in the deliberations.

9. *Michael Moodie*

A very important point is to underline the relationship between decision-making with respect to weapons of mass destruction and conventional weapons. Too often, both in academic conferences and in government circles, there is a tendency to compartmentalize those two issues in a way that is not realistic in terms of capturing the way decisions are made. It is important to recognize that relationship.

Having said that, to accept the characterization of the decision-making as being one in which weapons of mass destruction are being pursued by some countries because they are reacting to the build-up of conventional forces by American allies through US arms transfers is both dangerous and inaccurate. One need only remember that before the Gulf War Iraq, as it was pursuing a nuclear program, a biological program, and a chemical weapons program also had a larger tank inventory than either Britain or France. It was not a question of pursuing a weapons of mass of destruction program at the expense of, or in lieu of, an expensive conventional program. Similarly, North Korea's decision to pursue a weapons of mass destruction program was made at a time when the generally accepted view was that the conventional balance in the Korean peninsula was in the North's favor. It has been only within the last five or six years, because of some changes in the nature of the technology, and so on, in the South Korean forces, that people have begun to characterize the shift in the conventional balance in Korea as moving toward the South.

So, it is not necessarily the case that people pursue weapons of mass destruction programs in lieu of conventional forces. In fact, you could make the case that as often as not the two things occur much together. The reason that those countries of concern are highlighted is because they are pursuing both. We do not have criteria to identify or agree necessarily on the list of rogue States. Indeed it is a much more complex decision-making process that has been suggested.

Another point is that all of the discussants have emphasized the shifting nature of the market away from finished products to enabling technologies, whether it is information technologies or those technologies necessary for systems integration. That shift will pose a significant challenge for those people who are trying to define new ways to constrain, in particular, the conventional arms trade.

10. *Aharon Klieman*

One could question the utility behind the term *weapons of mass destruction*. Both historically and statistically ever since 1945, the weapons of greatest devastation have fallen more into the conventional, standard category. Virtually all of the presentations thus far have only reinforced the point that so-called "conventional" weapons have become increasingly sophisticated, intelligent, and therefore lethal.

This leads to the question whether we might not be well advised to reconsider our professional use and reference to the very term "weapons of mass destruction". A first option is to define the term sharply and most seriously, making it quite clear what falls into the notion and what is excluded from it. Secondly, alternatively, perhaps we ought to make the terminology more inclusive and acknowledge the fact that conventional weapons are, and continue to be, the weapons of greatest destruction. And lastly, perhaps we might just consider doing away with the term.

11. Edward Woollen

From a technologist point of view, the reason that we put precision in weapons is to minimize the numbers (the amount of destruction), not maximize it. The whole purpose for having the most precise seeker on the front end of a weapon is to hit only that single target you intend to hit with the smallest possible warhead and not to have any collateral damage: women, children, buildings, churches, synagogues, mosques, and so forth.

The concern you should show is that the term *weapons of mass destruction* should absolutely be used. It should be applied to those weapons that are used indiscriminately against civilians in the context of a war. They should be abhorrent. It is a very good term: *weapons of mass destruction*. Probably another way to say it is: *weapons of indiscriminate destruction*. Anybody who is buying and using those types of weapons has not, and cannot have, any defensive intent. There are perfectly good weapons to buy for defensive purposes. If you are buying *weapons of mass destruction*, you have an intention to work against civilian populations and not against other military targets.

12. Geoffrey Kemp

Most of the slides of very advanced technologies being provided to the third world are from Russian inventories. The question is, if you compare what the Russians are prepared to make available today and what the United States is prepared to make available today, there are some differences. There is not a slide for instance of stealth technology, some of the really sophisticated technologies that were made available for the United States forces during *Desert Storm*. I think there is still a distinction between certain constraints on the part of the United States at the very, very high level of technology and the range of technologies that everyone else is prepared to sell.

How much longer can the Russians afford to sell such sophisticated weapons at such bargain basement prices? Presumably, they are doing it right now because they have no alternative and the market mechanisms in Russia do not fully reflect the cost of producing these high technologies, but at some point, if the Russian economy becomes more normal, it would be very very difficult for them to give away weapons at this price. In this case, if the price rises to what might be considered the market price, how many people would really be able to afford these technologies in the next century?

13. *Aaron Karp*

In considering arms trade control, one does have to be very explicit about what one's objectives are. If it is to save money that can go into other purposes, that is feasible. If it is to save lives, however, it is very debatable. Limiting access to major weapons is unlikely to limit war; it may even make war worse. Warfare involving major weapons does not kill very many people. One only has to look at the experience in *Desert Storm* where 400 Allied troops died, half of them through their own carelessness. Iraqi casualties were not laughable, but most sensible estimates now are that somewhere under 100,000 civilians and soldiers died. This is not trivial, but it certainly is smaller than the rate of dying going on in ethnic conflict today where people are being killed with the most fundamental of weapons technologies (ancient) that look trivial, certainly compared to any of the modern weapons that we just saw on the slides.

If one wants to control killing, then one has to think very seriously about ways to embrace the small arms trade, especially the kinds of processes that Ambassador Petrovsky talked about in his presentation, embracing the private and black market for weapons. Then you will begin to save lives. However, I think it takes a great deal of imagination to think that conventional arms trade control - stressing major weapons alone - is going to have that affect.

14. *Shahram Chubin*

What is the intention of these transfers? If the problem is that weapons of mass destruction destroy massively because they are indiscriminate, then surely one could make the facetious argument that it might make sense to provide stabilizing technologies. That is, in regions where missiles are inaccurate, to provide greater accuracy in order to make sure that those missiles can be used in a militarily effective way rather than to be used in a militarily ineffective way.

15. David Markov

I do not agree with the idea of the high ends of technology being offered by the United States. In fact, it is a challenge for the United States. On the one hand the Secretary of Commerce Ron Brown says that the United States needs to sell weaponry overseas in order to convert. On the other hand, Boris Yeltsin and other individuals like Andre Kokoshin also say that we need to sell weapons overseas to convert. And if, in fact, you have a client base which is demanding certain kinds of weapons, and that is the only kind of weapons that they are willing to buy, it is a real challenge to the sellers to offer the kinds of technology that the people want to buy.

We are out of the mode of having thousands of heavy armored vehicles. We are probably into the mode of having antitactical ballistic missiles systems and other things of this nature being offered rather than the sale of large numbers of what I call "antiquated technologies" like T-55s and 54s and things of that nature.

What is happening is that the customers are really going to start to dictate in a way they have not in the last five years what will be sold, what the terms of the sale will be, and what the coproduction agreements will be. This is really what we need to keep our eyes on, and this situation is not going to go away. We are in a temporary respite until the next major regional conflict breaks out. Then you are going to see the world's arm suppliers rush to supply the two parties.

The fact that there are no ethics in the arms trade is beyond any doubt. Countries around the world are looking to convert their defence industries, are looking to take that revenue in some cases to place it into their own economies to convert. Countries such as Israel, Russia, China, etc. will do whatever it takes to make sales. They are looking to do whatever it takes to survive for that particular industry.

Part II

Political/Military Factors Associated with the Diffusion of Advanced Technology

Chapter 7
Global and Regional Security Concerns

Section I: Supplier Motivations

A - Sten Lundbo

At a high level meeting in The Hague on 16 November 1993, it was decided that the Committee on Multilateral Export Controls (COCOM) would be phased out as soon as possible, and no later than 31 March 1994. The COCOM countries are currently conducting negotiations with a view to establishing a new multilateral export control regime, but these negotiations are far from concluded. However, we envisage the establishment of a forum for control of sensitive dual-use goods and technology, as well as conventional arms. It is essential to ensure that the new regime does not duplicate the work of the existing multilateral export control fora.

The objective of the three existing regimes - the Australia Group, the Missile Technology Control Regime (MTCR) and the Nuclear Suppliers Group (NSG) - is to prevent the proliferation of weapons of mass destruction and their delivery vehicles. The export control measures that have been agreed on are not a substitute for disarmament and arms control agreement, but are designed to supplement and underpin the latter. Within this broad framework each regime has a specific target:

- The Nuclear Suppliers Group focuses on nuclear weapons,
- the Australia Group on biological and chemical weapons,
- and the MTCR on delivery vehicles for weapons of mass destruction.

Mention should also be made of the Zangger Committee, which has two objectives:

- to define what constitutes nuclear material and equipment, or material especially designed or prepared for the processing, use or production of special fissionable material,

- to consider conditions and procedures that govern export of such equipment or material, in order to meet the obligations of Article III.2 of the Non-Proliferation Treaty.

Since the Gulf war, the scope of these regimes has been considerably expanded.

A dual-use regime was negotiated within the Nuclear Suppliers Group between March 1991 and March 1992. Within the framework of the Australia Group, agreement has been reached to extend the export controls to biological agents and dual-use biological equipment. At the Plenary Meeting in Oslo in July 1992, the partners of the Missile Technology Control Regime decided that the regime should apply to missiles capable of delivering all kinds of weapons of mass destruction, not only to nuclear weapon missiles. This was necessary in view of the growing danger of further proliferation of weapons of mass destruction and of delivery vehicles for such weapons.

It should be stressed that export controls are in no way intended to prevent peaceful uses of sensitive high technology. Thus, the Guidelines of the MTCR explicitly state that they are not designed to impede national space programmes or international co-operation in such programmes, as long as they cannot contribute to the development of delivery systems for weapons of mass destruction. Similarly, the Australia Group countries have decided that their controls should not hinder normal trade in materials and equipment used for legitimate purposes. As regards the Nuclear Suppliers Group, its guidelines for transfers of nuclear-related dual-use equipment, material and related technology are not designed to impede international co-operation, provided that such co-operation does not contribute to a nuclear explosive activity or an unsafeguarded nuclear-cycle activity. In other words, the members of the supplier regimes control exports, but do not ban them. An application for export is only denied if there is reason to believe that the item to be exported would be used illegally for weapons purposes.

During the last few years the membership of the MTCR and the Australia Group has grown considerably. Both regimes now count 23 OECD countries, plus Hungary and Argentina, as members. The growth in membership, and the inclusion of Argentina and Hungary as the first non-OECD countries, are welcome developments. A number of other countries are interested in joining the Australia Group and the missile regime, including the Czech Republic, the Slovak Republic, Poland, the Russian Federation and

Romania. The Nuclear Suppliers Group comprises 28 countries, including the Russian Federation and the following Central and Eastern European countries: Bulgaria, the Czech Republic, Hungary, Poland, Romania and the Slovak Republic.

Members of the supplier regimes have devoted a great deal of effort to improving the understanding of their objectives and work among non-members. Their outreach activities have included bilateral contacts, missions of several Member States to non-partners, regional and international seminars, etc. As a result, a number of States that have not yet joined the regimes, or have no intention of doing so, have nevertheless implemented export control measures or are interested in doing so. In this way, the guidelines and policies of the regimes are gradually becoming international non-proliferation norms.

B - Comments

Michael Moodie

The new forum to replace COCOM will be a forum for constraining conventional arms. Is the new forum designating systems that are not to be sold? Is it going to control transfers on the basis of the overall guidelines that are developed, and how might those guidelines shape decisions with respect to transfers?

Rakesh Sood

Mr Lundbo mentioned that in this "new forum" there will be no list of embargoed items; then he went on to say that decisions will be made by individual countries on the export of these items. Does that assume a situation where a particular country would be more receptive to receiving end use assurances or issuing an export license for one of these controlled items, as compared to another country? Under such conditions, how would the harmonization work? Or, is Mr Lundbo implying that this will be less harmonized than the current COCOM structures which are in place? Are the guidelines supposed to be mandatory, or are the guidelines supposed to be indicative of the policy which is to be followed by individual exporting countries?

Ian Anthony

About the membership of the new forum: is it the case of the countries which are already discussing the creation of a new forum that they will choose specific countries to approach with a view to making them members, or will it be that you simply leave it open, and anyone who chooses to can apply, if they so choose and if they meet your criteria?

Another thing. A month or so ago Lynne Davis was quoted as saying that one of the countries that might be approached as a prospective member of this new forum is China. Did the United States raise that in any of the discussions? If so, is it at all a possibility for them to be a member?

Mahmoud Karem

I would like to seek clarification from Sten Lundbo on the relationship between this new COCOM, insofar as it deals with conventional weapons and the register of the United Nations on conventional weapons.

David Hobbs

Is the new forum likely to get into the area of providing assistance to countries which need help in developing their export control mechanisms? One of the problems if we bring in central and Eastern Europe is that they do not have a particularly well-developed structure for controlling exports. How do we expect to engage those countries in the new forum?

Marie-Hélène Labbé

You have mentioned the fact that China was following the MTCR provisions of 1987, but not these of 1992. It seems obvious, given the furnishing of missiles, namely, to Pakistan. Could you elaborate a little bit more on that?

Michael Moodie

What is meant by saying that the replacement for COCOM will be a forum for dealing with conventional arms transfers? Is it the intention to identify weapons systems that cannot be transferred? Is it to apply the guidelines developed for broader technology transfers specifically to conventional arms sales? If so, are those guidelines going to be at all useful given the imperatives that countries seem to have to transfer arms? Can we have a little bit more detail on this approach because, as he indicated, it may in fact be the first effort to do such a thing, and it would be useful to know more about it.

Sten Lundbo

I will first answer the question by Rakesh Sood because that will create a basis for the remainder of what I will say. In this new forum we will have no embargoes but rather agreed lists of controlled items which means that there will be less harmonization than in COCOM. The procedures in this new forum will basically be the same as in NSG, the MTCR, and the Australia Group. We have even discussed if we should have a "no undercut policy." The thinking is that there should not be a "no undercut policy".

With regard to the questions of Mr Moodie and Mahmoud Karem, I take those together because they deal with conventional weapons. I wished I could at this point elaborate more, but I cannot. We are in a situation where COCOM will be phased out on the 31st of March 1994. Ideally, the new forum should be established on 1 April 1994, but it will take more time. We have, at this point, concentrated on the procedures for dual-use, goods and technology. But regarding arms we have so far envisaged that the control will be limited to the seven categories of major weaponry in the UN registry (to which Mahmoud Karem referred) and also to some few items from COCOM's munitions list.

I envisage discussions and consultations on developments of global trends in arms transfers, but there will not be a great deal of harmonization in this area. There might, however, be separate consultations among a small group of members, which are the principal exporters of arms.

Specifically, Mr Anthony referred to the question of China and its possible membership. At this point, I see three basic criteria: first, having an effective export control policy; second, pursuing a responsible policy of non-proliferation, which means, in fact, being treaty participants in the relevant arms control treaties as well as implementing the guidelines of other export control regimes; and thirdly, being a supplier or a potential supplier of conventional weapons and/or high technology. This means that as members you would definitely have the COCOM countries, the 6 COCOM fully co-operating countries, Iceland, Central and Eastern European States, Russia and some of the CIS States. Two weeks ago I was in the Ukraine and in Belarus. There was great interest in the Ukraine and in Belarus for joining this new regime. Ideally, of course, we would like to have China as a member. These are personal observations.

Speaking on China and the MTCR and the differences over the 1987 guidelines and the 1992 guidelines, China has said, first of all, that it will not join MTCR because China did not take part in its establishment. Secondly, China has said that it will adhere to the MTCR guidelines of 1987, which means that it will control missiles capable of delivering nuclear weapons - missiles with parameters of a range of 300 kilometers and a payload of 500 kilometers. China has said that it will not implement the guidelines which were agreed on in Oslo in July 1992 which cover missiles capable of delivering all kinds of weapons of mass destruction with the parameters of more than 300 kilometers.

David Hobbs asked if this new regime would mean that the Member States would be involved in assisting new members in establishing export control systems. That is certainly the idea. In November 1992 we established what we called the COCOM Co-operating Forum (CCF) which has been engaged in such a process. Norway, for example, is now assisting Estonia, Ukraine, and Poland in establishing effective export control systems. Other countries are concentrating on other States. I hope that this process will continue in the new forum.

Serge Sur

You have alluded to the P-5 concertation. At the end of the Gulf War, the idea was raised to maintain consultations among the permanent members in order to control the non-proliferation policies, or at least to consider expert controls. Apparently such a process has progressively been deceptive.

Sten Lundbo

In London, in October 1991, the P-5 countries agreed on guidelines regarding the export of conventional weapons to the Middle East. These guidelines are very important. It was the first time that China has adhered to guidelines for certain limitations on export of conventional weapons with a focus on the Middle East. What happened was that during the presidential campaign President Bush said that the United States would sell *F-16* planes to Taiwan, after which China said it would no longer participate in the P-5 talks. However, China has said that it would still implement the London guidelines of October 1991. I hope that in the long term we will have China as a partner in this new regime.

Suha Umar

We are inclined to discuss what will happen to COCOM, who will be included, and will anybody be excluded. I wonder if we are missing the real point. Why are we trying to deal with COCOM at this stage? The answer looks simple. The most important technology exporters are especially very much engaged in technology-sharing with the countries that were the former targets of the COCOM regime. A lot of countries are trying to improve the capabilities of their conventional armaments, armaments covered by the seven categories of armaments in the UN registry. Whether this trend is favorable to world society as a whole or whether it will create problems cannot be foreseen for the time being. This is a thing for time to show all of us. Maybe there is a good side to it. It might get rid of the argument which was used in the case of Middle East wars in the recent past. This time when someone loses a war in the Middle East main exporters will not be afraid that its technology lost the war against the technology or armaments of the other side. After all, if the trend continues, all the armaments will have the same technology and even the same shape.

Edward Woollen

Some of the finest and brightest minds for advanced technology exist in places like China, India, Pakistan, Brazil, and Argentina. You have to consider a wide open regime for anything you are doing. If you close a regime, you are exclusive for all the wrong reasons.

If you are going to do a MCTR, if you are going to have to go through yet another series of "COCOM juniors," let us at least do it as a wide open regime. If the friendly nations that are going to use nuclear power for peaceful means want to joint a nuclear regime, they ought to be allowed to do so. If the users, and also the suppliers other than the large industrial countries, want to make weapons, want to joint a regime, they should be allowed to do so. That may put me at total odds with the NATO countries, but that is from a technologist viewpoint. They are equally as good, and in many cases better, than we are in some core technologies. Let's not ignore the ability to have them on our side.

Section II: Post-Cold War Regional Arms Control

A - *Ahmad Kamal*

For the better part of four-and-a-half decades we have lived in the shadow of the Cold War. This Cold War suddenly disappeared with the demise of the Soviet Union, and this led to great expectations that it would be replaced by an era of peace and prosperity, happiness, and milk and honey. Somehow that did not turn out to be so. Whichever way we look, problems seem to be increasing rather than decreasing. We have a dramatic proliferation of regional conflicts. We have widespread ethnic tensions around the world. We have the outright genocide that we are facing in Bosnia. We have a jump in refugee numbers which have increased by almost 40% in the past five years alone.

Is all this something that is new, or is it just that we have rediscovered something that existed already? The Cold War gave us the impression that regional problems did not exist, that everything had to be fitted into the grid of East-West tensions. Then when socialism crumbled we still have to answer the question of why it did, because this has been projected as the great victory of capitalism over communism; but time alone will tell, firstly whether communism and socialism are really dead, and secondly, whether it was not the internal contradictions of socialism which caught up with it, just as the internal contradictions of capitalism may catch up one day with capitalism itself. But the battle, nevertheless, appears to have been won; and the problem is that we cannot understand why there is no peace after the battle.

The Cold War had fitted us into a strait-jacket of alliances. It was easy to tell your friend from your foe. Suddenly, that is no longer possible, and we find that there are little pots boiling all over the kitchen. When we cool one down, another starts boiling over. Is it new, or is it that this is only a rediscovery, that all this is more of the same? For many of us who come from developing countries this situation is not a result of the end of the Cold War, it is that these tensions and these regional disputes had always existed, but that they were never the focus of people's attention.

- I -

For most of us it was our region that was the perimeter, the outer limit of our knowledge, the formative framework of our threat perceptions and our security policies. Even during the Cold War our threat perceptions and our security policies were limited to our respective regions only. Now why is it then that the West has suddenly discovered also that regional tensions exist? Certainly not because of the long jihad in the First Committee of the General Assembly, where we tried with great difficulty over two decades, and unsuccessfully, to sell regional disarmament as a concept; until suddenly, about two or three years ago, the penny dropped and everybody discovered that regional disarmament was something that was necessary. Why? A couple of very over-simplistic explanations could be to put forward as to the mood in which the Western countries find themselves and the dilemma in which they are placed.

- The first explanation is that, once the Cold War has ended, these enormous defence industries in developed countries find it progressively more difficult to sell hammers for 600 dollars a piece, or toilet seats for 250 dollars a piece. So they have either to scale back their production, and that is something that is very difficult, or they have to try to convert themselves which is just as difficult, perhaps even more difficult in an age which is getting progressively identified with an economic recession. So what do they do? They talk about arms control and about the need to cut-back sales even to erstwhile allies, but this is just talk. You find at the same time that the arms are available without difficulty around the world. The only difference is that the price has to be negotiated at a higher level.

- The second explanation is that the developed countries have suddenly woken up to the end of the Cold War, and to the fact that they have no enemy in front of them. It is a very unnerving thing if for 40 years you have been trained to react to an enemy, and suddenly there is a vacuum and no enemy in front of you. So you go round and try to look for one, or else create one. In fact, the more you look around, the easier it becomes to create one, and this is what is being done around the world. There is talk of this huge impending emergence of something called Islamic Fundamentalism. There are new problem countries which have suddenly appeared in the focus of our attention.

The creation of new enemies automatically results in another contradiction. Arms are pumped into the region, particularly to neighbours who are supposed to control these new enemies. Initially, one country has the edge in supplying arms. In the current case it is the United States which has the edge; we have seen charts which show how the market share of the US has jumped in the past two years since we have started talking about arms controls. But this is a temporary situation, because there are other producers of arms who are waiting and watching in the wings and who cannot relish the idea of allowing one country to monopolise 50% or 60% of the market share. So the economic multiplier comes into force. Ultimately over-supply results. A particular region gets glutted with arms, and somehow one has to wipe the slate clean and to recycle the process all over again. All this is quite profitable for the developed countries which are the major suppliers of arms. We might consider the interesting fact that somehow the Permanent Members of the Security Council seem to hold a near monopoly on the supplies of arms.

- II -

Now, given the confusion between these two explanations, both of which are relatively difficult to accept, there is a temptation to slide into isolationism. We see this as one of the most visible factors of the past two years. One talks with slogans of leadership, but one acts with isolationism, ineffectiveness, and limp responses to situations which require resolute and firm action. Bosnia is the best example because it is a critical case. It sits on the cutting-edge of all the principles that we have been trying to build-up and defend for 40 to 50 years, whether these are the principles of the prevention of aggression across international borders, the right of self-defence under Article 51 of the Charter, the collective security under Article 24, or the opposition to human rights violations, to ethnic cleansing or genocide. Everything that we have stood for is being negated in Bosnia, and yet all of us know how ineffective and almost effeminate the response to that situation has been.

Along with isolation, the other temptation is towards the simplistic solution of export controls. Let us just cut down arms. Let us not even talk about the underlying causes which led to the need for arms in the first place, and let us just apply export controls. That, in itself, creates new enemies, because if you deny the basic legitimate minimum to others, you push countries to the wall, and they begin to react irrationally. Even the most responsible countries react irrationally if they are pushed into corners. We have seen examples of that type of behaviour, not just in the developing countries, but at times in the developed countries as well.

The third temptation is something like the situation of the Sultan in Rimsky-Korsakov's "Sheherazade", where slumber takes over, and then suddenly the Sultan wakes and remembers that he is supposed to be angry. So there is a stormy outburst. North Korea is a good example, despite the oversimplification, where there is an irrational and angry outburst. We all know that, despite the dangers of the situation, the problem is not really in North Korea but in the temptation that the North Korea situation gives to one of its more powerful neighbours, because there, if you add nuclear capacity to their economic might, you get a very dangerous combination, so dangerous in fact that nobody is even willing to talk about it.

Now while the developed countries are going through this schizophrenic confusion, not knowing how to assimilate leadership with isolationism, the level of technical knowledge in developing countries is constantly increasing, because knowledge always goes forward; it does not go backwards. So in developing countries knowledge is developing, as is also the ability to assimilate the knowledge and the technical capacity. Where this forward move of knowledge is superimposed on regional tensions and on a desire to build up arms levels, you have a lethal combination, because there is even faster assimilation and faster concretisation. Once again, even responsible States have a tendency to behave irresponsibly.

- III -

The point is that security is certainly a desirable objective, but whose security are we really talking about? Is it the security of the few, of the developed countries? Or is the security of the many, of a global village in which we all live? It seems very odd that the underlying tone of the concept of security in this room is that of the security of one-fifth of the world's population, which somehow seems to take an arrogant precedence over the security of four-fifths of the world's population. We had always thought, at least we had always been taught, that democracy was a responsiveness to the wishes and the desires of the majority. If we then embark upon a path of selectivism, of unilateralism, of protectionism, of arms controls in this manner, then we are essentially being undemocratic, and it is this contradiction we have not quite been able to deal with so far.

Take the word "non-proliferation", which we have discussed now for 25 years. Consider the fact that "non-proliferation" has been given an aura of respectability, when basically what the word has meant is a license for some to have arms, and denying any to others. Non-proliferation has essentially been license to proliferate, because we know that in the 25 years of non-proliferation those who owned nuclear arms have multiplied their stockpiles many-fold. And yet the word "non-proliferation" is bandied around here as if it is motherhood and apple pie.

Consider again the problem we had with the definition of Transparency in Armaments. This was the debate that took place in the General Assembly two years ago. And despite the wishes of the large majority of the membership of the United Nations, the definition of armaments was limited to only those six categories of heavy arms which interested the developed countries themselves. Now we have heard that the quality of arms does not really determine the magnitude of the suffering that is caused. It is not the weapons of mass destruction, it is ordinary bullets and mortars, and relatively simple rifles, which have caused the greatest amount of suffering in the last forty years. Yet they are not covered in the register of Transparency in Armaments. Consider also the fact that the essential idea should be that comparisons of arms transfers should be based upon destabilising acquisitions of arms, or the acquisition of arms beyond legitimate defence needs, in other words, of their stockpiles. This is not a concept which is reflected in the Transparency in Armaments either.

Finally, from the point of view of developing countries, many of us have heavy crosses which we bear, in the way of unresolved disputes, in the way in which territorial borders were arbitrarily drawn on colonial maps. Just look at the map of Africa with its long straight lines cutting across ethnic expanses. All this leads to tensions and disputes, which are there all the time, just waiting to ignite and waiting to be noticed. Now they are ignored to a great extent, because CNN is not present everywhere. But please remember that of the 150-odd disputes we have had in the past forty years, all have been regional. All of them have been based on either an existing ethnic or territorial dispute, or on the desire of a local bully to exercise hegemony in his respective region. That is why disputes and regional tensions have to be addressed frontally. They cannot be pushed under the carpet. This requires a greater attention to preventive diplomacy than we have allowed ourselves in the past. That is what we should really be turning our attention to in this room.

B - Comments

Geoffrey Kemp

Ambassador Kamal talks about the "willful creation of enemies" and then about armaments being "pumped into neighboring States" who are expected to fight proxy wars. That is an extremely important statement, if it is true, because it raises all sorts of questions about the world we live in today. Without stating the countries you have in mind, or which countries are going to fight the proxy wars, I am afraid it is very tantalizing and titillating, but I need some harder data before I proceed to comment further on it.

The second point relates to this concept that has been mentioned three or four times now. Essentially, it is these low tech weapons that we see every day on television around Sarajevo that cause all the deaths, not high-tech. I think this is correct in one sense, but highly misleading in another. High-tech weaponry is extremely lethal if it hits the right target at the right time. What I think you will see historically is that the correlation between high casualties and low technology is a function of the duration of conflict. It is when conflicts go on for months and months and years and years, fought with mortars, artillery, and small arms that you get an extraordinarily high level of casualties. Short wars fought with high technology also tend to be extremely dangerous in the first two or three days, but they end very quickly; therefore, at the end of day perhaps they do not kill as many people, but I do not think we should kid ourselves that somehow high technology avoids casualties.

Ahmad Kamal

My statement that there is a search for new enemies, a search which is actually encouraging their birth and development even when none really existed before, has been challenged. I have been asked to produce chapter and verse in support. Let me give three examples of the this type of attitude that I am speaking about.

The West had a problem with the Soviet Union. It was an ideological problem. It was necessary to ring the Soviet Union with a group of countries which would constrain its ideological expansionism. In that process, one of the key links in the chain was Iran. Iran was heavily armed. It was over-armed. The Shahanshah of Iran referred to some of the attack helicopters as "expensive toys" which had been given to him.

The Shah fell because of an internal revolution which took place in Iran, and was replaced by what was perceived to be people with relatively long beards. That was now a danger because here was something new. People have forgotten, incidentally, that until a few decades ago every Prime Minister of France, for example, had a beard, but this fact was completely ignored, and these Iranian beards were suddenly seen as the emergence of some sort of new ethnic entity with red eyes and a curved sword which was to be called Islamic Fundamentalism. Now that had to be countered.

People fell backwards over each other (and people means the developed world's arms suppliers) to over-arm Iraq as a counterweight to Iran. I, myself, remember a conversation with the French in which we said, "Why are you handing the Iraqi's *Crotale* missiles because they are going to misuse them?" But the commercial argument was so important that there was no way the French were not going to sell hundreds of *Crotale* missiles to Iraq.

So who supplied Iraq with all these elements in the first place? It is so easy to talk of the over-arming of Saddam Hussein, but who is the guilty party? Is it those who supplied or is it those to whom the supplies were given? I leave it to you to examine your own consciences.

In wiping out the Iraqi arsenal, a marvelous system for the fastest recycling of 80 billion petro-dollars in history was implemented. Never have we seen such fast economic recycling of such a figure, but it was recycled by the marvelous technique of building up an enemy where I am not sure any existed. Now the money is being put into Saudi Arabia and Kuwait.

A second example is Bosnia. I keep coming back to Bosnia because Bosnia, I repeat, is a critical case in our judgment of western civilization and in our ability to stand up against a denial of the absolute fundamentals of civilized international behavior. Bosnia is being depicted as a humanitarian problem. It is not a humanitarian problem. Humanitarian action in Bosnia is being presented only as an excuse for not addressing squarely the basic problem which is one of aggression across an international border, which is one of ethnic cleansing, which is one of the right to self defence, etc. One has to salute the Jewish community which has really been the only community which has perceived consistently what is really at stake in Bosnia. Despite that, we somehow see Bosnia as some sort of a Muslim enclave being created in Europe. People were interested in Bosnia because it was a people being squashed by two aggressors, but it was never a problem of a Muslim entity. But, having made it into a problem of a Muslim entity, we are now creating a Muslim fundamentalism even in the heart of Europe.

The third example is the well-known example of Algeria. Algeria had an election. It was a free and fair election. A particular political party won that election. Somehow, again, this party was perceived as having long beards, and anybody with long beards is suspect in today's world. So, a huge campaign was mounted to say that perhaps the elections may have been democratic, but what we really need is stability. Never did we hear an objection to this denial of the results of a democratic election in Algeria as we would have heard had the ethnic community been somewhat different. The point that I am making is that we are somehow trying to create an enemy where I personally do not think any exists.

Hendrik Wagenmakers

On Bosnia, in intellectual terms, I would agree with Ambassador Kamal. Grave events are taking place there despite all our international co-operation and arms control and disarmament efforts. Sometimes we Europeans are accused of always knowing what is good for others. Making statements about this and about that and the whole thing. Then, when we have to do something in our own region, like Bosnia, it does not always go well. This greatly bothers me, I confess.

The examples that Kamal gives are interesting examples. One can debate the issue of Iran, Iraq, and Algeria. But now our colleagues from the subcontinent, great minds, are always expressing good thoughts in high quality English. However, Mr Kamal did not say "we have learned from all these things. We, from the subcontinent, we are going to do it better."

What do we read in our media? We read about all these weapons, missiles and what have you, going into Pakistan - in the same words like he used, "pumping arms" into the subcontinent. I would just, as a friend and colleague of Kamal's, like to hear how they in the subcontinent are going to do it better, so that we can learn from them.

Richard Grimmett

Our subject is regional security. Regional tensions have always existed, certainly during this century. It is fair to argue, as some already have, that the Cold War gave nations in the West an excuse not to address those regional problems. Now the former East-West conflict has been replaced, in some important ways, with a North-South conflict over what constitutes an important regional security matter.

The question is not: are regions now the focal point of conflicts? I think they are. But what is new about the post-Cold War situation is that not all regional conflicts threaten global security in general or the security of the West in particular. Stated bluntly, until a regional dispute develops into a direct threat to Western security interests as happened with Iraq's invasion of Kuwait, that dispute is not going to be addressed by the Western powers to the extent they might have during the Cold War period. Why is that the case?

Because the world is now witnessing a degree of intense, localized, nationalism to the degree that has not been displayed since perhaps the First World War, if not earlier. Bosnia is a prime example of the results of that nationalism. At the same time, there is no compelling international security threat in the Bosnian conflict that would lead Western European States or their allies to conclude that military intervention in Bosnia on a massive scale was justified at this time. This is true despite the revulsion in the West over the brutal killings and outrages against the civilian population in Bosnia we have witnessed.

A major complication in finding effective solutions to regional conflicts in the years ahead is that the revolution in communications technology has permitted citizens throughout the world to see almost instantaneous, and often horrible, events displayed on their television sets every night on news broadcasts. These images have often stimulated calls for leaders to take immediate actions, to provide a quick solution which just is not feasible. In nearly all of these cases, what is involved is an ethnic, religious, or political conflict that has deep roots in history and does not lend itself to an easy, comprehensive settlement. Yet, this dictation of foreign policy focus by CNN images seems likely to continue for the foreseeable future. This phenomenon of media-stimulated moral outrage will not likely lead to resolution of regional conflicts, but it will keep those matters only a newscast away from becoming a stateman's policy nightmare.

The emerging focus on regional conflicts is quite appropriate. But achieving solutions to any number of these conflicts is not as simple as some would have us believe. Certainly, swapping philippics against one another about them is not going to lead to their resolution. For, in the end, that activity just leads to continuing rhetorical counter responses that are not particularly useful.

Ahmad Kamal

What is the difference between Bosnia and Kuwait? We have two situations. Other than oil, can you identify a second point which is significantly different between the two cases? Bosnia has had statehood for close to several hundred years. Both of these countries are members of the United Nations. Both of them are aggressed from outside their frontiers. In the one case, there is a response that we know, and in the other there is the absence of response that we know. Why?

In other words, we come down to the question of the definition of security, which is what I was trying to say. What is security? Is it the security of oil supplies for the United States at cheap prices, or is security the absence of suffering and the creation of peace in a global village? If it is the latter, then I am afraid the responses have to be commensurate in both cases. That is what is lacking, and it pains me that after 45 or 50 years of a post-graduate, multilateral experience, everything that we have been doing, trying to frame multilateral collective security principles, that we should now be defining things in such a unilateral manner.

Section III: Regional Contexts and Perceptions

Shahram Chubin

This section will address three sets of issues. One is the context in which technology transfers occur. Another is the perceptions of regional States, though obviously there are as many perceptions as there are States in any particular region. And thirdly, the impact, insofar as one can speak at a certain level, of transfers of technology and arms on regional security.

I - Context

In this context there is a continuing demand where there are funds and there are endemic conflicts. It is clear also in the post-Cold War period that there is a renewed need for self reliance among States and doubts among former allies about commitments, or question-marks about the continuing commitments. There is greater supply of competition, greater spare capacity, new suppliers, much greater emphasis on commercial competition among all suppliers with the exception of the United States, the only supplier that tends to look at things strategically. There are also fewer restraints on local conflicts and correspondingly a greater need for indigenous balances. There is also the emergence of new and destructive and longer-ranged technologies, advanced conventional weapons, the diffusion of weapons of mass destruction and more focus on these two, and particularly the latters' capabilities by supplier States. There is also the inexorable diffusion of science and, to some extent, technology throughout the world: communications, computer and other revolutions including the global economy, the mobility of labour, and so on. And there are finally more efforts at creating supplier regimes, transplanting COCOMs into the North/South context and various other efforts to strengthen existing regimes.

There is also an increasing intermeshing of regional, global, or if you like, global order issues. What North Korea does in the Korean peninsula affects not only the regional balance, but also the nuclear proliferation incentives worldwide, or certainly the lessons drawn. Policies and technology transfer, it seems to me, are conceived bi-laterally, but have regional and global connotations as well. And similarly denial or supplier regimes are conceived globally but have clear regional implications, at least in theory.

One cannot speak very usefully at a high level of generality or abstraction and we need to bring issues to concrete cases. But obviously the structure of the region is important. Between the Korean, the South Asian, and the Middle Eastern case there is similarity and they are comparable. Essentially there are two camps, in two cases two States. In the Persian Gulf there are more than two States, they are what we call multiple axes, and here it is far more complicated. In this latter case, not only are the regimes in principle vulnerable but as we have seen in recent times, alliances are subject to reversal.

In all of these cases technology transfers are seen with their political connotations as well as for their practical utility. That is as part of a currency of a political relationship that either exists or does not exist. It is either good or bad, whether in the supply or in the denial, particularly of US supplies. The recipients thus see access to arms and technology variously. Some see it as a matter of a right to obtain advanced technology, a means of keeping up, being competitive and developing, requiring experience and familiarity with technology, as well as for the national security purposes defined rather more broadly and finally for the narrower specific defence purposes that particular technology might serve. In specific cases, US supplies to Israel, Saudi Arabia and South Korea, technology transfer is part of a general defence relationship. In fact, it is the equivalent of a defence commitment in cases where technology is denied particular States, as is quite often, because political relations are particularly bad with that State.

II - Recipients' Perspectives

Now in terms of the recipients' perspective, there are a number of disjointed points to make. Obviously, access to technology is important where States cannot develop their own comparable systems, cannot do it feasibly or cannot do it economically. There is a parallel, but very distinct point, which is that the costs of advanced conventional capabilities are rising rapidly and this may well increase incentives for off-setting systems which are not so costly, such as the consideration of weapons of mass destruction in some areas.

Recipients, however, tend to ask for technology transfer as a component. They are not happy any more with finished systems. And that leads to co-production, local production, licensed production and weapons systems which are then made available locally; Israel and South Korea are cases. We have seen that in certain cases recipients upgrade, adapt, retrofit equipment and then transfer it: Iraq and its missiles; Israel and its *Jericho* which was originally a French programme. We have seen actually in cases of circularity where the US or France provides Israel with technology, Israel develops it; it goes to China and then ends up somewhere in the Gulf. Few regional States are totally dependent on one system. Diversification of sources of supply is prudent where technically and financially feasible. And we have seen this in the Gulf States where Kuwait has been fast rearming, but diversifying at the same time. Saudi Arabia has always had diversified sources of supply.

So recipients do not simply rely on one weapons system or one supplier but they tend, but for the specific cases mentioned earlier, to focus on one supplier because of their defence commitment. It is worth mentioning simply that the US controls not only its own supply directly, but it also tends to control, through its legislation, supplies of components in third countries' weapons systems, and not necessarily weapons systems, but technology that might have utility for, let us say, a transport plane that might be used militarily. Obviously recipients seek to use the gaps between the US and other States' standards to gain access to technology, which they then seek to replicate domestically. They seek to loan it and restrict definitions of dual-use, to exploit the commercial competition by dangling other commercial deals and incentives to play on the tradition of some States like Germany, for example. They seek to transfer technology, and not simply completed systems, or else to depict the United States' vigorous application of standards as vindictiveness or impunitive.

Now, most suppliers are motivated by commercial considerations, not regional security. We saw this in the Gulf War of 1991 when many suppliers supplied both Iran and Iraq simultaneously, and that did not exclude China, North Korea and Brazil; it was not just the Soviet Union that got involved, or just European countries. The effect these supplies have on regional politics obviously depends upon the region itself. In seeking to maintain a qualitative edge in an asymmetrical situation, as the United States has in the Near East with Israel and to some extent now in the Gulf, and Saudi Arabia, it of course guarantees infusion of vast arms into the region, something, I think, Ian Anthony was pointing to this morning.

It may act more directly as a balancing power in a region. The United States, for example, in both South Korea and in the Persian Gulf, is not only a supplier of arms, it is also a physical presence. It may provide off-setting systems. The *Patriots*, for example, are in South Korea, in Israel and in Saudi Arabia and the *Arrow* in Israel eventually. And there is even now discussion about the possible supply of technology that may be stabilising after the fact, that is, for example, after nuclear proliferation occurs, finding a technology that will harden command and control and stabilise the situation.

It is clear, though, that suppliers' influence comes from supply and not denial. There are legions of cases where denial was practised and little control was exercised thereafter. South Africa is a good example. Iran in the 1980s is a good example, not simply because it shifted from Western sources of supply to Eastern sources of supply, but also the composition of the arms it bought changed. When it was supplied by the West it had no missiles; when it shifted to the Eastern bloc it began emphasizing missiles, a whole string of missiles: Stinger missiles from Afghanistan, *Scuds*, *Silkworm*, and possibly even *Cruise* missiles. And it is also clear that the cut-off of supplies to regional countries often encourages those States to go single-mindedly for new sources. Pakistan in 1965 was even-handedly cut-off in the middle of its engagement with India. Unfortunately, India did not have supplies from the US, so Pakistan considered this discriminatory and went off for new sources of supply.

III - Impact on Regional Security

Now, what about the impact of new supply and new technologies on regional conflict? Firstly, it seems that these are unlikely to be used optimally. They are probably neutral in terms of the probability of war, and they are fairly certain to leak, as we saw with Afghanistan and *Stingers*. And they tend to force the acquisition of equivalent or compensating technologies: Iran's missiles versus, perhaps, Saudi Arabia's F-15s. There is very little or no control of the subsequent use of the weapons that are supplied. We have seen that, as in the case of Israel and missile technology via China into the Gulf, new technologies may or may not increase the destructiveness of war. On the one hand, they may be more discriminating in terms of the targets acquired. And it is certainly true that most casualties of war come from conventional weapons. But it is also true that new technologies do tend to increase the number of participants and may reach new targets through aerial refuelling, over-the-horizon missiles, AWAC's and C-3 systems. Missiles might also increase pre-emption incentives and widen conflicts.

The impact of supply of technology and arms to regions on regional security obviously then depends on the region and the political context. In theory it can under-gird, buttress regional security when significant balances exist and where these are combined with tensions. But it can just as well encourage quantitative and qualitative arms races. Each of these cases can be made in the Middle East, Persian Gulf, the Koreas and South Asia. In general, such infusions can buy time for political settlements. However, they do run the risk of discouraging one party among the regional States from an inevitable and necessary regional accommodation, which is necessary for regional security. India, for example, long argued that the US assistance to Pakistan falsely equated Pakistan with India.

A supposedly industry-biased report was put out by the National Academy of Sciences in 1990-1991 on US export controls in the changed global environment. It noted, "Much technology that we might like to control has spread so widely and is produced so extensively that its control is no longer feasible. The reality of much of today's high-tech world, especially in computers and micro-electronics, somewhat less so in other areas like aircraft and engines, is that once a technology is used substantially in one military equipment it may become by nature virtually uncontrollable." Now, there are clearly a lot of questions here about applicability and enforcement and the slippery definitions of dual-use items. There are also questions about the ability of the United States to act unilaterally and effectively as opposed to punitively. The ability of multilateral supplier regimes to agree on anything apart from the lowest common denominator is also another question.

The final question is the balance between the national, global and regional approaches to these sets of problems. Most security problems are regional. Even more so, our definitions of regions are becoming more elastic depending on the issue. Global approaches, for example to non-proliferation, have problems associated with them. On the one hand North Korea is an important regional as well as global precedent. On the other hand, uneven or selective enforcement of this norm leaves some regions imbalanced and exposed. Export controls ultimately may arrest and increase the cost of weapons development. They will buy time and the use of this time for conflict resolution is as much the responsibility of regional States as it is that of the outside powers.

Chapter 8
Security Considerations in the Middle East: A Regional Perspective

Section I: An Iranian Approach

Javad Zarif

With the end of the Cold War, international politics have undergone a fundamental transformation. No student of international politics could have been adequately prepared for the events of the past several years. These events have undoubtedly altered the structure of power and influence in the world. Bi-polarity has given way to a transitional State, not clearly identifiable as uni- or multi-polar, at least temporarily.

In the aftermath of the Cold War, problems connected mainly with the legacy of past erroneous approaches and perceptions continue to challenge our common efforts towards a better world order. Nowhere, perhaps, is this more evident than in the Middle East. The destabilizing approaches in this region, coupled with biases and misperceptions about the region, remain almost unchanged. In an era of limited attention to the root cause of conflicts and security problems, it is high time to evaluate seriously the adverse impacts of these approaches on regional security, and to develop constructive and comprehensive policies with a view to building a solid security structure for the region.

Allow me now to reflect on two fundamental issues related to regional security, namely the proliferation of weapons of mass destruction in the Middle East region and the security dilemma in the Persian Gulf area. But before that, let me just make one or two general observations about the wider picture.

The underlying problem in the Middle East is the unresolved question of Palestine and the unrealized human and national rights of the Palestinian people. Most, obviously not all, of the security concerns and threat perceptions of various actors in this region are rooted in this problem. It follows that a comprehensive, just and lasting solution to this underlying problem will remove the most significant obstacle to regional stability, thus helping to arrest the dangerous spiral of the arms race, particularly in the area of weapons of mass destruction. It also follows that such peace and stability is, or should be, the desire and objective of all.

It is our contention that a "peace process", as distinguished from, and in fact as opposed to, a process of "force, intimidation, suppression, submission, and surrender" has never been embarked upon in this region, despite the television episodes of the last two seasons, or perhaps as illustrated by the same episodes. Whatever its short-term result, it is evident that surrender by a few will not alter security and threat perceptions of an entire population. Thus, instead of leading to peace and stability, it will only entrench the same threat perceptions leading to further insecurity and instability.

In such a complex situation, in which various and competing political, economic, strategic and ideological interests come into play, weapons of mass destruction not only present a dangerous escalation, but also a major impediment to a comprehensive settlement. The objective of non-proliferation as a component of total elimination of nuclear weapons and other weapons of mass destruction has assumed added significance in the new international environment. Given the sensitivity of the Middle East region, it is essential to direct all efforts to make this region, once and for all, a zone free from any weapons of mass destruction. This is particularly imperative because of the following realities of this region:

1. The region has been fraught with several cases of aggression, occupation and expansionism;
2. Various types of weapons of mass destruction, most notably nuclear weapons, can be and are produced in the region by Israel;
3. Only a few in the region, prominent among them Israel, have long-range delivery capabilities, enabling it to target almost any Middle Eastern capital with weapons of mass destruction;
4. Chemical weapons were used extensively and with little initial adverse international reaction by Iraq during the 1980's;
5. A number of regional actors, including both Israel and Iraq, have failed to sign one or more important international disarmament instruments, most importantly NPT and CWC.

In spite of this, no genuine effort has been initiated to meet this serious challenge. Indeed, major nuclear-weapon States, who are the most active advocates of non-proliferation, have found no reason to object to Israel's production and stockpiling of weapons of mass destruction, tacitly exempting it, despite its record of reckless expansionism, from the emerging international non-proliferation regime. This has prompted the argument that a deliberate and conscious policy is in place to maintain a permanent threat against the security of regional States.

This approach and the perceptions it has fostered have in themselves increased the potential for further proliferation of weapons of mass destruction in the Middle East. In fact, the threat posed by possession of nuclear weapons by Israel and its failure to accept the NPT and IAEA safeguards has given rise to non-accession to international instruments prohibiting weapons of mass destruction, most notably CWC, by a number of States in the region, including those with formal diplomatic relations with Israel.

Thus, the pursuit of a discriminatory policy of selective proliferation rather than non-proliferation by nuclear-weapon States constitutes a major threat to peace and security in the Middle East. It also curbs the advancement and success of any disarmament initiative in the region. In the larger context, the persistence of nuclear-weapon States in this attitude would run the risk of gravely harming the NPT which comes up for review and possible extension in 1995.

In this context, due attention should also be paid to the legitimate prerogatives of States Parties to the NPT for the peaceful application of nuclear energy. In reality unfortunately, States Parties to the NPT, who have fulfilled their obligations under the treaty, have become subjects of mounting political and economic pressure coupled with a propaganda and misinformation campaign launched by some nuclear-weapon States, and even by Israel, the most prominent NPT outlaw. The former's attempts to gain access to this technology for peaceful use have been unjustifiably suppressed. This has left the impression that the NPT has failed to serve the legitimate aspirations of its signatories in addition to its broader failure to curb proliferation.

The prospect for non-proliferation of nuclear weapons, particularly in the Middle East, can be improved only when its most vocal proponents, the nuclear-weapon States, adopt a comprehensive, non-selective and non-discriminatory policy based on a single set of standards and stop discriminating between friendly and unfriendly countries when it comes to proliferation. Towards this end, it is essential to take constructive and practical steps including

1. Placement of all facilities and installations in the region under the safeguard mechanisms of the IAEA; and
2. Accession by all regional States to all international disarmament instruments particularly the NPT, CWC and BWC.

Let me now turn to the issue of security in the Persian Gulf. This is an area of particular economic and political importance for the world, but, in spite of the urgent need to forge new security structures for the region, appropriate measures in this regard have yet to be precisely defined and developed. Indeed, there are mutually reinforcing elements which still nurture tension and precipitate instability in the region. Among these one can highlight the lack of confidence, insufficient dialogue, substantial foreign military presence and the excessive and unwarranted imports of advanced and sophisticated conventional weapons particularly from major arms exporting countries.

Unbridled and unwarranted conventional arms build-up coupled with the widespread military presence of foreign powers in the region not only undermines regional efforts towards strengthening security and co-operation in the Persian Gulf, but also precipitates insecurity perceptions in the region. These perceptions naturally encourage destabilizing incentives and in turn may generate a spiralling crisis.

In a hysteria fanned and exacerbated by one country or another, and based on an approach founded on rivalry and competition rather than mutual security and co-operation, the smaller States are induced or compelled into relying on foreign forces or underwriting military expenditures of others in the misplaced hope of creating for themselves a security shield against perceived enemies. Taking into account the geo-strategic characteristics of our region, it is evident that an approach based on rivalry and competition would eventually lead to fostering new imbalances and providing the capability for concealed ambitions to surface and menace the region.

For an area which has experienced two devastating wars within one decade, it is quite plausible to conclude that only a regional security and co-operation arrangement among countries in the Persian Gulf free from reliance on foreign powers can guarantee long term security and tranquillity in the region. Towards this end, countries in the region must promote dialogue, increase co-operation and enhance mutual confidence in their foreign relations, including with their neighbours in the Persian Gulf. In time, this will be translated into arrangements under a United Nations umbrella that will guarantee regional security. Indeed, the underlying principle in any sound approach should be co-operation among the regional countries in areas of common interest on the one hand, and confidence-building in areas of historical concern and mistrust on the other. This approach stands in contrast to the formation of competing blocks, which would naturally entrench and exacerbate historical divisions and rivalries.

For Iran, the Persian Gulf signifies vital national interests. Its critical importance for Iran's security and economic development is self-evident. All major Iranian commercial ports are located on the Persian Gulf through which more than 90 percent of Iran's trade flows, including its oil exports. Iran, with the longest coast on the Persian Gulf and the Gulf of Oman, has historically equated its own national security and economic prosperity with security, stability, tranquillity and free flow of oil and international commerce in the Persian Gulf area, and thus acted as the force for stability. In this context, Iran has allocated a mere 1.5 percent of its national budget for defence, and has had the lowest military purchases in the entire region. A glance at some figures makes the point even more clear.

In the last two years of the imposed war (1987-88), the total figure for Iran's import of armaments stood at less than $1.5 billion. Comparable figures for Iraq and Saudi Arabia were $8.2 billion and $5 billion respectively. In the following three years, the gap between Iran and the other two widened even further. Iran's total military imports bill for the 1989-91 period was $2.8 billion, while those for Iraq and Saudi Arabia had jumped to $10.3 billion and $10.6 billion. In 1992, Iran's military imports dropped to less than $850 Million. It is illustrative to point out that Iran's total military spending constitutes only a fraction of a single Saudi-US aircraft deal of $9 billion.

In order to arrest the spiralling arms expenditure, thus taking an important step to foster greater confidence as well as development, we should study and present concrete and workable proposals that seek to limit arms inflows into the region including:

- Measures that limit and reduce the waste entailed in excessive military expenditures;
- Steps that increase transparency, aimed at building confidence among regional States;
- Measures that put a cap on arms transfers to the region.

In arriving at a ceiling, limitations and hopefully subsequent reductions, a baseline will have to be agreed upon. This would reflect each State's relative weight and needs, which could be clarified in regional discussions. Whatever the approach, whether by limiting military budgets (expenditures), arms transfers, or specified weapons systems, the aim would be to eliminate a source of tension and to contribute towards regional security.

In the strategic region of the Persian Gulf, where major arms suppliers do not show sympathy and interest for genuine security and long-term stability of the region, only dialogue and co-operation among regional States coupled with positive inducements can secure a greater chance of success for pursuit of security and stability in the area. Creation of a forum by regional countries in the Persian Gulf, in which security issues, threat perceptions and other concerns could be aired can be a good and modest first step in this important endeavour.

Section II: Responses

Peggy Mason

I was particularly encouraged by the references to the need to promote dialogue. If I understood correctly, the language that was used, and did not seem to be hinged on any other preconditions, involved co-operation in areas of mutual interest, plus confidence-building in areas of longstanding sensitivity. Then there was the further comment made near the end in respect to arms transfers and the thorny question of what is excessive or too much.

This concept of a base line that would have to be developed seems to concern an emerging consensus in the arms control and regional security working group about a need for some kind of arms reductions in a balanced way. My question really is: is there any thinking that has elaborated on what this balance might constitute, given the situation of, if I might be blunt, the one and the many in the region?

Javad Zarif

The important first step is to agree to start the debate. If we start the debate, we can raise the different issues and the different concerns, some of which were just mentioned. All of these issues can be raised. That is why we think a forum, a regional forum, to discuss these ideas could be a good first step. It cannot be the end result, but it would be a good first step.

Ian Anthony

Is the Iranian government considering submitting a report in the framework of the United Nations Register of conventional arms for the calendar year 1993, the second year of the Register? Given that most of your primary suppliers are participating in the Register, it is difficult to see what you have to lose.

Javad Zarif

Actually, there are two issues involved regarding the UN register of arms. The first issue is the theoretical problem that a number of countries had with the proposal, with its limitations, and with its planned ways of limiting weapons, etc. The resolution does not cover enough. It was short in areas that were of interest to a good number of Third World countries, including weapons of mass destruction. But this is a theoretical question.

There is a practical side; there are practical problems for transparency. One-way transparency will not lead to confidence-building; it would invite aggression. Transparency should be comprehensive and global. Iran is prepared to provide a reply to the request by the Secretary General within the next few months, but we want this reply to be seen in the context of all regional replies. That is, we want the replies to remain confidential for as long as other regional States fail to present similar reports on their arms transfers. In that way we can start on the road to what is confidence-building, rather than simply inviting aggression.

Amit Bhaduri

Do you think that the question of building confidence in the region and building confidence in a larger global scale are complimentary in the case of Iran, or are they very often not complimentary? Do they work in the same direction: regional confidence-building and global confidence-building?

Javad Zarif

Regional confidence-building can be a good first start. It cannot run directly opposed to the global trends. That is, global trends cannot go in the direction of mistrust and exacerbation of crises, while at the same time we trying to build confidence in the region. The first important and essential step, a step that is attainable for our region, is to start a regional dialogue on confidence-building. I think that step is attainable and can start early.

Serguei Batsanov

From the Iranian perspective, what region are you talking about? We really deal with a very interesting region, however you define it. In these terms, in terms of confidence-building, in terms of arms control, in terms of supplying data for the UN arms register, etc., what kind of region are we talking about?

Javad Zarif

In my statement I addressed two regions in which we are members: that is the Middle East and the Persian Gulf, our more immediate neighborhood. There are also other regions in our thinking. One is the central Asian and the Caucasus region, comprising Iran, Pakistan, and Turkey (minus some countries in that region). The economic co-operation organization is, in our thinking, another way for fostering regional confidence and co-operation. In terms of arms transfers and the UN register of arms transfers, we are speaking about a wider presentation of ideas, a wider presentation of the statistics on arms purchases in our region, where our security concerns could also be addressed.

Richard Grimmett

You emphasized what appears to be a declining level of weapons purchases by Iran. You also mentioned your concerns with arms purchases by other States in the Persian Gulf region. Are we to understand that you feel in the current circumstances - in the absence of new regional initiatives to limit the sale of more weapons to the Persian Gulf region - that you expect Iran's arms purchases to remain at a low level, despite the threats from others that you perceive exist in your region?

Javad Zarif

If I understood your question correctly, I think if we establish the forum for discussion, everything will be discussed and debated within the forum in order to establish the base line and go on from that point. In terms of our policy with regard to arms purchases, the policy of the Iranian government is to maintain a very low level of defence replenishment (because of the problems we had in the war) and to put more of our limited resources into the area of economic development and reconstruction of the country, including manpower (in terms of the military forces).

Ahron Klieman

As an academic, I do not see the utility in using a forum such as this to replicate many of the one-sided presentations heard in various international negotiating forums. I find it incredulous to hear that the unresolved question of Palestine constitutes the single foremost security threat to the region from a spokesman of a country which was a direct participant in the Shatt al Arab in the War of the Cities (involving conventional weaponry), which was a concerned onlooker to the Kuwait aggression, and which witnessed the initial stages of the 1975 Lebanese civil war, all three of which were unrelated to the Palestine question.

Second, in my humble opinion, the major threat today to peace and security prospects in the region is not so much the weapons of mass destruction narrowly defined as the nuclear option, and Israel's reported nuclear option, specifically, but rather the insistence upon depicting the Sadat initiative, the Madrid peace process, and most recently and most notably, the

Oslo format, as instances of submission and surrender, rather than the acts of inspired statesmanship and initiative which, in truth, they really represent.

Edward Woollen

This question is on terrorist weapons. The most pernicious of weapons are not expensive, they are quite inexpensive. An aircraft bomb, a car bomb, chemical weapons, biological weapons are all quite cheap. There is a fear in the West about these weapons as really the global problem, not the big high-tech stuff. The high-tech stuff you can see and spot the control.

Raytheon recently had to move equipment that we were selling to Iran. In fact, we just sold our air-traffic control to Iran from Canada. The reason we had to do it from Canada is because there was a misunderstanding about the intentions of Iran and other countries in terms of suppressing use of terrorist weapons. Can you help us with the way that we can really begin to suppress on a global scale those most dangerous of weapons, which really attack women, children, and innocents? Is there some way that maybe Iran could take a leadership role and suppress that type of activity? I think that would put to bed this problem or concern - and I will call it confusion - that, for some reason, some countries are interested in terrorist weapons as a low cost solution to the high-tech things that occur next door.

Javad Zarif

There are two elements involved here. One is the proliferation of chemical weapons which can possibly be used by terrorist groups. This concern was raised by Iran during the 1980s when we were victims of chemical weapon attacks. We had no way of getting international attention concerning this use of chemical weapons against us. So, we said that these weapons could be used tomorrow against you by any terrorist group in an attempt to arouse some sensitivity in the world while we were being bombarded in our cities by chemical weapons.

The question of fighting terrorism requires a depoliticized international approach to deal with terrorism on equal footing throughout the globe. If you take that approach, then Canada is prepared to provide to Iran aircraft security machinery or equipment in order to combat terrorism and, at the same time, discourage terrorist groups which are involved in terrorist operations elsewhere. If you have a wider definition of terrorism and people who are involved in terrorism rather than simply specifying as terrorist those who are fighting against our own particular interests, then we might have a better chance of having a crack at this international global problem, rather than simply using terrorism as a slogan and to belabor a point with our adversaries.

Shahram Chubin

I wondered if we could not take, even if we share or do not share your analysis, your prescription somewhat further. It seems to me that you were talking about one region, the Persian Gulf, for one range of issues, and then the global approach on another set of issues. I wonder whether it is not worth asking whether there may not be some utility in looking at existing approaches that are at least on the table.

One approach is the regional multilateral talks on arms control. Although not necessarily part of the unacceptable peace process, I think there are States uninvolved in the peace process who are involved in those multilateral talks. The other is a nuclear-free zone approach, which was after all originally an Iranian-Egyptian proposal many years ago. The nuclear-free zone approach, it seems to me, could only buttress the IAEA approach; it is not an alternative to it. It is also a regional approach, but it may be a way in which you might get other parties in the region who are concerned involved. I wonder if you could comment on that.

Javad Zarif

The second issue is an easier issue. Iran has continuously supported the nuclear weapons free zone in the Middle East and now stands with Egypt on the question of the Middle East as a zone free from weapons of mass destruction. I alluded to this in my statement, although I did not want to state that in 1974, it was actually Iran which originally suggested the idea of a nuclear weapons free zone in the Middle East. We still support that idea. We are prepared to engaged in serious dialogue within the UN system to promote that idea, as we have done in the past with our Egyptian friends.

As far as the conferences are concerned, we have to start from the same starting point. That is participation of all States in the region (of everybody in the region) in the treaties and international instruments prohibiting weapons of mass destruction, as well as submitting all facilities in the region to the IAEA safeguard mechanisms. That would be the first step toward beginning a discussion.

John Simpson

There is a general issue central to this topic: the right of individual sovereign States to decide not to export technology, not to make exports to other sovereign States. I just wonder where you see States drawing a line between their own judgments on these matters, which are very much within their rights of sovereign States, and their commitments to transfer technology under international agreements. To put it another way, which has precedence, Article 1 of the NPT or Article 4?

Suha Umar

There was a reference in your statement and also in your replies regarding the need for a dialogue or a forum where security issues would be discussed among the regional countries and where confidence-building measures could also be taken up. I share that view. This should be the only way to a balance in the region which would bring peace and stability. On the other hand, we know that there is another process going on which is making good progress in these fields. Do we need to take any steps which would facilitate your participation in this process, or would you be willing to plan to start your initiatives independently from this in order to be able to put together such a forum as you have in mind so that you can have the possibility of discussing these issues? Thank you.

Javad Zarif

One very brief comment about the second question. The forum I suggested was as far as the Persian Gulf is concerned. That forum is lacking, and we need to start from there. I am a bit more modest in my aspirations. If we can stick to our immediate neighborhood, we will be better off.

As far as the first question is concerned, every sovereign State has the right to decide who will be its economic and technological partners, but we have to keep in mind that we give up some of our sovereignty when we join international agreements. That is the give and take process of international relations. We cannot simply insist on others giving up portions of sovereignty with regard to Article 1 of NPT, yet insist jealously that we want to maintain our portion as far as Article 4 of NPT is concerned. That is one part of the issue, but I think the issue is broader than that. It is not simply a sovereign State deciding not to import or to allow technological transfer in the area of nuclear energy to another State, but a State actually having to campaign to prevent others from doing the same thing. That would certainly be outside the realm of that very jealous interpretation of sovereignty which would prevent people from gaining access to nuclear technology and prevent suppliers from allowing a State to complete and finalize an already in-place project with IAEA present at the project and able to inspect it on any interval it desires. That is a totally different issue.

Chapter 9
Middle East: Security, Confidence-Building and Arms Control

Section I: Presentation

Mahmoud Karem

- I -

Many scholars have long argued that the Middle East is *sui generis*, that it has repeatedly brought the world to the brink of a nuclear war and that it harboured the most insoluble of all modern time conflicts. Recently, we have seen encouraging signs, and for the first time ever, negotiations between the parties. A specific track for arms control and regional security (ACRS) has been operating. Participants are engaged in a constructive effort to discuss a host of problems and a plethora of issues ranging from regional security, confidence-building, arms control measures, risk reduction centers etc...

Following three formal plenary sessions, under the co-chairmanship of the United States and Russia, as well as several workshops and inter-sessional (in between plenary meetings) it has become evident that the region for the first time was initiating a fundamental treatment of arms control issues. Events proved that parties moved away from an academic conceptual, if not theoretical, treatment of the topics on the agenda to a process of gradual and more business like substantive treatment.

This gradual change in positions advocated by the parties made possible for the first time the consideration of issues varying from arms control measures, in the proper sense, such as the implementation of the Mubarak 1990 initiative on the establishment of a zone free from all weapons of mass destruction in the Middle East, to the deliberations on measures to restore confidence and salient verification models. This gradual shift underscored a discernible trend, namely that arms control efforts may be discussed in tandem with confidence-building measures (CBM's) and that both should not be seen as mutually exclusive. This in itself may soon enable the parties to

133

commence identifying concrete measures. For the first time the United Nations was invited to participate in those meeting, thereby paving the road towards a future expanded UN role, especially in the fields of verification of arms control agreements in the region.

With the context of (ACRS) lectures, seminars and background papers were presented. The format itself allowed parties the chance to interact in order to remove divergencies in the interest of promoting arms control and security in the region, and the use of this forum to reach agreement on specific measures. Additionally, extra regional parties offered valuable assistance. The United Kingdom, for instance, offered to host a challenge inspection demonstration; Denmark offered to host a live CBM demonstration on monitoring a military manoeuvre. Other key states offered to shepherd a few areas such as a proposed joint US-Russian effort to study non-aggression undertakings, Netherlands on the establishment of a communication center, and Canada on the establishment of a rescue naval center in the Red Sea with the participation of Israel, Saudi Arabia, Egypt and Jordan.

In between the plenary sessions of ACRS several inter-sessional events took place. The first, two workshops hosted by Austria from 19-21 October, 1993. These workshops dealt with long-term objectives of the arms control process and declaratory CBM's. Additionally, Turkey hosted a workshop on exchange of military information and pre-notification of certain military activities in Antalya on 4-6 October 1993. Twenty-three delegates from five regional countries and representatives of the co-sponsors (USA and Russia) and the host country participated. The workshop recommended to the ACRS working group that the parties to the process study and consider the above-mentioned areas and identify the different stages at which they may be implemented, and to present their concrete suggestions on these matters at an expert group meeting for further formulation, taking into consideration security sensitivities and concerns of all participating parties. In this respect, it was seen that higher priority should be accorded to areas that are widely considered to be of a non-sensitive nature and which could be implemented in the initial stages of the process.

In July 1993, Egypt hosted a specialized workshop on "Verification of Arms Control Agreements and Confidence- and Security-Building Measures,"and in February 1994, a working group on a "Conceptual Basket". Granted, not all parties in the Middle East have joined this process, but I am confident that the accumulated experience will benefit all the parties and help charter an edifice of security and justice for the future.

- II -

Perhaps one of the biggest remaining challenges confronting the Middle East is arriving at a definition of security after such a long period of animosity and armed confrontations. Parties remain seized with the objective of realizing if not maximizing national security. The challenge we face now is to demonstrate to the parties that security can be achieved through means other than through arms. Additionally, it has become evident that defining a security regime for a volatile region such as the Middle East is a great challenge. Security in our region is not only security achieved through arms or defensive capabilities. Security in the Middle East is closely intertwined with stability, justice, water requirements, self-determination, economic considerations, etc... This is not to say that progress in one should be contingent upon progress in another or that one issue should be held hostage to the other. On the contrary, for as we have seen; we now have special separate tracks for water, environment, arms control... etc. Naturally, all these issues are interrelated and remain tied to a broader network aimed at realizing a comprehensive peace in the region. In this respect the Middle East is not much different from Central Europe which faced this problem before. Conventional wisdom forced regional European actors to segregate the issues by establishing different baskets under the aegis of peace talks for confidence-building and security in Europe. In a study headed by the late Swedish Prime Minister Olof Palme, comprising eminent figures and entitled *"Common Security: a blue print for survival"*, (1983: 10), the Study stated:

> Linkages between arms negotiations and political events should be avoided. Disarmament efforts do not move forward in a political vacuum. They must reflect political interests and the political order and are thus an integral part of international relations. However, it is important not to construct, as a matter of deliberate policy, linkages between particular negotiations to limit specific aspects of the arms race and international behaviour in general. The task of diplomacy is to split and subdivide conflicts rather than generalize and aggregate them. Linking them into broader issues tends to limit, rather than broaden, the scope for diplomatic manoeuvre. Progress in arms negotiations is not a reward for either negotiating partner; it is a means for both to capitalize on their common interest in security and survival. At the same time it must be recognized that significant movement towards disarmament will proceed only

with difficulty in the absence of broader political accommodation. The two interact and must move together. They can aid one another in facilitating progress, but neither can proceed very far without progress in the other. Just as arms negotiations would fail in the absence of political accommodation, so too would movement towards more co-operative political and economic relations come to an end without concurrent progress towards stabilization of the military balance and reductions in the size of armed forces.

However, if we are to deal with and analyze our present security setting in the Middle East we can identify a few salient parameters.

The first centers around the endemic intra-regional perspective of opposing security structures, concepts and perceptions. This is important in order to understand the full scope of achieving security in our region. Regional wars with global implications took place in 1948, 1956, 1967 and in 1973. Additionally, the Middle East is at present entering a different level of analysis, that of a qualitative rather than quantitative procurement for arms or as some scholars have argued, a race for a "qualitative edge". The independent commission on disarmament and security stated in the study *Common Security: A Blue Print for Survival* (1983:5):

> Technology imposes other costs as well. The advanced technologies incorporated in modern weapons mean that the domestic burdens of armaments are great - not just the use of enormous sums of money, but the diversion of scarce resources, particularly highly skilled individuals and also materials, from solving social problems. Thus, a second irony is that the more we strive for security from external threats by building up armed forces, the more vulnerable we become to the internal threats of economic failure and social disruption.

Examples of such a qualitative edge is Israel's reaching into outer space by launching satellites, the development of a new anti-missile system (ARROW), and practising an undeclared nuclear posture of psychological deterrence, introducing super computers, proliferation of weapons of mass destruction and their delivery systems apart from astronomical regional military expenditures, and procurement from national production. All these factors conformed the present security setting and add obstacles to peace efforts.

Second, against this background it is imperative to present an analysis of what seems to be an emerging arms control, arms limitation global regime in order to fully comprehend its relationship with a future Middle East security setting. In the recent years several attempts aimed at regulating the flow of weapons to the region have begun and meetings between the five major weapons exporters succeeded in laying the turf for the implementation of guidelines in order to limit the flow of weapons to the region. The five began consultations in Paris in 1991, and as a result we saw the Paris declaration by the five. Naturally, countries in the region followed these meetings with suspicion and feared that the results may lead to a situation of asymmetry in the region. The thesis is that any regional disarmament regime and machinery which aims at limiting, preventing the proliferation, prohibiting, or inhibiting arms transfers must proceed taking into consideration the political realities of the region, the need to achieve security in its wider definition for all parties and at lower level of armament, the right of all States to live behind secure and recognized boundaries, as well as arriving at an agreed and mutually acceptable definition of national security.

- III -

What then are the possible basic pillars, as we see it from our part of the world, of such a possible and emerging global arms limitation and arms control regime?

1. More genuine efforts need to be exerted to convince significant nuclear threshold countries to join the Non-Proliferation Treaty (NPT). Declaratory statements calling on threshold States to join the NPT are not sufficient and must now be coupled with concrete direct contacts as well as action-oriented steps designed to achieve the universality of the NPT regime before its extension in 1995. The topic of non-proliferation must be forced on the agenda in the Middle East and Asia. Conferences dealing with non-proliferation and security must be convened to emulate progress already achieved in Latin America and especially by non-NPT States Argentina and Brazil. The fact that a few States have chosen to withstand international pressures to join the NPT is a serious flaw that needs to be redressed especially in light of the fact that the NPT has been in *de facto* existence since 1968. Some scholars argue that the NPT has harboured several nuclear threshold countries and has given them a safe haven to develop their nuclear capabilities by allowing them the benefits of the non-proliferation regime without their formal accession notwithstanding that other regional parties renounced the nuclear option and acceded to the treaty thereby shouldering

their commitments and obligations. It is essential, therefore, to address in a symmetrical and balanced manner, the rights and obligation of all States vis-à-vis all the legal instruments comprising the juridical regime of weapons of mass destruction namely, the NPT, Biological Weapons Convention and the Chemical Weapons Convention.

2. In recent years the world community has shown an increasing appreciation of the significance of transparency and openness in international relations and the positive impact it could have on international security and world prosperity. While it is valid to assert that transparency and openness emerge as the model and future wave in arms control and disarmament efforts, especially in the present international milieu, its treatment is being conducted with a Eurocentric perspective and without taking into consideration the different basic characteristics of different regions around the world. Certainly, basic tenants of the European model may be emulated elsewhere. In the Middle East, for example, a region that has undergone the turmoil and suffered the destruction from several wars in the past forty years, it may become difficult to start with an ambitious program of openness and transparency involving all the parties due to the existence of an unresolved political conflict. One further example to elucidate the difference: whereas the concept and doctrine of deterrence was a key tenet of European security, in the Middle East war-fighting and war-winning strategies are central. In Europe deterrence was possible because, within the east-west framework, it was used to preserve and maintain the *status quo* outlines and implemented in treaties and agreements. In the Middle East, on the other hand, the *status quo* is not acceptable and hence encouraging deterrence thinking in the region is a serious matter, for it may force parties in the region, who are helpless in the face of an unavowed Israeli nuclear capability, to resort to obtaining or developing weapons of mass destruction in an attempt to create a situation of parity. The Iraqi case is a classic example underscoring such a theoretical underpinning. International costs and efforts to diffuse this situation have levied an astronomical toll on world financial resources. Additionally, statements have emerged from Iran, including one by its deputy president, to this effect. In 1992 Ayatollah Mohajerany, the Deputy President asserted:

> Because the enemy has nuclear facilities, the Moslem States too should be equipped with the same capacity. Moslems should strive to go ahead.

Hence what we need to underline at present is the necessity of engaging in a deeper examination of the lessons learned from the European model and agreements aimed at securing military stability, the applicability of such models and modalities in order to draw from this large body of knowledge, guidelines and tailor-made lessons. One of these measures should be to revisit standing arms control initiatives such as the Mubarak Plan (April 1990) to rid the Middle East of all weapons of mass destruction.

Concomitantly, it is important to dissipate regional fears that a scheme for transparency and openness, regulating arms transfers, might only lead to the disarmament of needy States and the establishment of regional giants enjoying massive indigenous production and large conventional weapon stockpiles, as well as a qualitative edge, which offers them a leverage over the other regional actors and neighbours.

3. Securing transparency and consultations, not only between and among the supplier States but also between the supplier and the recipients, is necessary to increase confidence. After all it must be remembered that States, weary of seeking to protect their national defence requirements, national industries and development plans, need to be reassured of the purposes and objectives of these high level closed consultations between exporter States.

During the same time and while we are witnessing the consolidation of groups such as the missile technology control regime (MTCR), designed to combat the dangers of the proliferation of ballistic missiles, we also witness that Iran has recently purchased from North Korea medium range, 1,000 km missiles, which place many Arab capitals in jeopardy. Additionally, a recent study confirms this fact (*Non-Proliferation Review*, fall 1993, p. 57). For instance, in the category of missiles in service, the study reports that Egypt has missiles with a range of 280 km while Iran possesses missiles in the range of 600 km. However, in the category of missiles in development Egypt, the study asserts, is developing a missile in the range of 450 km, while Iran is developing a system that is more than double the range of the missiles developed in Egypt, *i.e.*, in the range of 1,000 km. This asymmetry creates a situation of imbalance which forces regional actors to refuse the *status quo* and increases international apprehension with the MTCR regime guidelines that aim to legitimize such a disequilibrium. This conflicting procedure creates doubts behind the rationale of such control regimes and forces regional actors to rely on extra-regional powers for arms supply which runs counter to the basic objectives of the major weapon suppliers destined to regulate the process and diminish arms sale to areas of regional tension.

The same could be said of other groups which have been created in the past few years. Take for instance, arrangements such as the ones destined to review the existing nuclear export control policies of supplier States such as the Zangger committee, the nuclear supplier group, which met in Warsaw recently, as well as the Australia group, on harmonizing ways and means to prevent the proliferation of chemical and biological weapons and conforming national export policies on chemical weapons dual equipment and biological weapons related items and components. Naturally, recipient States with peaceful uses as well as chemical industries need to be consulted and briefed on the purposes of such closed meetings as well as their outcomes.

- IV -

However, it could be argued that the Middle East is also different in terms of the arms control proposals that have been advanced by the parties. Some of these proposals have gained intra-regional support over a long period of time. This makes the Middle East different from South Asia, for example, which has on its agenda arms control proposals that do not enjoy regional consensus.

Two of the salient proposals that have accrued international recognition in the Middle East arms control endeavors are the 1974 initiative for the establishment of a nuclear weapon free zone in the Middle East, and the 1990 Mubarak plan to establish in the Middle East a zone free from all weapons of mass destruction.

As has been discerned, the establishment of a NWFZ in the Middle East has been the subject of active consideration by the United Nations General Assembly every year since 1974. The resolution calling for the establishment of this zone in the Middle East is the only one that has provoked positive developments within the framework of the United Nations, ultimately reaching the degree of a consensus resolution in 1980. This is of cardinal importance since it tool place long before the initiation of the peace talks and when Israel only enjoyed the recognition of Egypt as the sole Arab country exchanging diplomatic missions with her. The members of the General Assembly, as stated in the resolution, overwhelmingly commended the application of a NWFZ in the region, and recognized that the establishment of such a zone enjoyed wide support in the region which in turn evolved into a consensus. Hence, the first prerequisite (intra-regional support) for establishing the zone was assured. The General Assembly did not limit itself to an endorsement of the initiative nor to sanctioning its necessity or acceptability by the States of the region. On the contrary, the General Assembly, mindful of the dangers inherent in the situation, both for the region and the world at large, remained constantly seized with the matter. Several series of practical measures emerged to promote the realization of this objective in order to keep open the option of establishing a NWFZ.

Among the first set of measures were a recommendation to the States of the region to refrain, on reciprocal basis, from producing, acquiring, or in any other way possessing nuclear weapons and nuclear explosives; or from permitting the stationing of nuclear weapons or nuclear explosive devices on their territory, or territories under their control, by any third party. Among the second set of measures aimed at generating momentum toward the establishment of such a NWFZ, were an invitation to the countries concerned to adhere to the NPT, an invitation to the countries of the region to declare their support for the establishment of such a zone in the region, and to deposit these declarations with the Security Council for consideration as appropriate, and an invitation to the nuclear-weapon States to render their assistance in the establishment of the zone.

On the other hand, another initiative for the establishment of a zone free from all weapons of mass destruction was geared towards averting the implications of the proliferation of weapons of mass destruction and their components to the Middle East. In essence, this initiative constituted one of the endeavors aimed at realizing export control mechanisms at this early stage of time. Events proved that many countries, some western, were responsible, due to lax export control measures, for supplying lethal components to countries in the Middle East. The three basic tenants of the Mubarak initiative aim to prohibit all nuclear, chemical and biological weapons in the Middle East while requesting States to make an equal and reciprocal commitment to honour the prohibition as well as a commitment to the application of verification measures.

With the entry into force of the Chemical Weapons Convention in January 1995, as well as the NPT extension conference in May 1995, both initiatives gain topicality. It is hoped that the necessary measures as well as the modalities for the implementation of both plans will be duly discussed between the parties in the Arms Control and Regional Security (ACRS) Forum for the Middle East. One necessary component should be to agree on the definition of the zone as well as its geographic boundaries. In the context it may be necessary to approach this exercise with flexibility in order to accept salient political realities which may allow for the evolution of a geographic definition of the region. Some scholars call for starting with a narrow definition of the region by allowing it to widen as the regime proves more successful. Others, in dealing with different categories of weapons in the Middle East, have called for a narrow approach while stating that when dealing with weapons of mass destruction, a large territorial definition as well as a wide geographic extent is compulsory because of the far-reaching and transboundary implications of such weapons of mass destruction.

In conclusion, as has just been demonstrated the Middle East is rich with arms control proposals, enjoys a special track for arms control where it may be possible not only to address these initiatives, but also to allow the parties to interact and understand the perceptions and security preoccupations of one another. Indeed the process may be long and arduous, but it has already begun.

Section II: Comments

Aaron Karp

You did not condemn the various supplier groups - NSG, MTCR, et al. - outright. Rather, if I understood you correctly, you think that, with some changes, Egypt could accept the existence of these groups. In particular, you wanted more consultation before and after meetings and perhaps some tailoring of the control lists, but you were not opposed to the existence of the groups outright.

Mounir Zahran

About the supplier groups motivations and the repercussions on regional security, it is not a matter of condemnation or praise for such groups. These groups do trigger suspicion and mistrust. The most practical way to address these suspicions and mistrust is to associate the users and the recipients of *the respective technologies in the relevant* groups. For the nuclear suppliers group, those who are interested in that technology for peaceful *purposes should* be invited to join. For the Australia Group, likewise; those who are interested in developing their chemical industries for civil purposes *should also* be invited, and so on and so forth.

Mahmoud Karem

I would like to add that we should not group all regimes together and afford them an equal treatment. I think each is somewhat different from the other, not only in terms of the category of equipment with which they are dealing, but also in their nature, historic background, number of participations, etc. However, if we get into an elaborate discussion of Egypt's view *vis-à-vis* each and every single regime, I think it is going to take endless time. The message that I wanted to convey has been delivered, mainly a message concerning the spirit in which these regimes operate. Many countries have problems with the secrecy, with the opaque nature - the closed nature, if you will - of the operating mechanisms that these regimes use. This is precisely the message that I wanted to deliver and I think it has been understood. We hope that these disparities will be remedied in the future. There should be universal application of transparency.

One additional point: the Middle East is different, and it is more different now than it was in the past because we now have a structured process of arms control negotiations taking place. These negotiations are taking place in a very co-operative spirit. Credit for that co-operative spirit goes both to Israel and to the Arab countries that have chosen the difficult task of sitting around the table addressing questions, presenting proposals, listening to others' positions and fears, trying to solve all the problems facing the region. Granted, these problems may not be solved in the near future. We know that this is a long process, but at least it has begun in a very constructive atmosphere which again makes the Middle East different from many other regions around the globe.

Chapter 10
Impact of the Gulf War on States' Behavior and Attitudes Toward Advanced Technology

Section I: Technology and the Gulf War: Lessons to be Drawn

Geoffrey Kemp

It was inevitable that in the aftermath of the Gulf War, which was the most viewed conflict in modern history, everybody would go back to square one and start to assess what impact this war had on their own military capabilities, and what it means for the future of warfare.

1. Clearly the war revealed the enormous vulnerability of relatively modern societies like Iraq to modern weapons. Societies that are heavily dependent on electrical grid systems and modern communications systems are vulnerable to precision bombardment. The war also demonstrated the highly accurate capability of modern missile systems, those delivered without aircraft and those delivered from aircraft, to hit fixed co-ordinate targets. It also showed it was difficult to hit targets that could move, particularly the SCUD missiles.

There was some weaknesses revealed in the war which were most obvious in the communications arena. Modern warfare involving very high technology communications systems is itself vulnerable to overloading circuits which, in turn, made communications sometimes vulnerable to security lapses at some points in the Gulf War. The co-ordination between the United States Army, Navy, and Air Force was so bad that co-ordinates and updated targeting lists had to be carried by hand because the services could not talk to one another.

Of the things that went wrong with the Allied operation, they were primarily in the communications field. The friendly fire that killed almost as many American casualties as the Iraqis did, in part, was a failure of communications. One of the most profound lessons of the Gulf War, for at least the industrial powers, was that in its aftermath we became much more sober about Iraq's potential to build nuclear weapons. While there was some discussion of this before the war, you will remember that as late as October and November of 1990, when George Bush highlighted the potential danger of an Iraqi nuclear program, he was roundly criticized for trying to hype and exaggerate the threat posed by Iraq as an excuse for going to war.

Yet in the war's aftermath we not only discovered that the Iraqis were farther ahead than anyone had imagined, but that aerial bombardment including the extraordinarily high number of missions conducted by very accurate airplanes and missiles could not deal with the problem. It had to be dealt with on the ground by UN inspectors. So one of the clear lessons of the Gulf War for the status quo powers, at least, is that a country like Iraq (with co-operation of willing suppliers from the advanced world) could make enormous strides at developing a nuclear weapon under the very eyes of the International Atomic Energy Agency. Hence one of the major foci of the post Gulf War era has been to highlight the problem of proliferation.

2. But if you take out of the proliferation equation Iraq and North Korea, and the concerns about Iran, Libya and Syria, the proliferation problem would not get the attention that it is getting today. People may dispute this because of what happened with the break up of the Soviet Union, but Iraq and North Korea have set a precedent which is now being followed in the non-proliferation circles. The non-status quo countries - those that were in awe of the use of American technology during the Gulf War - have drawn quite different conclusions. In fact you can make the argument that precisely because non-nuclear technology was so effective during the Gulf War at defeating Iraq, which was the most highly armed country in the Middle East outside Israel that in the future you either have to match the capability of an industrial power like the United States with the same types of technology, or you have to develop nuclear weapons.

If you are in this category of countries, one of the most persuasive arguments in favor of developing a nuclear option is that without some equalizing weapon system capability, there is no way you can stand up to the onslaught of modern high tech non-nuclear weaponry. If you go through the list of countries that have drawn lessons from the Gulf War, implicit in a lot of the statements you hear from Third World Ministries of Defence is an assumption that the Gulf War strengthened the case for nuclear weapons.

After all, what was the issue that would truly have changed the nature of the conflict? It would have been if Saddam Hussein had had a nuclear weapon. This surely would have changed not only the debate about whether to go to war, but the nature of the war itself. So, the absence of an equalizing force on the part of Iraq was a lesson picked up by Iraq's neighbors.

3. As far as the lessons learned by other countries, in the case of the *Russians* there has been a great deal of study done on the Gulf War in part because it was predominately Russian equipment that was destroyed by American equipment. And, the question is would this have been typical of what would have happened in Central Europe if NATO and Warsaw Pact had fought each other? There is a school in Russia that says "yes." There are others who say "no." They agree the Gulf War had very little to do with the performance characteristics of Russian or Soviet systems, it had an enormous amount to do with the ineptness of Saddam Hussein and the way in which he used that technology.

One country that did not radically change its views as a result of the Gulf War, was *China*. The Chinese were modernizing their vast military establishment before the Gulf War, and the Gulf War reinforced that trend. What the war suggested was that those in China who still believed that human factors could offset technological superiority were dealt a setback. If you look at what the Chinese have been up to since the end of the Gulf War, particularly their intense efforts to buy at very good prices the high tech Russian equipment that was mentioned this morning, you could see that the modernization of the Chinese military establishment has not only been boosted as a result of the Gulf War, but this may well be one of the most important developments in international relations in the years ahead. China's military modernization is bound to have a profound effect on East Asia, South Asia and possibly even Russia itself if a new leadership came to power.

On the Indian subcontinent the lesson one is a rather apocryphal one made by former Indian Chief of Staff, who said after looking at the results of the Gulf War, "Well, at least that shows that India should never go to war with the United States unless it has nuclear weapons."

For *Israel* the war had some very profound implications. First, the Iraqi surprise attack on Kuwait - and it was a surprise to everybody including most of all those Arab diplomats that were telling the Americans right up to the last minute that Saddam was bluffing - that shows you still can have surprising events in the region. Once the war started, the Israelis learned the hard way that even a World War II type technology, such as the SCUD can have a devastating effect upon a highly industrialized modern society that wishes to minimize its casualties. It was not the effect of the SCUDS on military targets or even civilian targets that had such a profound effect on Israel, it was the psychological impact and the economic impact. Studies have been done showing that the Israeli industry lost billions of dollars of high tech orders. Industries literally had to shut down for days and days at a time because of gas masks, shelters, and the fear of chemical attack.

Located next to the theater of operations it was quite obvious that the *Iranians* would draw a very profound and important lessons from the War. Iran suffered double indemnity. It fought an eight year war with Iraq. The first two years went extremely well and the Iraqis were expelled from Iranian territory. Some have said that Iran should have then declared victory and worked out a peaceful agreement. But no, Khomeni wanted to carry the war across the Shatt al Arab and overthrow the Saddam Hussein regime, relying on human wave tactics and the Koran. After six more years of particularly vicious fighting, Iran was defeated and humiliated by an Iraq that was armed by most countries of the world (but not the United States). The Iranians then witnessed the enemy that had just humiliated them lose in a decisive battle. Consequently, Iran has gone through a major reappraisal of its own requirements and it is evident that Iran is now stressing high technology, professionalism, and reliance on skills rather than raw manpower. Some would also argue that Iran can now make a powerful case for considering weapons of mass destruction.

The Arab countries of the Gulf also learned the lesson that you need high technology. The best evidence of this is the extraordinary proliferation of arms sales to the GCC countries since the war. We could debate whether these are weapons that have been foisted on these countries by rapacious western salesmen, or whether or not the countries themselves were truly fearful of what the Iraqis nearly did, and are now taking out an insurance policy in the event that Iran becomes a more serious threat to security.

The GCC countries are very sanguine about what they are capable of and what they are not capable of in the high tech field. Possibly, with the exception of the Saudi Air Force, there is no really effective fighting force within the GCC - absent a strong American presence. So what you see here is rearmament for the GCC to build up a capability that would withstand either an Iraqi or an Iranian offensive alone. But jointly with the US then, of course, it is quite a formidable force.

4. Some more futuristic observations. Countries want to upgrade their capabilities, but there are limits to how far they can go because of manpower constraints or because of financial constraints. But there are now new theories that are emerging concerning the deeper lessons of the Gulf War. These have less to do with the accuracy of Stealth fighters and their missiles and Tomahawk cruise missiles than they have to do with the new importance that communications systems and information systems played in the whole management of that war.

Consider the development in nonlethal weaponry and the capacity to destroy targets without necessarily killing a lot of people. New weapons permit the destruction of communications systems through precision bombing or electromagnetic pulses to wreck electronic systems. There is a new concept known as cyberwar - a concept developed at the RAND Corporation, which argues that in the future the initial phases of most wars will be about attacking each other's information systems. The country that has the technology to destroy the enemies information system, destroys his ability to position his forces and his information and knowledge of the battlefield.

So the irony may be that one lesson of the Gulf War is that the super high tech that people now want to buy may be irrelevant, or very vulnerable, unless you have the parallel capabilities and the information systems to destroy it. This is what William Perry, the new Secretary of Defense has referred to as the "reconnaissance - strike capability," a capability he believes that will remain in the hands of a few industrial powers for a long time to come.

Section II: Comments

Amit Bhaduri

We have heard about offensive and defensive weapons in conventional technology. In information systems, has there been any attempt to classify which kind of information can be used specifically for offensive purpose and which can be used for defensive purposes? Certainly, something like this should be attempted at least. I do not know if it is a complete blind alley, but I would like to hear.

Michael Moodie

Is there any discussion of what might be called the "psycho-political" impact of the Gulf War, particularly on the attitudes of States potentially involved in regional conflicts toward their alliances or involvements with potential external sources of support?

You could make an argument that, in fact, a spin on the Indian General's comment is that the lesson of the Gulf War is that if you have nuclear weapons you will not even have to fight the United States. This is not only because the possession of nuclear weapons may change the political calculations in Washington with respect to the costs and benefits of intervention, but also because of the impact on the attitudes of potential American allies, or the side on which the United States would be intervening. It would not be US territory that would be subjected to the threat of weapons of mass destruction, but the territory of those allies on whose territory US forces were going to operate.

So, the desirability of providing bases of the kind that Saudi Arabia, and other States, made available during the Gulf War may be recalculated by those allies as a consequence of the presence of weapons of mass destruction.

John Simpson

The first question is really an extension of a point that Geoffrey Kemp made. Have we now, as a consequence of the Gulf War, actually arrived at the rather paradoxical situation that it might be perceived to go in the United States' interest to press for total nuclear disarmament? If it has overwhelming superiority in the conventional armament area, and if, therefore, the equalizer is going to be other States having nuclear weapons, then it would logically follow that it would be in the US national interest to have complete nuclear disarmament.

The second question is more a puzzle than anything else. Looking at what we understand about weapons acquisition processes, it appears that one of the things that has driven the weapons acquisition process over the last 40 years has been the East-West conflict, insofar as weapons developed in the Western States have tended, to some extent but not entirely, to be geared to combating weapons that were believed to be being developed in the East and vice versa. My puzzlement is that if we do not now have an East-West conflict, then where is the technological dynamic to come from in weapon procurement? Where are the stimulii going to come from for new weapons? What sort of new weapons are we actually going to look for, and who is going to look for them? Is one of the implications of this new situation that the technological dynamic, or the military dynamic, for weapons procurement is in future going to come from regional conflicts? It is going to be from indigenous States in the regions wanting particular capabilities, rather than from any central strategic relationship.

The third question comes back to another point that Geoffrey made. Is one of the implications of information technology or communications technology seeing the case of high tech warfare that satellites become increasingly central to military capabilities? And equally, that the ability to destroy them becomes increasingly important? Therefore, is there a need for some type of very clear arms control regime in the area of satellites. How are we going to handle this whole field when it would appear that militarily this technology is going to become more and more critical, yet at the same time, we know that these satellites are actually very, very vulnerable.

David Markov

My comments are linked to a point that Mike Moodie made in an earlier reference to the fact that if nuclear weapons are brought into the theater and hold hostage those bases in the country from which US or coalition forces would operate, the very fact that they have nuclear weapons can greatly complicate mobilization. One of the lessons from *Desert Storm* is not to give the allies or coalition forces in any future engagement 4-6 months to mobilize, but to have nuclear weapons to hold those bases hostage.

Two other points on anything that the Third World learned, or other lessons learned, regarding training or logistics: clearly these were two areas in which the allies and the coalition forces excelled.

Michael Brzoska

One question concerns the time before the war, or at least the liberation of Kuwait. If I remember correctly, there were quite a wide range of predictions of how well the war would go. People predicted 6,000 casualties and these kinds of things. How has that changed? Is there now the impression that one can be more confident about how things will go, or is this still something to be reckoned with? You do not know how future conflicts will go.

One comment is that those countries that are not going to fight the United States, or plan to fight the United States, who are taking the lessons you have more or less outlined, are really developing their military capabilities in the wrong way. It may not be possible for them to do advanced military operations as well as the United States did. They might be planning to fight the last war again and not the war that might be more appropriate for them.

Geoffrey Kemp

Offense/defence information systems go both ways. You could not make a distinction between offensive and defensive weapons except in a most abstract way, and I think the same thing would apply for information systems. They can and will be used for both purposes integrally.

About the psychological impact. It was terribly important, particularly to the United States. Particularly important was that the war was won with so few casualties. If you want one reason why there is such hesitancy about Bosnia and why Somalia created such chaos with Bill Clinton, it has to do with American casualties. The United States has gotten use to winning wars with very few casualties. For any President to put US troops into a quagmire like Bosnia without knowing how many casualties there are going to be is an extraordinarily difficult political task in this day and age, and one that is not going to go away. It is one of the things that limits the effectiveness of American diplomacy, diplomacy backed up by the use of force.

On whether or not the lessons will have an impact on Allies: without Saudi Arabia we could not fight another major Gulf War and could not have fought the last one. I am not sure how much the Saudis would be influenced by nuclear weapons in the future. They have so much to lose if Saddam

Hussein is breathing down their neck. The Saudis will not wilt under the threat of a nuclear weapon, although I might be wrong in that because, essentially, the Kingdom itself would be destroyed if the United States were not there to protect it.

I personally believe that the case for nuclear disarmament is strengthened if you accept the premise of all the high flaunted things that modern technology can do and if you assume, for the foreseeable future, that the predominant adversaries the United States will face will be essentially small or regional powers in areas such as the Middle East. However, if you see a much more gloomy picture of the world, one that has Russia and China re-emerging in different forms as potentially global problems for the West, and this is not unrealistic, then I would argue that there would be extraordinarily strong pressures to retain nuclear superiority in the United States for the foreseeable future.

About the time factor in *Desert Storm*. This, of course, was absolutely critical. We had the luxury of 6 months. In most wars you do not have the luxury of 6 months, if 6 weeks, or sometimes not even 6 days. The impact that this had, of course, was on the ability of the allies to fight a ground war with massive superiority. The time factor was less obvious in the context of the air war. We brought to bear air power very, very quickly. So long as you have prepositioned bases in the Intercontinental Hotel, as was the case in Saudi Arabia, and as long as you have a very friendly environment in which to get your Navy and Air Force to the theater of operations, then the time factor is less important. Of course, if you deny yourself the ability to bring in ground forces, you are clearly going to change the nature of the war. Had we had to rely entirely on air power, then we would have to have been a lot more destructive and more ruthless about the use of air power and that might have raised enormous political consequences for the allies.

- About the predictions: a lot of very famous reputations were ruined based on predictions made about what would happen in *Desert Storm*. Thousands of casualties, 10's of thousands of casualties. Was this unique? The United States should not be overconfident about the lessons of *Desert Storm*. This was unique although a lot of the operational experience is not unlike the type of operations you would experience in the future if you were fighting a desert war against an enemy that did not have the same capabilities as you have.

What are the lessons for other countries? It seems that other countries in the Middle East will draw precisely the same lessons that the United States did. If you are going to fight another Middle East war and the United States is not there, you would like to have as near to the US capability as you can get. I would imagine the Israeli Air Force is now upgrading as quickly as it can to make sure it has the type of capabilities that it did not have at the time of *Desert Storm*.

Part III

Economic and Technological Considerations

Chapter 11
Exports and Defence Jobs/Industrial Base in Industrialized States

Section I: A Russian Approach

Guennady G. Ianpolsky

The Russian Federation State Committee co-ordinates the fulfillment of orders to meet defence needs, and controls the activities of such branches as aircraft, space-missiles, shipbuilding, radiotechnical, optical devices, armament, ammunition, special chemistry, telecommunications and electronics industries.

Russia has inherited three-quarters of the former Soviet Union's defence-industrial potential, created to ensure military parity in global confrontation.

Today this potential is represented by 2,000 enterprises, which employ more than four million people. The defence industries have more than 600 scientific research centres, design bureaux and test facilities which employ about one million people. In other words, this constitutes a basis of industrial technology for the whole of Russia.

- I -

For three years, already, the Russian defence industries have been undergoing a process of *demilitarization*, which has resulted in the following: the share of the civil production output has increased from 50% up to 80%, while the share of the defence production output has decreased to 20%. The State orders for defence research works and armament acquisition were drastically reduced by 70%. The defence industries' production accounts now for less than 10% of the total industrial output in Russia.

Russian defence enterprises manufacture all types of products apart from just nuclear arms. They produce 100% of the whole output of civil airliners, helicopters, cargo and passenger ships, and optical devices; 92% of equipment for light industry; 76% of equipment for processing agricultural products; 83% of medical equipment; 98% of refrigerators, tape-recorders, as well as the greater part of computers, TV-sets, motorcycles, and sophisticated consumer goods.

The demilitarization process, which is in principle positive and necessary for Russia, has at the same time destabilized production in defence industries and influenced the fate of a quarter of the country's population. The most dramatic situation has arisen in 70 cities and towns that have a high concentration of defence industries.

According to the economic reforms elaborated by the Russian Government, with the participation of our Committee, defence industry enterprises are given selective and minimum support through budgetary subsidies, preferential credits, and other measures. However, during the transition to a market economy, with price liberalization, inflation and increase of the State debt for fulfilled orders, the financial situation of the defence enterprises has become critical. The year 1993 has seen a continuous decline of defence industry output (as well as of Russian industry as a whole). The rate of decrease has reached 19%. An average salary in the defence industry has been 70% of that in civil industry. Employment in the defence industry has decreased by 600,000 people, including 100,000 in science and research fields.

The deep reforms that have begun in Russia's defence industry proceed from the guidelines of Russia's new military doctrine with regard to economic realities. The world experience has proved that direct State support and governmental management, provided for the defence industry, are necessary to ensure security and independence for the country.

The State Committee on Defence Industries has developed a concept of a State industrial policy concerning the defence industry complex. The priorities of this policy are as follows:

- support of science and research achievements;
- development and production of effective and competitive arms and military equipment in priority fields;
- reasonable limitation of military equipment types to be developed;
- minimization of production expenditure for military equipment;
- restructuring of defence industries on the basis of specialization, unification, and the use of versatile and dual-purpose technologies;
- renewal and development of industrial co-operation with the Commonwealth of Independent States (CIS);

- full use of defence industry export possibilities;
- State support for diversification and conversion.

It is supposed that necessary financial funds will be accumulated from the federal budget, enterprises' own funds, and available extra-budgetary sources. In this field we count on foreign investors, too.

- II -

Our most competitive goods today are arms and military equipment, as well as advanced scientific products and technologies. That is why we aim to restore and strengthen our position on the world arms markets. I would like to emphasize that Russian arms export is under strict governmental control.

In 1993 Russia's arms export was two thousand million dollars, which is fifteen times less than the USA's export. The shares in arms exports to developing countries were as follows: United States, 57%: France, 16%: Russia, 5%. As we see, Russia appears to be outside the arms exporters.

Taking into account the present conditions of the Russian defence industry, arms exports constitute an important source of additional assets for the amelioration of its financial situation and the realization of diversification and conversion. All this is with a view to increasing stability in society and reducing social tensions. The present level of armament exports allows a small group of defence enterprises to sustain themselves.

The return of Russia to the world arms markets is a vital objective supported by the State. To reach this objective we need new approaches, as follows:

- to put competitive military equipment on the market;
- to ensure broad participation of leading designers and enterprise managers in marketing activity;
- to organize the display of military equipment, including at international exhibitions;
- to alter approaches to providing spare parts and maintenance services for users;
- to simplify the contracting process.

- III -

We see another source of financing, necessary for diversification and conversion, in foreign investors' participation in our major projects and programmes.

The Russian Government has approved fourteen Federal Conversion Programmes. For example, the Aircraft Development Programme concerns the development of airliners and helicopters conforming to international safety and environmental requirements, which allow the improvement of airliner and helicopter effectiveness by at least three times. We also expect the completion of a new IL-96-300 jumbo-jet, the TU-204, TU-334, and other new generation airliners.

American and British companies take part in some projects in the framework of this Programme. We also have foreign partners in a number of other programmes.

The conversion programmes are mainly aimed at saturating our internal market.

In the past two years our defence enterprises have prepared, together with foreign companies, 600 projects concerning the creation of new types of competitive goods for the world market. Contracts have already been concluded on 20% of these projects, and will soon be concluded on some 25% of them. Among these projects one might mention the following: the development of microlasers and integral optics together with the German Ienoptic, the development of a hydroplane together with the Italian Alenia, telecommunication satellites launched by the Russian Proton carrier as part of the American Iridium Project, and finally, the promotion of ceramics and composite materials technologies to the USA market.

Foreign partners are welcome to participate in our conversion programmes and projects, with the aim of creating new types of competitive civil products.

For a number of enterprises under conversion we acquire licences and "know-how" from leading foreign companies to produce competitive durable consumer goods. This will allow us to keep jobs.

We realize that foreign investors' activity greatly depends on governmental support and guarantees, as well as on investment insurance. We also realize that foreign investors prefer to deal with private business.

- IV -

The defence industry in Russia is undergoing privatization on a great scale. Today more than 600 defence enterprises are no longer State-owned: they have been transformed to joint-stock firms, which have set up a number of trade companies, holdings, as well as financial and production groups. We expect that, by the end of this year (1994), we shall have 60% privatized enterprises in the defence industry.

All these efforts open more opportunities for the investment process.

To build up stable and secure international relations, solutions have to be found to abolish discriminatory restrictions in the fields of commerce, economics, science and technology, and to ensure equal access for Russian products to the world market. We count on the understanding and support of the world community in all the above-mentioned issues.

The Russian Federation State Committee on Defence Industries is closely co-operating on these issues at all levels, and is ready to receive representatives of companies and official bodies in order to establish business contacts with our enterprises and joint-stock companies.

Section II: A US Approach

Edward B. Woollen

The purpose of this text is to examine the economic and technological factors that are driving defence manufacturing and exports/imports, and more specifically the economic and technological factors that are driving capital equipment manufacturing and exports and imports, as sold to governments.

1. Governments around the world buy capital equipment with taxpayers money. They buy power plants, hospitals, telecommunication equipment, air traffic control equipment, transportation equipment, and so forth. Private companies - Raytheon being one of them along with a number in Europe, a number in Russia, a number in China, a number in Brazil, and other places around the world - supply those needs, and they supply them to the specification of the buying country.

Now this sounds like Business 101, but included in government procurement programs are military systems. To be frank, there is very little difference, other than special preference and funny laws in some places, in the buying habits of governments for defence equipment versus buying air traffic control equipment or vessels traffic control equipment or even airports or hospitals. Most governments issue a product specification. Contractors who choose to compete in the capital equipment market make competitive bids on a transaction by transaction basis or a project by project basis. We then win or lose the competition.

It is not difficult to figure out that if one is in the heavy capital equipment business, they are automatically desirous of being a global supplier. The idea of exporting defence equipment is nothing new. Raytheon has been exporting air traffic control, defence equipment, power plants, and so forth for about 30 years. It is a mistake to think that defence companies suddenly found the export market when their own defence budgets went down. It is sort of like some of the other things that people began to focus on, but it has been going on for a considerable period of time.

Now, [here is] the dynamics of how a company works. Each of the defence contractors compete in narrow sectors and has a relatively narrow number of competitors. In Raytheon's case, we compete in defence electronics against [similar] suppliers from Europe (who are quite good), [suppliers] from Russia, from China, from Brazil. This competition is normal, and competition is healthy. We are comfortable with it and accustomed to it. We also compete, by the way, in other sectors: power, petro chemical plants, pharmaceutical plants, etc.

There was a slide put up that says it is now a buyers' market. It is always a buyers' market. There is always crisp and hot competition in a free and open society. We find air traffic control and power plant construction to be as competitive as selling missile systems. The dynamics that we face for selling power plants or air traffic control or missile systems are approximately the same. By the way, they are about the same scale in size and procurement, and they take about the same length of time. There is nothing particularly unique about selling conventional weapons to your own home customer, your own government, or the governments of countries around the world.

2. Now, let me talk about what drives contractors crazy. What we do not like that you government people do to us. That is probably worth putting on the table. First, most of us respect our competitors. My biggest competitor in the United States in missile electronics is Hughes Aircraft and a company called Loral; my biggest competitor in Europe is probably Thompson. We all know each other; we all respect other; we compete in hot pursuit and at the end of the day one of us wins and the others lose. We usually will drink a beer and move on to the next one. That is the normal process of competition. It is no different when we compete for power plants against Bechtel, the DASA group or, in the case of the Japanese, Mitsubishi.

What drives us crazy is when our own collective have a different set of playing rules regarding exports in the international market. It is not pleasing to me when I'm in hot pursuit of a contract against one or more of my non-US suppliers for my government to preclude me from selling the same product which is available from a European, Russian, or Chinese source. I am eliminated from the market. I do not even get to the starting gate. I would appreciate if the industrialized nations agreed on what we are going to have. We subscribe to GATT, so let us agree that we are going to allow free and open competition in every economic sector.

The second concept is that all relevant technology is dual use. There are a lot of people making a lot of money talking about dual-use technology. All relevant technology is dual-use and all relevant technology is proliferated worldwide. Technology flows freely around the globe, and the old idea that you can put up a false barrier is a total mistake. We build pharmaceutical plants and chemical plants. We at Raytheon also build and maintain nuclear power plants; we are the largest biotech plant producer in the world, and we also make military electronics. Most people are not aware of our civilian-oriented businesses.

It is impossible to know before you build a chemical plant or pharmaceutical company whether that end product will be combined with two or three other end products to make chemical weapons. It is impossible to know in advance whether that plant will be used to produce a biological weapon. By the way, those same pharmaceutical plants can also built plastic and chemical explosives. It is also impossible to limit the numbers of computational devices that are available around the world. It takes a first generation equivalent of a 386 PC CPU to run an AMRAAM missile. The 386 computer chip has long been released for sale to the world. That is more than adequate to put into a small aircraft with a global positioning system to create a flying bomb.

Therefore, this government approach to order-by-order export control is ludicrous, expensive, and totally counterproductive. We would rather see a different approach. If the purpose is to sanction a country for being a "bad" actor, then put the political sanction on that country. Or, if a supplier country is a bad actor, then put comprehensive political sanction on the supplier country rather than trying to do it transaction by transaction. That process has never worked; it is not working now, and it will not work in the future.

3. Another thing that drives us crazy is that when we all go to the plate we try to supply a product, whether it is a power plant or a missile system, to that government and user for the lowest possible competitive price. What is good for that country is that five or six suppliers bid on a project and if we hotly and fairly compete, the winners are the taxpayers in that country. That market is disrupted when the supplier country's government decides to intervene in ways that are probably inappropriate in a moral sense and certainly cause us problems. Let's cover them.

Number one is when, in a hot competition in a third country, a supplier government decides to fly their prime minister in for a special meeting in that country or the supplier country flies in a minister of foreign affairs or economy and says, "If you do not buy from me, I will sanction you by not buying from you (something at the political level)." What you have now is a distortion in the market.

A second thing that distorts the market is government official corruption. You can go into many countries in the world where it is allowed for a contractor to have a local representative who is paid on a commission basis. But what is a reasonable commission? On a system that costs 10 to 100 million dollars, which is probably the standard transaction cost of most military systems, you can argue that a commission up to 1/2 to 1 percent, or even 2 percent, for the representative is probably reasonable payment in return for his hard work in the country. However, to find commissions, allowable commissions, of 10 percent, 15 percent, 25 percent and 40 percent (and we see them frequently), we say wait a minute. A 40 percent commission on a $100 or a $200 program [is a lot of money.] What is that representative going to do with all that money?

We who are in the business understand the game called "passing white envelopes" to the evaluation committee or buying off ministers. It is done all the time, and what it does is distort the market. Now, since we are use to it, it is sort of like a common joke. We try to get our government to send the Ambassador to counter [the graft], because it distorts the market. However, the loser is the taxpayer in the country of choice. Again, it does not matter whether it is a power plant or an air traffic control system, an airport or a missile system; that kind of distortion negates the intent and potential benefits of competing for a project.

Specifically, on military systems, there are about 25-30 countries who buy sophisticated military systems: the high-priced ones, the aircraft, missiles, electronic countermeasures equipment, and so forth. There are about 25 countries who buy the high end systems. Those countries are very specific; they are very well regulated. Everybody knows who they are, so you can decide to sanction or to remove sanction from those 25 or 30 and you probably have a good control of the world, or at least of the sophisticated defence systems market.

4. The systems we sell are not generally the ones that are used for killing people *en masse*. In this day and age, the most destructive weapons are the car bombs and the aircraft bombs and the other similar weapons. We got into an argument about weapons of mass destruction. Probably a better word is weapons of *indiscriminate* destruction. There is not much difference between the damage a plastic explosive on a 747 can do to about 300 people and a *SCUD* attack. They both are capable of killing approximately 300-350 people indiscriminately. They are *both* weapons of mass destruction. One can be bought in the market for about $50 while the other one can be bought for about US$ 300,000. The lowest cost missile will cost you $100 thousand because I will put a very expensive seeker on the front end that hopes not to kill 300-400 people. Instead, I hope to kill perhaps 5 - the people in a tank.

Thus, there is a significant difference in the kinds of weapons that you ought to consider when you talk about weapons proliferation. We contractors will leave that to you who are specialists in that area, but I would ask you to consider very carefully the fact that the most *deadly* weapons in a post-Cold War environment are the least expensive. Anthrax developed in your backyard costs nothing; chemical weapons developed by taking the output product of three of my pharmaceutical plants costs very little to put into combination. As I said, plastic explosives put in an airplane loaded with happy passengers on their way to and from holiday costs very little, too. Those are the weapons of mass destruction. Those are the weapons of terrorism. Those are the weapons on which we should be concentrating.

5. All of my supplier friends, certainly every American supplier and every other major supplier that I know of, will tell you freely and openly to whom we are selling, when we are selling and to whom we intend to sell in the future. We will be glad to share that information with any and all relevant governments, not only our own. We would like to continue to sell those systems as openly and freely as required when governments call.

Let me just close by saying that companies like Thompson, Hughes, Alenia, and Raytheon intend to remain in the supplier of capital equipment called defence electronic systems. We believe that it is an important market. We believe the countries have a sovereign right to their own defence, and we believe that the political body, including those here, can decide to whom we can and cannot sell. We will abide by those rules. Once you set the rule book though, let us have a hot competition that is in the best interest of the taxpayers.

Chapter 12
The Problems of Defence Industrialization for Developing States

Luis Bitencourt[1]

The point of departure must be a brief review of the factors that characterize the relevance of these industries. We will consider the latest changes in the global defence environment, then conclude with the identification of the problems and possible consequences. Before starting, I think it would be safe to remember that, in the defence market, what is a problem for one State is frequently the solution for others... or, at least, for those interested in controlling weapon proliferation.

It was during the last two decades that the defence industries of some developing countries were noticed on the world weapons market.

Although they have only achieved the modest status of secondary actors among the stars (the western Super-Powers, mainly the United States, and the USSR), these industries have conquered a market niche that has been characterized by low and medium technology weapon systems. Their customers, basically third world countries, were attracted by good sales packages, availability, easy access to components, better possibility of technology absorption and, mainly, more independence in relation to the dominant Super-Powers.[2]

The rise of the weapons' industry in developing countries was pushed, primarily, by regional rivalries. In, or out, of the Cold War influence, those rivalries have motivated the establishment and the enlargement of the first defence industries. Commonly, it happened with strong support of the respective governments. For most of them, the search for external markets was an immediate consequence brought on by the expensive costs of those

---

[1] The author is Director of the Brazilian Presidency of the Republic's Center for Strategic Studies and Advisor for International Relations of the Faculdades Integradas da Catolica de Brasilia. The points of view expressed in these remarks are the responsibility of the author.

[2] See Amit Gupta, "Third World Militaries: New Suppliers, Deadlier Weapons", *Orbis: A Journal of World Affairs*, Winter 1993, pp.57-68.

industries, highly dependent on components imports and R&D investments. Thus, besides countries such as China and India that had already considerable defence industrialization, there appeared on the stage Brazil, Israel, South Korea and North Korea.[3]

Third world countries would become the main market for these suppliers. Not surprisingly, their sales success was associated with Middle East tensions, particularly the Iran-Iraq War. The end of the conflict brought the developing countries' industries similar problems to those brought by the end of the Cold War to the Super-Powers' industries: reduction of procurements, a surplus of weapons on the market, contraction of industrial bases, conversion to civilian lines, etc.

Evidently, each State is affected differently as a function of its respective defence industrialization capability. And that is defined by the perception of threat, the access to financial resources, the existence of a diversified industrial basis, the domestic procurement budget, the status of domestic education, and eventually, the existence of Super-Power support.

The combination of demand contraction and the increase of weapon systems' availability drove many industries to bankruptcy. The severe difficulties faced by many of these industries, mainly the export-oriented, could suggest that the defence industrialization of the developing States has achieved its limit. Nevertheless, in spite of the crisis in the sector, some new suppliers have made their appearance. Weapons "made in" Iran, Taiwan, Indonesia and several others, particularly from Pacific Rim States, have been fighting for customers.

It is far from clear that the developing countries' market share was very small compared to the traditional suppliers. Individually, however, the arms production capabilities of many States have expanded and become more sophisticated, *i.e.* more lethal. The combination of sales of finished weapon systems with the transfer of the underlying technologies, and even the infrastructure for indigenous production, has been the largest part of the defence bargains.

A critical factor in the defence industrialization of developing States is the domestic defence budget. Some flourishing defence industries, such as those of Brazil and Australia, for instance, have been struck harshly by the

---

[3] Cf. US Congress, Office of Technology Assessment, Global Arms Trade (June 1991), p.6.

small procurement budget of their armed forces.[4] It is well known that, commonly, the viability of defence industrialization is guaranteed by strong State involvement, sometimes through the direct ownership of the industries for alleged strategic reasons. The Embraer from Brazil and the aircraft industries in India, Taiwan and Singapore are good examples of that.

I - The Defence Industrialization Environment

The end of the Cold War has brought wide-ranging effects on the global weapons' market. Several of them are affecting the developing States' defence industries. The pattern of international relations and trade relations have suffered the impact of the decreased East-West tensions, followed by the increase of hostilities among ethnic, religious and nationalist groups.

The main effects can be summarized as:

- the end or diminution of Super-Powers' support and subsidies for some countries;

---

[4] In the Brazilian case, the Lilliputian military budget, on the one hand, and the transition to democracy, on the other, would have deep effects on the defense industry. One can conclude that the reduction of the military budget was a natural consequence of the absence of real threat: there are no visible security risks or border problems for Brazil. This fact is correct, but the conclusion is wrong. It is true that the improvement of the relationship between Brazil and Argentina put an end to the historical, yet discrete, rivalries between the two countries (This sounded like the end of the "regional Cold War") and the war hypothesis of both countries vanished into thin air. Today's problem sounds much more like the effect of the economic crisis mixed with the crisis of the decision-making model, not as yet defined. Indeed, for around 25 years, Brazil was run according to a decision-making model that suffered a long erosion process, suddenly to be thrown into disarray by the Fernando Collor administration. A new pattern has not yet been completely built. Even the notions of sovereignty and national security, which could be used to support a higher domestic weapons' demand, were extremely abraded and are scarcely shared by the civil society. Finally, the disbandment of the civilian sectors, formerly responsible for strategic defense definitions at the political level, made it difficult to issue a defense policy, even minimally shared, and thus legitimated by society. This strategy would be essential for the definition of the amount of governmental support for the defense industries, that could be justified by "strategic reasons".

- a surplus of older equipment from both the former Warsaw Pact and NATO nations for "sale"[5];
- the possibility of a spread of advanced knowledge with some experts from the Super-Powers' defence industries looking for new jobs;
- the possibility of having more aggressive US weapons' sales (pressures from the defence industrial base X Governmental conversion strategy)[6];
- new conflicts' pressure on weapons' demand.

The Persian Gulf War and Operation Desert Storm have also influenced the defence industries of developing States. The most impressive effect was the demonstrative one: it showed the superiority of advanced-technology weapons, and the utility of missiles and anti-missile systems. Nevertheless, for the defence industries of developing States the most effective consequence was the closing of that market for them, and the enlargement of the domination of US and European producers. On the other hand, the high cost of advanced weapon systems encouraged the search for joint ventures and other forms of association by the developing States, as a way to overcome technological and market hindrances.

II - The Problems

All these variables have affected differently the defence industrialization of developing States. Some of these industries, the export-oriented first and, specifically, those directed towards the Middle East market, are facing very hard times. Others, benefited by domestic expenditure or pushed by the economic boom, were untouched by the macro-economic crisis. In the first group are the Australian and South American industries; amongst these is the

---

[5] Christopher K. Hummel, "Ukrainian Arms Makers Are Left on Their Own", RFE-RL Research Report, 14 August 1992, p.36, describes the attempt of Russia to sell the MIG-29 to Switzerland, and the sale of the Su-27 to China. More recently it was reported that Ukraine offered China an aircraft carrier and put the 19 Tu-160 strategic bomber on the market.

[6] See Jacques S. Gansler, "Transforming the US Defence Industrial Base", *Survival*: The IISS Quarterly, Winter 1993-94, pp.130-146.

Brazilian defence industrial base.[7] In the second group are China, India, Indonesia, Singapore, Thailand, and North and South Korea.

Regarding the possible implications of these problems on the macro-economic situation of the developing States and their social implications, the question is rather open.[8] To some countries, the importance of defence industrialization is high. Indeed, it is important in the saving of scarce foreign currency, in making possible the mastering of new technologies and, sometimes, in the starting of an industrialization process through military investment. However, we must concede that the effect of industrialization is weak because the military technology spinoff for the civilian sector is very narrow. The social argument is based on the unemployment effect. Again, considering strictly the question of providing jobs in the developing States, compared to the situation in the same sector of the developed States, the transference to the civilian sector is relatively easy because of their low specialization.[9]

---

[7] The causes of the Brazilian defense industry crisis have been summarized by the official sectors as
 - Reduction in the international demand for weapons caused by the economic recession and the end of the cold war;
 - Reduction in the capital of industries due to the artificial parity between the Brazilian currency and the dollar;
 - The international embargo against Iraq;
 - Suspension of the payments from Iraq;
 - Frustration over the procurement of 1,200 heavy "Osorio" tanks to Saudi Arabia, putting ENGESA out of business;
 - The Gulf War gave absolute dominance of the Middle East market to the United States and some European producers.
 - Shortages in the Brazilian military budget frustrating the possibility of domestic demand.
 (Interview with Gen. Div. Werlon Roure, Director of the Diretoria de Material Belico/Brazilian Army Staff, 01/17/94.)

[8] This is one argument frequently used by defense industries in crisis. They argue that there are many more jobs connected with the defense industries due to the junction with the thousands of direct and indirect suppliers.

[9] See Jacques Fontanel, "Effects for Developing Countries of the East-West Disarmament Process" in Serge Sur (ed.), *Disarmament Agreements and Negotiations: The Economic Dimension*, UNIDIR, 1991, pp.132-133.

Anyway, the claim of these export-oriented industries does not seem efficient. Those that have survived and that are in a better situation today have achieved it through their potential to produce civilian outputs.

From the technological point of view, the question suggests some sensitive approaches. Although it is clear that the low-technology market share is overcrowded, the developing countries consider the production of more sophisticated systems a permanent challenge. The Persian Gulf War showed the impact of advanced weapon systems and raised the question of the high investment costs. But, also consider the fact that if Iraq had more sophisticated systems, the Western human and material costs would have been much higher, and the duration of the conflict would have been longer. It gives a new dimension to the question of conventional disarmament. Furthermore, it brings into focus the perceived capacity of some developing countries, in both the missile and nuclear fields, with respect to the available controls. That brings the question of controls dramatically under the spotlight.

As we can see, the conventional disarmament field promises to become critical during the next years. The difficulties in establishing the control regime during the Cold War will appear an easy task, compared with the complexity of designing agreements and control instruments for conventional armaments: there are many more actors, the capabilities are highly differentiated, and there are no more automatic alignments. To the developing States' defence industries, the existing control regimes are basically discriminatory and bureaucratic. In the first instance, control instruments are seen to be disguising the real commercial objectives, and there is an enormous preoccupation with the Super-Powers' capacity to pressure international organizations in order to make them accommodate their own interests.[10] The second is due to the incapacity to distinguish specific

---

[10] As stressed by K. Subrahmanyam, "In July 1991, the five permanent members of the UN Security Council, which are also responsible for 85 percent of the world's arms exports, undertook to exercise restraint on arms sales. (...) The United States has booked orders for $40 billion of arms sales to the Gulf area since the end of the Persian Gulf War. It is also to sell 15 F-16 aircraft to Taiwan": "Export Controls and the North-South Controversy", The Washington Quarterly, Spring 1993, Vol. 16, No 2). See also Jacques Gansler: "Industry leaders have support in their worldwide quest for sales from labor interests, who fear loss of jobs without foreign military; from the armed forces, whose members want, they say, to 'maintain the defense industrial base for the future,' and by the politicians of both the executive and the legislative branches, who fear loss of votes unless defense factories are kept

characteristics among the developing States, according to their records, their policies, and the nature of their societies and national ethos.[11] Apparently, the solution to this grave problem rests less in broad global deals, and more in incentives for regional agreements capable of discouraging the existing regional rivalries.

Another sensitive theme, and frequently defined as a "problem" connected with the defence industrialization of some developing countries, has been the relationship between "access-to-outer-space" and missile developments, which embodies the issue of dual-use technologies. Again, here we have ingredients of a difficult association: between the legitimate effort of the developing States to obtain important technologies, the purely commercial interests, and the possibility of using the same technology in weapons with a high lethal capacity. What is more evident here is that today's control philosophy seems outdated and excessively tied to the former security order.[12] Although some positive outcomes have already been observed in some developing countries, initiatives to adjust the internal legal frame to the controls' framework have been taken, and are on course.[13]

Finally, there is the nuclear question, that requires a somewhat distinct approach. The peculiarities of this theme do not favour its consideration as an industrialization factor of the developing States. However, it is brought to the discussion by the constraints on the dual-use components that have sharp implications for both the defence and civilian industries. In this case, to some developing States, it appears that the nuclear agreements consider the question as a global generic threat rather than a problem of aggressor States. Lately, this argument has been enriched by the critics who argue that the

---

busy. These special interests use the national security argument as the basis for their claim of 'protecting the industrial base' through arms sales around the world.", *op.cit.*, p.108.

[11] See K. Subrahmanyam, *op.cit. passim.*

[12] For a detailed discussion, see Péricles Gasparini Alves, "Access to Outer Space Technologies: Implications for International Security", UNIDIR, 1992, New York, 150p.

[13] Brazil is a good example. Several structural and legal measures have been taken, ultimately aiming to demilitarize Brazil's space program (Brazilian Complete Space Mission) and some "end user certificates" have been agreed. One critical problem here, that is very common to the developing countries and familiar to the whole disarmament context, is the lack of academic debate on the question. On this respect, see Marcos Castrioto AZAMBUJA, "Desarmamento - Posições Brasileiras" in Temas de Política Externa Brasileira (IPRI), Editora Ática, 1990, pp.177-193.

International Atomic Energy Agency (IAEA) safeguards are insufficient and that the Nuclear Non-Proliferation Treaty (NPT) can be used as a cover for a nuclear weapons program - see Iraq's and North Korea's (both Treaty signatories) efforts to acquire nuclear weapons.

III - Conclusions

The interpretation of the problems of defence industrialization for the developing countries can be made from several perspectives. First, there are two panoramic perspectives, strongly interrelated and blended in the overall context: the one of the entrepreneur, the weapons industry, interested in profits; and the one from the State's point of view (that is, as the State is an abstract element, it is usually represented by its military, and based on defence needs perception).

From the angle of the developed countries, the main tendency is to maintain their dominance of the market and technologies, particularly in this context of general contraction of procurement. Here, we cannot ignore the possibility of pressures and lobbies on the respective government administrations, usually on the grounds of unethical conduct, over the use of the State political power for the benefit of specific entrepreneurial objectives. Here lies the enormous contradiction, that some developed countries are, simultaneously, the main arms producers and the leaders of the non-proliferation efforts. From this perspective, also, the problems of the weapons industrialization of developing countries are, in general, reasons for happiness.

From the perspective of the developing countries, we have seen that the title "problems" should not be attributed broadly to arms industrialization. While in some regions the levels of production and technology have gone down sharply, particularly where it has been dependent on external demand, in others, because of regional rivalries, there has been an increase in quantity and sophistication. The critical problem, arising from this perspective, is the growing mistrust surrounding the control regimes. These are frequently viewed as a sort of disguise used by developed countries because they are seen as having a higher influence on the organizations interested in non-proliferation, and can thus keep their dominance of the market.

Finally, in terms of the institutions in charge of the control measures, we cannot say that their job is a simple one, for reasons of those very different and conflicting perspectives. Despite modest successes in the design of global agreements, in the register of conventional weapons and in the oversight capabilities, there is still an increasing trend to have sophisticated weapons available in crisis areas. In truth, it is very difficult to convince arms producers that there is some difference between selling buttons and selling weapons.

Finding the fair formula to reduce the actions of some, without bringing benefits to others, is a very complicated exercise. It is this, however, that we have found to be the most effective up until now. And what appears clear is that, in the regions of the world where countries, in building up confidence measures, have achieved successful treaties, arms production and proliferation have consequently been reduced. Considering this evidence, one important factor in the disarmament equation should be support lent to the establishment of regional agreements, as a way to reduce regional rivalries. This has been proven to be more effective than measures designed to control access to new weapons or production capabilities.

Chapter 13
The Role of Technology Transfers in Economic Development

Section I: Co-operation for Weapon Technology Transfers and Technological/Economic Development

Kensuke Ebata

In the post-Cold War era, it is impossible to define a single, clear-cut ideological or economic bloc to which the transfer of weapon-related technology could be restricted or banned.

The new regime, to replace COCOM, is intended to control exports of goods other than those covered by international control regimes for weapons of mass destruction and missile technology. It is also planned to include in it most, if not all, of the countries that possess advanced technologies useful for producing not only mass destruction weapons and missiles but also conventional weapons. Today, many newly industrialized developing countries possess such technologies. This underlines the need for an internationally - accepted weapon technology transfer control regime.

- I -

However, there are several complicated and difficult problems to be overcome before an effective control regime can be established. The first challenge is to specify the types and levels of technologies to be controlled, because they vary in accordance with each country's situation. For a certain country which is not technologically advanced, the restriction of even a very basic technology might be effective in countering that country's ambition to develop a nuclear weapon. For another country, which is fairly technologically advanced, the restriction of only very advanced technologies would be effective to slow the development of a small, light-weight nuclear warhead for a ballistic missile. But it might be impossible, from the technological point of view, to prevent that country producing a nuclear bomb and eventually developing a small, light-weight nuclear warhead.

Appendix 1 gives examples of security export control items and regions specified by the Japanese Ministry of International Trade and Industry (MITI). Four fields of goods related to so-called mass destruction weapons and weapons themselves require approval from MITI for their export to any country in the world. Other fields of goods, such as advanced materials and electronics, require MITI's permission only for export to specified countries. The number of such countries has been increased by the dissolution of the Soviet Union. The countries to be included will vary in accordance with the world and the country's situation at the time. For example, a country's political leadership can be changed in one day by a coup or by other factors. The tight control of export to South Africa has been considerably eased since the economic sanctions on that country were lifted in October 1991. On January 25th of this year, the Japanese Government removed the restrictions on the export of four-wheeled vehicles and computers to South Africa, and excluded the Czech Republic and Slovakia from the list of countries subject to COCOM control. In this way, frequent review and adjustment of the countries subject to the control is required.

In Japan sixteen items are specified in the weapon export control law; eighteen are specified in the nuclear-related technology export control law; two items are specified in the chemical weapon-related technology export control law, and 26 items are specified in the missile-related technology export control laws. The number of items in each field tends to increase with the advance of technologies. And again, the levels of technologies of concern are influenced by many factors. This is especially the case where dual-use technologies are involved. Appendix 2 gives some examples of dual-use technologies which can be used for both commercial goods and weapons, and indicates how difficult it is to control such technologies. Some export control regimes specify the tensile strength of carbon fibres subject to control. Very high-tensile strength carbon fibres can be used for manufacturing missile structural components and cylinders for gas-centrifuge uranium enrichment processing. However, even low-tensile strength carbon fibres, which conduct electricity, can be used as a weapon in themselves. In the Gulf War, the United States Navy employed a number of *Tomahawk* cruise missiles. Some of them were equipped with carbon fibre-filled warheads which dispersed a large number of carbon fibres over Iraq's electrical switching and transformer substations to cause short circuits. Japan produces about 95% of the world's carbon fibres today.

If we banned the export of carbon fibres and automated machine tools, not only Japanese manufacturing corporations and trading companies but also many importing countries would be in a difficult position. No country should hinder another country's technological and economic development and welfare as long as it does not threaten world security. It is the duty of technologically and economically developed countries to seek the common prosperity of all countries of the world. The technological development of a country will accelerate its economic development, enlarging its purchasing power and making it a larger market for exporting countries.

At the same time, very complicated measures are required to achieve an effective weapon technology transfer control regime. Appendix 3 shows how the number of security export control laws have grown in Japan in the last seven years. Both industries and governmental organizations concerned are now required to conduct a long, exhaustive and costly process before being able to approve a product for export. This process might reduce the competitive power of the exporting country in international trade and prevent the importing country from achieving rapid technological and economic development. A country which has less tight security export control laws will have an advantage over a country which has more stringent control laws.

In September 1992, MITI established the Security Export Control Committee under the Industrial Structure Council, an advisory body to the Minister of International Trade and Industry. After holding six meetings on security export control policy, the 19-member ad-hoc committee, which includes this speaker, finalized its report on 25 March 1993. The report, entitled "The Future of Security Export Controls", is attached as Appendix 4. This is the first official and comprehensive proposal for Japanese security export control policy, and it sets out directions for future action.

The report explains the current situation and key issues, and stresses the importance of developing an effective international export control framework. To this end, it calls for Japan to play an active role in three areas: (1) coordinating multilateral export control regimes, (2) restraining the transfer of conventional weapons to countries of concern, and (3) assisting other countries, particularly in Asia, to establish their own export control systems. Also it is necessary, in implementing security export controls, to give due consideration to minimizing obstacles to healthy economic development.

The committee pointed out difficulties for export controls in identifying the end use and end users of goods, which sometimes fall outside the area of the exporting country's authority. So, to promote international co-operation in security export controls, Japan will work to build a consensus on concrete measures in this policy area in various international fora, such as meetings under multilateral export control regimes. Not many countries in the world today understand the importance of security export controls.

As a first step, last October Japan held a regional export control seminar for Asian countries. Representatives of trading, foreign affairs and customs services of the six countries of ASEAN, South Korea and Hong Kong participated. At the seminar, MITI, along with representatives of the United States and Australia who were co-sponsors, explained the importance and necessity of the establishment of effective security export controls, and the current state of multilateral export control regimes, and advised on practical measures for conducting effective security export control. The latter includes export controls legislation, licensing, inspection and customs operation.

MITI has also been providing training courses for officers in charge of export controls, upon request. Administrators in charge of export controls from Mongolia and Vietnam received such training in October/November 1992 and March 1993, respectively.

MITI is going to expand the list of invited countries to include former republics of the Soviet Union, and plans to host a one-week seminar on security export controls early this March in Tokyo. To support such efforts, MITI has established the Export Control Support Center in the Center for Information on Strategic Technology (CISTEC), an extra-departmental body of MITI. The CISTEC was established in 1987, in the wake of the Toshiba Machinery Incident, as the main institution for security export controls in the industrial sector. Three expert staff are assigned to the Export Control Support Center for administrative work such as arranging security export control seminars and sending export control experts to various countries to offer advice. A total of 40 million Yen (about US $360,000) has been requested in the FY1994 budget for the operation of this support centre.

- II -

Needless to say, it is necessary to co-operate internationally on measures for multilateral co-ordination and harmonization, such as information sharing among member countries and the development of common international guidelines for implementation of export control. The ultimate goal is to consolidate the various control regimes into one simple multilateral regime. Otherwise, many more complicated export controls will be required and the number will have to be increased. Japan is now working to strengthen the international control of conventional weapons exports for countries of concern.

Again, however, there are some difficulties and issues to consider. For example, self-sufficiency in weapons for self-defence is any nation's inherent right and ideal ultimate goal. Japan itself is the second largest arms importer in the world in terms of money. Export controls for conventional weapons should be careful and selective.

Cultivating awareness of the importance of security export controls in technologically advanced countries, including Japan of course, is also very important. Without the co-operation of each manufacturing and trading company, an effective export control is virtually impossible. Japan has had several bitter experiences. In some cases the exporter, either the manufacturer itself or the trading company, deliberately violated the relevant laws. In some cases the exporter was not aware of the violation of any laws. In the latter cases, tightening export control laws and procedures might help to ease the problem. In both such cases, if the exporter did not realize the effect of exporting such technologies, cultivating awareness of the importance of security export control would be of value. This is one of the major roles of CISTEC.

Japan has a very peculiar situation, in that few companies have even a basic knowledge of weapons. For almost half a century, Japan has been trying to close her eyes to the weapon field, except for a small number of defence industries. Thus, knowledge of weapons is insufficient. Not many scientists, engineers and trading staff know how their products can be used for weapon production, and what the result will be if such technologies were in the hands of some bad guys.

Several Japanese electronics companies are manufacturing small, lightweight GPS (Global Positioning System) receivers. Even commercial GPS receivers can give you your position with an accuracy of within 30 metres. The GPS is now becoming popular for precision-guided weapons. Not many countries in the world today, probably less than ten, can produce compact, inexpensive, high-performance GPS receivers, but a large number of countries, surely in double figures, can put the receivers into their missiles, for example as a guidance system for cruise missiles.

A joint committee of Government organizations and civilian companies to promote the use of GPS was established in Japan in late November 1992. This was led by the Ministry of Post and Telecommunications. More than fifty Japanese companies, including electronics, automobile and trading enterprises participated in the committee: the Committee of the Satellite Positioning System. Its purpose is to study the expansion of civilian applications of GPS, but this will also increase the possibility of the spread of GPS receivers to many countries, which makes it easy for them to obtain such high precision navigation systems.

There are very many difficult problems ahead of us in the world of security export controls. Nevertheless, technologically advanced countries should continue to try to find effective export control systems. Although this is purely the speaker's opinion, in establishing such export control systems, technologically advanced countries should make utmost efforts not to hamper the technological and economic advance of developing countries.

Appendix 1

Goods Subject to Security Export Control in Japan

	Goods	Export region
1	Weapons	All
2	Nuclear power related	All
3	Chemical weapon related	All
4	Missile related	All
5	Advanced materials	Specific*
6	Machine tools	Specific
7	Electronics	Specific
8	Computer	Specific
9	Communication related	Specific
10	Sensors, lasers	Specific
11	Aviation related	Specific
12	Maritime related	Specific
13	Propulsion	Specific
14	War materials	Specific
15	South Africa related	South Africa**

* Specific countries include Afghanistan, Albania, Armenia, Azerbaijan, Belarus, Bulgaria, Cuba, Czech, Slovak, Estonia, Georgia, Kazakhstan, Korea (except the area governed by Republic of Korea), Kyrgyzstan, Latvia, Lithuania, Moldova, Mongolia, Poland, Romania, Russia, Tadzhikistan, Turkmenistan, Ukraine, Uzbekistan and Vietnam.

** Economic sanctions on South Africa were lifted in October 1991 and a considerable number of items have been deleted from the list of prohibition, except weapons themselves which are banned to export to any countries by the Japanese Government policy. On 25 January 1994, four-wheeled vehicles and computers were deleted from the control list.

Appendix 2

Some examples of dual-use technology applications to mass destruction weapons.

Machine Tools (various industrial machining)
• Producing gas centrifuge machines for uranium enrichment

Carbon Fibers (composite materials such as tennis rackets)
• Structural component of missiles

Trimethanolamine (non-freezing coolant for engines)
• Raw and processed materials for chemical weapons

Freeze-dry Processing Machine (food processing)
• Biological weapons producing equipment

Appendix 3

Increase of Export Control Laws and Items in Japan

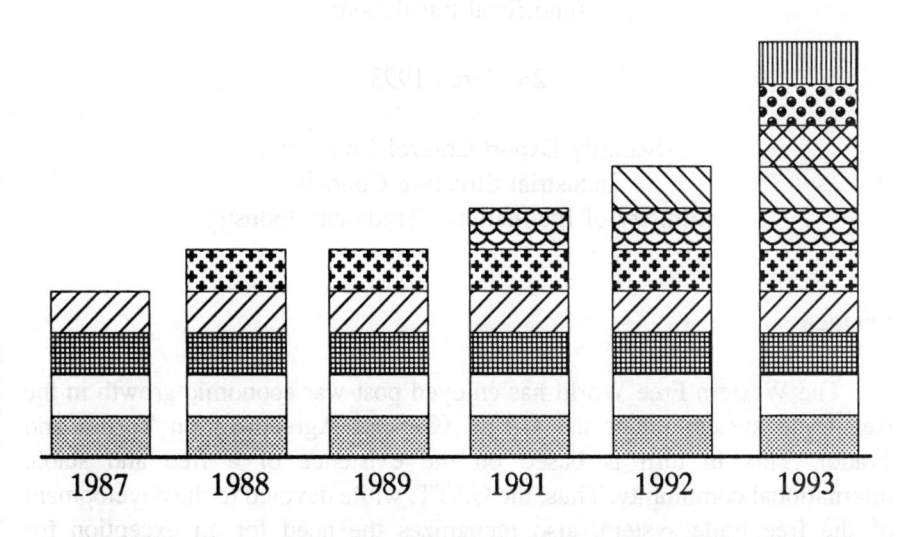

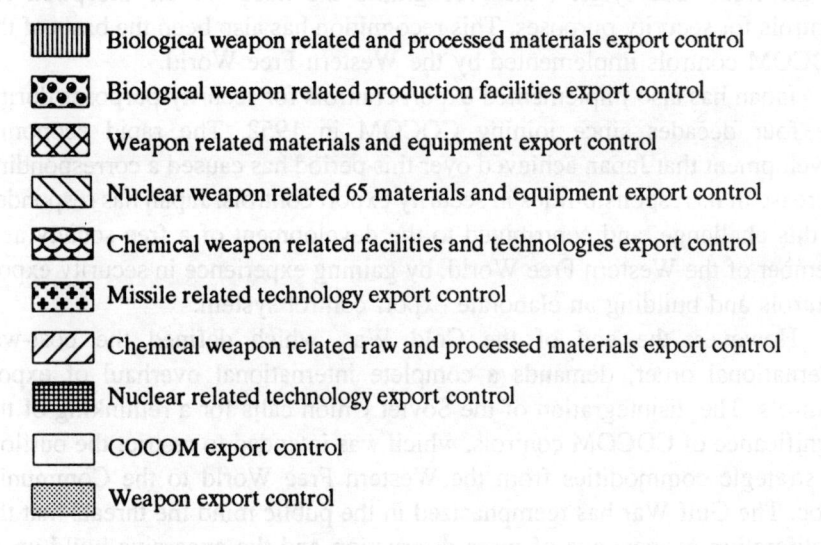

1987 1988 1989 1991 1992 1993

- Biological weapon related and processed materials export control
- Biological weapon related production facilities export control
- Weapon related materials and equipment export control
- Nuclear weapon related 65 materials and equipment export control
- Chemical weapon related facilities and technologies export control
- Missile related technology export control
- Chemical weapon related raw and processed materials export control
- Nuclear related technology export control
- COCOM export control
- Weapon export control

Appendix 4

The Future of Security Export Controls
(unofficial translation)

25 March 1993

Security Export Control Committee
Industrial Structure Council
Ministry of International Trade and Industry

Preface

The Western Free World has enjoyed post-war economic growth in the free trade system under the GATT (General Agreement on Tariffs and Trade). This in turn is based on the existence of a free and stable international community. Thus, the GATT, while devoted to the development of the free trade system, also recognizes the need for an exception for controls for security purposes. This recognition has also been the basis of the COCOM controls implemented by the Western Free World.

Japan has also implemented export controls for security purposes during the four decades since joining COCOM in 1952. The rapid economic development that Japan achieved over this period has caused a corresponding increase in its responsibilities in security export controls. Japan has responded to this challenge, and contributed to the development of a free society as a member of the Western Free World, by gaining experience in security export controls and building an elaborate export control system.

However, the end of the Cold War, which defined the post-war international order, demands a complete international overhaul of export controls. The disintegration of the Soviet Union calls for a rethinking of the significance of COCOM controls, which was intended to restrict the outflow of strategic commodities from the Western Free World to the Communist Bloc. The Gulf War has reemphasized in the public mind the threats that the proliferation of weapons of mass destruction and the excessive build-up of conventional arms pose to global security. It is in the face of these changes in the security environment that efforts are being made to transform COCOM and reinforce non-proliferation export controls. Security export controls are at a major turning point.

As a major producer and exporter of high technology products, Japan's responsibilities to global security through its export controls are great indeed. Reinforcing export controls and other efforts in its economic activities to achieve world peace are an area in which it is most appropriate for Japan to play a role commensurate with its status as a major economic power.

There is a need to develop an export control policy in Japan that meets these changes in the international environment and befits its role in international politics, based on a fundamental rethinking of its current policy.

The Industrial Structure Council established the Security Export Control Committee in September 1992, and conducted the first intensive debate in Japan on this issue. This report makes proposals on the future of security export controls, based on this debate.

I. International Trends Surrounding Security Export Controls

1. Changes in the Security Environment

International developments on security issues since the end of World War II evolved within a "stable" global order, *i.e.* the Cold War, structured around the United States and the Soviet Union, the two Super-Powers with vast differences in political and economic structures.

With the progress in reforms in the Soviet Union and East Europe, starting with *Perestroika*, the East-West relationship has changed from confrontation to co-operation. Western countries are providing assistance to the Eastern countries in their move towards democracy and the market economy. In this process, the dissolution of the Soviet Union, one of the two main protagonists of the Cold War, in late 1991, brought a definite end to the Cold War structure, causing major changes in the international political scene.

Specifically, there are concerns about the emergence or aggravation of regional disputes concerning territorial claims, resource availability, ethnic conflicts, and religious antagonism, that had been suppressed during the Cold War by the presence of the two Super-Powers, as new threats to global peace and security. Such concerns are becoming reality in some regions, including the Iraqi attack on Kuwait, and disputes in former Yugoslavia and the former Soviet Union.

The Gulf War, and other developments in the Middle East in the post-Cold War era have brought to the surface moves to possess weapons of mass destruction, i.e. nuclear, chemical and biological weapons, and their delivery systems, i.e. missiles, and to rapidly build up conventional arms. It is feared that these trends will be linked to regional disputes, leading to further regional instability.

In the face of these trends, international efforts are under way to build co-operative relationships to prevent the proliferation of weapons of mass destruction and missiles, and the excessive build-up of conventional arms.

2. Transformation of COCOM

The traditional role of COCOM was to ensure the security of the Western Free World by preventing the outflow of strategic commodities to the former Communist bloc. This rule is disappearing with the end of the Cold War, and efforts are under way to deal with a new issue: responding to new regional threats.

In May 1992, the United States proposed that COCOM member countries and proscribed countries co-operate in dealing with new strategic threats. This proposal was taken up in November 1992, as the first meeting of the COCOM Co-operation Forum, which afforded an opportunity for dialogue between COCOM members countries and proscribed countries. Such attempts to adapt COCOM to a new strategic environment through co-operation between member countries and proscribed countries indicate a major turning point for COCOM.

3. Reinforcement of Multilateral Export Control Regimes

There has been a renewed awareness after the Gulf War that the proliferation of weapons of mass destruction and missiles and the excessive build-up of conventional arms pose a threat to global security, and that appropriate export controls for dual-use items which may contribute to this are important in meeting this threat. This understanding was confirmed, for example, in the Political Declaration at the Munich Summit in 1992. The last few years have seen the rapid development and reinforcement of export control regimes through the expansion of their membership and controlled items.

(1) Nuclear Weapons

The NPT (Treaty on the Non-Proliferation of Nuclear Weapons), with 156 parties, and the NSG (Nuclear Suppliers Group: 26 nuclear supplier countries) Guidelines have provided the framework for export controls on nuclear related goods and technologies. The accession of China and France to the NPT in 1992 brought all Nuclear Weapon States as defined in the NPT under its fold.

In addition, it was agreed at the NSG meeting in April 1992 to control the export of dual-use goods and technologies which can be used for the development and manufacture of nuclear weapons. Japan is taking the initiative in developing international guidelines for this purpose, and has agreed to act as the point of contact.

(2) Chemical Weapons

As for chemical weapons themselves, the Gulf War spurred the move towards an early agreement on the Chemical Weapons Convention. In 1992, the UN General Assembly adopted a resolution recommending the signature and ratification of the Convention. More that 130 countries have already become signatories. A major feature of this Convention is its provision for wide-ranging and strict verification measures, including challenge inspections.

Export controls on chemical weapon precursors have been implemented since 1985 through the Australia Group, consisting of the major suppliers. In 1992, chemical weapons-related equipment also came under control. The membership of the Australia Group has also been expanded, for the original 15 to the current 24 countries.

(3) Biological Weapons

The Biological Weapons Convention has been in force since 1975. In addition, in December 1992, the Australia Group agreed on the lists of human pathogens, animal pathogens, and biological dual-use equipment.

(4) Missiles

Export controls on delivery systems for nuclear weapons and related equipment and technologies have been imposed since 1987 under the MTCR (Missile Technology Control Regime), consisting of the major suppliers. Membership has expanded to 23 countries. After the Gulf War, in 1992, the restrictions were expanded to cover any delivery system for weapons of mass destruction, including chemical and biological weapons.

(5) Conventional Arms

In 1991, the five major suppliers of conventional arms, the United States, Russia, China, the United Kingdom, and France, conducted discussions, and, in October of the same year, agreed on the Guidelines for Conventional Arms Transfers. The UN General Assembly in its 1991 Plenary Session adopted a resolution for the establishment of the UN Register of Conventional Arms. In addition, in November 1992, the G7 agreed to apply export controls on dual-use items which could be used for the production of conventional arms in Iran, Iraq, Libya and North Korea, to which the G7 had already forbidden the export of conventional arms themselves. Discussions are continuing to enhance the effectiveness of such controls.

4. Reinforcement of Export Controls in Developed Countries and Assistance to Other Countries

(1) Reinforcement of Export Controls in Developed Countries

Based on the international recognition that the prevention of the proliferation of weapons of mass destruction and missiles is essential to global peace, developed countries, in addition to implementing export controls based on international agreements, are undertaking measures on their own to reinforce security export controls, to fully control exports from a security point of view.

The United States, the United Kingdom and Germany have added items which may contribute to the development or production of weapons of mass destruction and missiles to their lists of controlled items.

These countries have also introduced export controls using the "know" standard, and other countries such as Australia are also considering such introduction. Controls using the "know" standard subject export of goods other than those on their lists of controlled items to approval by administrative authorities when the exporter "knows" that they will be used to develop or produce weapons of mass destruction or missiles.

They are also taking measures to develop security export control systems within firms. Germany, the United States and the United kingdom have announced guidelines for export controls within firms. Germany requires firms to designate a person in charge of security export controls.

There are other efforts to strengthen the administration of export controls, such as reinforcing the relevant institutions (Germany has established a Federal Export Office), and increasing security export control personnel. Germany has taken further drastic measures to strengthen security export controls. It has twice increased prison terms, fines and other sanctions on unapproved exports, and beefed up monitoring by giving the federal agency for export control and customs investigations authority to open letters and other mail and to conduct wiretapping.

(2) Assistance to Other Countries to Establish Their Security Export Control Systems

The expansion of export controls to a wide range of items, together with industrial development, has brought countries, such as countries in the former Soviet Union, East Europe and Asia, into the scope of supplier countries of controlled goods. This has led to the recognition of the need to establish security export control systems in these countries in order to implement internationally effective security export controls on a co-operative basis.

Japan, the United States, the United Kingdom, Germany, Australia and other developed countries have given assistance to countries in the former Soviet Union and East Europe, and countries in Asia such as the Republic of Korea, Vietnam, Mongolia, in the establishment of their security export control system. Hungary and other countries receiving this assistance have shown growing awareness of the importance of security export controls, making initial efforts to establish security export control systems and participating in multilateral security export control regimes.

II. Japan's Security Export Controls: Current Situation and Issues

1. The Current Situation of Japan's Security Export Controls

Security export controls are an exception to free trade. Since joining COCOM in 1952, Japan has exercised export controls on COCOM controlled goods and technology. It has also imposed strict controls on the export of arms.

The Toshiba Machinery Co. case in 1987 created a renewed awareness of the importance of export controls from a security viewpoint. This resulted in the amendment of the Foreign Exchange and Foreign Trade Control Law to fortify criminal and administrative sanctions on violations, the reinforcement of export controls administration, and other measures to strengthen the export control system. CISTEC (Center for information on Strategic Technology) was established as the main institution for security export controls in the industrial sector, and has worked to raise awareness of security export controls and disseminate relevant information. In response to a request from the Minister of International Trade and Industry for the strict enforcement of export control laws and regulations, the industrial sector has worked to develop in-house control systems through such measures as the establishment of compliance programs. Such efforts and experience gathered over the past four decades have led to the establishment of a system, including the development of security export control experts in the public and private sectors, which provides export controls that meet international standards.

There is recent wide recognition in Japan of the importance of non-proliferation export controls, that is leading to active ongoing efforts in this respect.

2. Future Issues

(1) The Need for Detailed and Sophisticated Controls

COCOM controls could achieve their objective if all the exports of proscribed items to proscribed countries were banned in principle, regardless of the end use of goods to be exported. If this retarded economic development in the proscribed countries, this was accepted as an inevitable side effect.

On the other hand, non-proliferation export controls are aimed at preventing the proliferation of weapons of mass destruction and missiles, and the excessive build-up of conventional arms. If such export controls obstruct economic development of countries subject to control, this will invite their economic isolation, which could actually be a negative factor for regional security. Therefore, non-proliferation export controls should be implemented with restraint so that they will achieve their objective, and should not retard the economic development of countries subject to control.

Thus, in implementing non-proliferation export controls, unlike COCOM controls, it is necessary to confirm the end use of goods to be exported, which in turn calls for detailed and sophisticated controls.

However, when the government implements such export controls, activities beyond the border where Japanese authority cannot reach, must be taken into consideration in making decisions. This is making it more difficult to enforce controls. Exporters also face various difficulties in checking on the business activities of the recipients of the exports.

(2) The Renewed Need for International Co-operation

In COCOM controls, there is a clear and detailed understanding on the implementation of controls, covering proscribed countries and items and procedures, and a well-established secretariat.

However, non-proliferation export controls, which are seeing recent and rapid expansion, are implemented through co-operation among a large number of countries to deal with the risk of proliferation of weapons of mass destruction and missiles and the excessive build-up of conventional arms, and do not reflect ideological confrontation like COCOM controls. Therefore, the positions of participating countries may diverge because of differences in their perceptions of countries of concern, and their diplomacy. As a result, there is insufficient international agreement on the details for implementation, such as the means and criteria for determining that the goods in question will not be used to develop or produce weapons of mass destruction and missiles. Unlike COCOM controls, this has created broad areas where each country must exercise its own judgment. Thus, without international co-operation on co-ordination and harmonization, such as information sharing among member countries and the development of common international guidelines on the implementation of export controls, there is the danger that the controls will not be fully effective.

(3) The Need to Expand the Scope of Export Controls

Traditional export controls by developed countries have generally established lists of controlled items through international agreements. However, since the IAEA inspections after the Gulf War disclosed Iraqi efforts to develop nuclear weapons, there is a growing international consensus over the need to place goods other than internationally controlled items under export controls. In the United States, the United Kingdom and Germany, this has already led to the implementation of controls on the export of such goods. Other countries such as Australia are also preparing to introduce such measures. Since Japan is a major supplier of manufactured products, there is a concern that its products may be used to develop and produce weapons of mass destruction and missiles, which is creating a growing awareness that Japan must act expeditiously to take new measures in addition to existing controls.

III. Future Security Export Control Policy

1. The Role of Security Export Control Policy and Its Significance to Japan

(1) The Role of Security Export Controls in Overall International Security Policy

Maintaining global peace and security requires comprehensive efforts in such areas as strengthening the rule of the UN, developing regional security frameworks, diplomatic efforts such as the promotion of dialogue between parties to regional disputes, eliminating destabilizing factors through economic co-operation and other efforts, and arms control and disarmament. Export controls for security purposes are an important part of arms control. However, they are to be used in unison with other policies to achieve peace, and should not be considered a policy that can by itself completely prevent the proliferation of weapons of mass destruction and missiles, or the excessive build-up of conventional arms.

Besides, export controls for these purposes, unlike economic sanctions, are not aimed at constraining ordinary economic activities in the countries subject to export controls, but are intended to prevent the possession of weapons of mass destruction and missiles or the excessive build-up of conventional arms. Indeed, it is often important to prevent their isolation and eliminate regional destabilizing factors through economic development in these countries. In some cases, it may be appropriate the extend technical and economic co-operation to such countries. It is necessary in implementing security export controls to make due considerations so that obstacles to healthy economic development will be minimized.

(2) The Significance of Security Export Controls to Japan

As a major producer and exporter of manufactured goods, Japan is facing an increasing need to build a more effective security export control system that will prevent the use of Japanese products in the development or production of weapons of mass destruction and missiles. This responsibility is evident, in view of Japan's reliance on a free and stable international community.

Japan has imposed strict controls on the export of strategic goods. It is necessary for Japan to continue its efforts to implement effective security export controls. Based on such achievements and efforts, japan must co-ordinate its security export control policy with other security policies, and call on the co-operation of the International community in security export controls and seek their understanding and consensus. This is the main role that Japan must play.

2. Japan's Role in the International Community

(1) Co-ordination of Multilateral Security Export Control Regimes

In order for controls to be effective, supplier countries must implement them on the basis of a common understanding and common principles. This calls for efforts to share security-related information through international exchange, and to develop clear guidelines to internationally harmonize their implementation.

With the agreement of biological weapon-related agents and equipment in December 1992, the control mechanism for weapons of mass destruction and missiles now covers all areas. However, since controls related to nuclear weapons, biological and chemical weapons and missiles have been discussed under different regimes, problems have surfaced, such as the differences in the elaboration of the guidelines, as well as membership.

In order to promote co-operation essential to the effectiveness of international export controls, Japan must play an active role in promoting harmonization and co-ordination among the various regimes, including sharing information on and evaluation of threats posed by countries of concern and other security issues.

Consolidating existing security export control regimes with the aim of deepening common understanding on security issues including evaluation of countries of concern and promoting harmonization and co-ordination in various export control areas more efficiently should also be explored.

(2) Promotion of International Controls on transfer of Conventional Arms

There are various difficulties in controlling the export of conventional arms. Unlike weapons of mass destruction, whose production is, in principle, internationally recognized to be banned under treaties, some say that it is inappropriate to restrict the export of conventional arms across the board, since controls will directly affect the right to self-defence, as well as security, of the countries subjected to constraints on their access to conventional arms. Moreover, supplier countries of conventional arms consider export controls on such arms to be a matter of their own discretion, as an important part of their national security policy. Because of this, in controlling the transfer of conventional arms in the post-Cold War world, although efforts are under way to increase transparency through the newly established UN Register of Conventional Arms, there still is no international agreement on a means of restricting the transfer of them.

However, the transfer of conventional arms to countries and regions, where there are concerns that new disputes and aggravation of existing ones, could pose threats to global security. There are various international moves to prevent this. It is desirable to build on this, and control the transfer of conventional arms in some form of international co-operation. Moreover, although export controls on dual-use goods related to conventional arms have been discussed within the G7, this has meaning only if the transfer of conventional arms themselves is internationally controlled. Japan should call on other countries for international co-operation in strengthening the control of conventional arms exports to countries of concern.

(3) Assistance to Other Countries to Establish Their Export Control Systems

In building an effective international framework for security export controls, it is important to ensure the participation of countries in the former Soviet Union, East Europe and Asia. To this end, it is important to seek their basic understanding of security issues, and encourage their development of security export control systems and their participation in multilateral export control regimes, by dispatching expert missions, holding seminars, accepting trainees and other means.

In the former Soviet Union in particular, the outflow of weapons continues because of the domestic situation, including falling domestic demand for weapons, delays in the conversion from military to civilian production, and the desire to earn foreign exchange. There are concerns that this will be a destabilizing factor for global security. As one response to this state of events, there is an urgent need to establish security export controls in the former Soviet Union. Japan should also actively assist the development of such controls in those countries.

Asian countries, led by NIES (newly industrialized economies) and ASEAN (Association of Southeast Asian Nations) member countries, are enjoying rapid economic growth, and are expected to become major suppliers of manufactured products. Thus, there is an urgent need for their participation in the international security export control regimes. In this respect, it is important for Japan to seek their full understanding of the necessity and desirability of security export controls and encourage their participation in the international security export control regimes. Japan must actively co-operate in helping them rapidly establish their own control systems which is a prerequisite to this participation. We believe that strengthening political and economic ties in Asia through such efforts will contribute to enhancing security in this region.

3. Reinforcing Japan's Export Control System

(1) Future Export Controls

(A) Introduction of new export controls for the prevention of the proliferation of weapons of mass destruction and missiles.

The IAEA inspections after the Gulf War and other events have led to growing international concerns that goods other than internationally controlled items will be used to develop or produce weapons of mass destruction and missiles. Japan, as a developed country, must co-operate with other countries to implement export controls for such items, so that they will not be used to develop and product weapons of mass destruction and missiles.

Implementing export controls for such items by the traditional export control method, *i.e.* subjecting all exports of controlled items to approval by the administrative authorities, would require exporters to obtain approval for an enormous amount of goods directed to controlled destinations. Since this would impose an insupportable burden on exporters, it is necessary to limit the subject of controls. To this end, it is necessary to introduce a new method of controls, which subjects to controls only cases where there is a possibility that such goods will contribute to the development or production of weapons of mass destruction and missiles.

(a) limiting controlled destinations and items

In implementing such controls, it is appropriate to keep them to a minimum by limiting controlled destinations to those where concerns are that there may be activities related to weapons of mass destruction and missiles, and by refraining from controlling items which have little possibility of materially contributing to such development and production.

(b) developing clear and objective standards

In implementing such controls, relying on subjective factors, such as whether the exporter "knows" or "has reason to know" that goods to be exported will be used to develop or produce weapons of mass destruction or missiles, may lead to uncertainty for exporters and obstruct normal export activities. This is because it will be unclear to what extent an exporter must confirm usage and other factors to ensure that he can be absolved of responsibility if and when the goods are in fact used to develop or produce weapons of mass destruction or missiles. Therefore, in order to clearly define the responsibility of the exporter it is necessary to develop clear and objective standards to determine whether or not the transaction is subject to controls, based on the possibility of use for the development or production of weapons of mass destruction and missiles.

More specifically, it is essential to set objective standards to determine whether or not the business activities of the end user are related to the development or production of weapons of mass destruction or missiles.

In setting the methods and standards for determining the applicability of controls to individual transactions, it is necessary to conduct full deliberations, based on how transactions are actually conducted.

(c) the need for international co-ordination

It is also necessary to ensure international fairness and effectiveness through international efforts to harmonize implementation and other aspects of the controls.

(d) assistance to small and medium enterprises

It is desirable to assist small and medium enterprises in gathering security-related information, as well as to actively provide advice, consultation and other assistance in developing their compliance systems.

(B) The implementation of focused export controls by streamlining procedures

In order to make export controls more efficient as a whole, it is necessary to focus export controls by streamlining controls, including existing ones, where possible, and concentrating the available resources in the administrative authorities and firms on highly sensitive cases.

Currently in Japan, all destinations are subject to export controls aimed at the non-proliferation of weapons of mass destruction and missiles.

However, there are countries such as the United States which apply simplified procedures for exports to certain countries which are members of international export control regimes. Concerning exports to countries such as the United States, which implement export controls as strictly as Japan does, since there is little possibility that such exports will be diverted to countries of concern, easing controls on such exports, focusing controls on exports to countries of true concern should be considered.

As for firms with effective security export control systems, consideration should be given to facilitate matters for such exporters by simplifying export approval procedures, under the condition that they strictly enforce compliance programs.

Moreover, it is important to further streamline export licensing procedures and related documents in general.

(2) Further Improvement of Private and Public Systems

(A) Improving administration

The increasing importance of non-proliferation export controls is expanding the scope of export controls, and calls for increasingly detailed controls. This requires administrative reinforcement of security export controls. Specifically, it is necessary to enhance efficiency through further use of regional bodies and other means, increasing personnel, and training officials with high degrees of expertise matching the complexity of controls.

In addition, it is important to further reinforce ongoing efforts to introduce computer systems in export licensing procedures, in order to raise the efficiency of licensing applications and examinations.

(B) Establishing compliance systems in firms

The effective and efficient implementation of security export controls requires not only efforts to develop the necessary administrative authorities, but also sufficient attention and controls by the firms that are engaged in exports. Specifically, it is necessary for each firm to clearly define lines of internal responsibility, such as by designating a person in charge of export controls, and to further strengthen in-house examination, auditing and other aspects of its export control system.

Each industry should develop guidelines that fit the specific characteristics of that industry, to build efficient and fair compliance systems applicable to its individual businesses.

To assist these activities, CISTEC (Center for Information on Strategic Technology) should expand such activities as collection and analysis of information, response to requests for individual consultations, and education. Reinforcement of such aspects as personnel and finances in hoped for.

(3) Collecting, Analyzing and Providing Information

In non-proliferation export controls, information on security matters, such as development plans abroad for weapons of mass destruction and missiles, the military activities of various countries and sensitive export cases, plays a major role in examinations by authorities and decision-making in firms. It is becoming increasingly important to collect such information from a wide range of sources, and analyze it, to appropriately implement controls.

(A) Collecting, analyzing and providing information in the administrative authorities

It is necessary to collect and analyze information necessary to security export controls, including overseas information on weapons of mass destruction and missiles, and to develop the means to effectively utilize relevant information gathered by ministries and firms. Consideration should be given to having the authorities use such information in their examinations and in responding to requests from exporters. It is also necessary, however, to give consideration to the existence of limitations to public disclosure because of diplomatic and other considerations.

(B) Collecting and analyzing information and education in firms

Some firms, because of their business activities abroad, have opportunities to obtain overseas information necessary to security export controls through their overseas offices and other sources. It is hoped that these firms will actively collect, analyze and effectively use such information.

In order to raise awareness, not only in the export control departments, but also in the sales departments of firms, it is necessary to do such things as enhancing education in firms, and conducting seminars and training through export-related industrial associations.

Conclusion

This report proposes the basic philosophy of security export controls and future directions thereof, taking into account global changes in the security environment. We hope that appropriate policies based on the proposals will be implemented expeditiously.

When the government implements security export control policy, it is most essential to obtain the understanding and co-operation of the general public, as well as exporters. It is also important to closely co-ordinate efforts within the government, including information sharing among the ministries and agencies concerned. Moreover, the government should make efforts to raise the effectiveness of policy measures by fully explaining Japanese security export control policy to other countries, and taking a leading role in international efforts for co-ordination.

The proposals in this report provide an overview of future security export controls. Needless to say, there is the need for further and more detailed consideration of individual policy measures. Especially in introducing new controls to prevent the proliferation of weapons of mass destruction and missiles, it is necessary to conduct deliberations taking into full consideration the actual situation surrounding transactions, and to provide a sufficient lead-time.

Moreover, it is expected that there will be further, major changes in the international security environment, including the countries of concern. It will be necessary to reexamine security export control policy, recognizing that those changes will alter the premises of such policy.

Finally, we wish to State our hope that this report, the first attempt, by the Industrial Structure Council, to focus Japanese thinking on security export controls will act as a catalyst in deepening public understanding of security export controls, and enhancing Japanese security export controls.

Security Export Control Committee

Kensuke EBATA	Defence Commentator (*Japanese Correspondent, Jane's Defence Weekly*)
Riyako GODAI	Commentator (Freelance Writer)
Yoshihiro HARADA	Managing Director, Toray Industries
Yoshihiko HIROOKA	Managing Director, Sumitomo Chemical Company
Hideo HIROTSU	Executive Vice President, Mitsubishi Heavy Industries
Ryukichi IMAI (Chairman)	Former Ambassador for Arms Control and Disarmament
Toshi KITAMURA	Representative Director and Executive Vice President, Hitachi
Shinichi KITAOKA	Professor, Faculty of Law and Politics, Rikkyo University
Taiichiro MATSUO	President, Japan Machinery Exporters' Association
Hiromichi MIYAZAKI	Former Ambassador to the Federal Republic of Germany
Toshihiko MORITA	Executive Vice President, Sumitomo Corporation
Kinji NAKABAYASHI	President, Nagoya Tsusho Kaisha
Jin NAKAMURA	Editorial Writer, The Yomiuri Shinbun
Seiki NISHIHIRO	Defence Advisor
Yoshihisa OHJIMI	President, CISTEC
Hiroto OHYAMA	Professor, Faculty of International Trade, Tokyo International University
Naoaki OKABE	Editorial Writer, The Nikkei Shinbun
Yoshikazu TAKAISHI	Managing Director IBM Japan
Eiji UEMURA	Professor, Faculty of Law, Seikei University

Section II: Intellectual Property Rights, Technology Transfers and Economic Development: The Case of Agriculture and Defence

Amit Bhaduri

The links between technology transfer, laws relating to intellectual property and economic development are many and extend in several directions. The complexity of their interlinkage is reflected even in the simplest of patent laws. Intellectual property rights protected by patents have contradictory objectives to serve. On the one hand, in order to reward the innovator or the first applicant, he is granted almost monopoly rights over the innovation for a limited period of time, which slows down the pace of *diffusion* of technology. On the other hand, however, without such a reward scheme based on monopoly right to the innovator, the incentive to innovate weakens, thus affecting the *generation* of new technology. Patent rights imply both a balance as well as a tension between the generation and the diffusion of technology in any market economy.

1. The commercial reward based on the monopoly rent from innovation materializes through the market. Adam Smith's old dictum that "the division of labour (*i.e.* technology) is limited by the size of the market" still holds. By and large, the bigger the size of the market where the technology can be used, the higher the level of reward. Consequently, commercial innovators, especially multinational firms, would prefer freer trade in goods and services, enlarging their market, while at the same time wishing to maintain control over the diffusion of their technology. But free trade in commodities often embodies the results of technology which makes imitation and "free-riding" possible to various extents. Thus, the tension between technology generation and its diffusion implied in usual patent laws reappears in a new guise: the tension between the desire for free trade in goods coupled with tight control by the producer over the technologies producing those goods. And, the North-South tension on technology transfer centres precisely on this, because developing countries view easier and cheaper access to innovation or new technology as a necessary instrument for their rapid economic development, while the innovating multinationals would like to avoid what they consider

as "free-riding" on the technology they developed, usually at considerable cost and risk.

2. The tension between the North and the South becomes even more acute due to the quantitative dimensions of the problem. Almost all new technologies in their commercially recognized forms are developed in the North, while many of them are needed urgently also in the South. Of the world stock of patents in force at the end of 1990, which was about 3.9 million, OECD accounted for 85 percent with three major actors: the US (30% of patents; 5% of world population and 28% of global GDP); EC (26% of patents; Europe's total 40% with 15% of population and 37% of world GDP); and Japan (14% of patents with nearly 3% of population and 14% of world GDP). Moreover, no less than 80% of the patents issued in developing countries are granted to foreign innovators; whereas 95% of these patents are never used for local production.[1] In short, the overwhelming percentage of patents in force in developing countries has a *pre-emptive* nature. They are intended to stop local firms from using and "free-riding" on technology developed commercially in the North.

Since innovations also tend to be correlated positively with the per capita income of nations in a rough manner, the question of freer access to technology and its transfer generates much tension in a world marked by uneven income and wealth distributions. Naturally, private firms and corporations need to have the profits from their innovations protected. But, if past experience is any guide to the future, freer multinational foreign investment flows alone would hardly mitigate the problem of technology transfer; past trends of pre-emptive patenting can proceed with rather ineffectual international flows of direct private foreign investments.

The problem could be partly overcome, if significant parts of the R & D costs, especially in agriculture, were publicly funded in developed countries. The spectacular example of this was the high-yield variety seeds leading to the so-called "Green Revolution" in many developing countries. The rapid international diffusion and adaptation of high-yield variety seeds was possible mostly because it was largely publicly funded. In contrast, recent developments in biotechnology and the just concluded *General*

---

[1] L. Auriol and F. Pham, "What Pattern in Patents", *OECD Observer*, No 179, December 1992/January 1993, pp. 15-18.

Agreement on Tariffs and Trade (GATT) do not point to any solution in this direction. Major developments in biotechnology, related especially to agriculture, are largely *privately* funded. Private investors, understandably, need to have their innovations commercially protected by controlling their diffusion through free-riding. This means that the bio-technologically improved or engineered seeds have to be mostly commercially purchased from the foreign innovating multinational firms. This may not only be difficult due to the foreign exchange constraint in many developing countries, but it also takes away from the farmer his control over the production process.

To illustrate this with an example, in India 80% of seed supply - its reproduction, exchange, local adaptation by breeding etc..., is today within the farmer's direct control.[2] This may not be tenable any more when seeds are commercially purchased. Moreover, agricultural scientists in developing countries will not be able to adapt biotechnologically improved varieties to the local conditions without first paying hefty royalties, which would set up further barriers to even small innovations essential for the South. Thus, the need to control technology diffusion by commercial innovators in the North results in blocking innovative and adaptive needs of the South. For instance, the "collective knowledge" of farmers - the seeds they have developed through in-breeding and the experience of generations also becomes problematic in the new situation. The 1978 UPOV (Union pour la Protection des Obtentions Végétales) convention recognized farmers' rights to save seeds, but only for their own use. Any breeder starting with any protected variety cannot commercialize his results. There is little protection for the seeds the farmers have collectively improved over the generations, while there would only be protection for the improved varieties developed commercially by the multinational corporations.

3. With public investment everywhere playing a less important role in research and development in a more liberalized world, development by closing the technological gap has become an even more difficult task. But in this otherwise bleak picture, there may be a ray of hope, insofar as the end of the Cold War era has drastically reduced the justification for defence-related expenditure. If this opportunity is seized by both the developed and

---

[2] *Nature*, Vol. 366, 16 December 1993.

the developing countries, more innovations and related scientific efforts can be publicly funded.

In the North this means two things. First, it means redirecting the course of technical progress from the development of weapon systems to efforts at developing and adapting technologies which have beneficial effects also in the South. We emphasized the case of agriculture, precisely because it must have a high priority in the South, and can have a compatible objective in the North only through public funding. Second, it means a more transparent attitude to "trade and aid". Instead of ever linking aid (say) to defence exports, it would be mutually more beneficial if public funding of research useful to the South is treated as a form of aid.

In the South, this means less reliance on military means, including import of expensive weapons, and their development at home for solving regional conflicts and tensions. Rather than following this indirect and often dubious route for acquiring technology through defence spending, developing countries could develop their technological capabilities more purposefully if they also collaborate in the development of technologies which are beneficial to them, and are mostly funded publicly by the North. Such collaboration is possible when the North avoids the commercial benefits of technological domination and countries of the South are able to avoid a false sense of "national pride" which is wrongly equated with military strength. These are not easy political choices. But we might go some distance if we at least know what to choose.

Chapter 14
Discussion

1. *Ian Anthony*

What you asked for from an industry point of view was two things: the first one was a world where governments do not intervene in the trade in weapons for political reasons. That is never going to happen. You cannot have that if that is what you want. The second thing you wanted was a world where there is a market which works according to perfect competition. You really cannot have that either, because if you are going to have a world where the market works according to perfect competition, we can already say who the winners and losers are going to be, and the losers will not accept that.

However, there still seems to be a very important role which industry can play in the broader discussion of control in collaboration with governments. If there is going to be a control regime, at least for major conventional weapons, then it is going to be necessary for someone to define the universe of technologies which are associated with conventional weapons. That is something industry can do better than anyone else. If there is going to be a control system, it is probably going to be based on quite large and easily identifiable objects. What is so important is to identify the technologies that are necessary to make those large systems work. That is something that industry clearly can do. It is a role somewhat similar to the role that industry played in the formulation of the Chemical Weapons Convention.

2. *Edward Woollen*

First of all, there is no such thing as a perfect world, but you can liken how governments buy capital equipment. Governments buy power plants and generally allow free and open competition in the countries that are the beneficiary of that. Governments buy weapons systems. By the way, you can deny the shipment of a power plant or a pharmaceutical plant or any other sort of capital goods. You can deny those things politically, and I subscribe very strongly to sanctions against a country. I also subscribe strongly to the

G-7 partners. Let's stick with the G-7 plus Russia, plus China, to act together. I very strongly support political control, political sanctions against misbehavior in the world environment. What I would like to see is not lack of political control. Of course, you need it, but I would like to see, just like we do in the economic sphere, where the G-7 open and close together in an economic sphere and where the G-7 nations, the industrialized nations, open and control on other issues. They ought to open and control on armaments. It is not appropriate for the US to be closed on delivery of offensive weapons to a country and Russia to be open. Not in today's environment. It is totally inappropriate behavior. It is also inappropriate behavior for the Europeans to be open where the Russians and the Americans are closed. If we are going to have a global community, let's have one. Regarding control regimes, I have real trouble with this concept of segregating technology in weapons systems.

Let's take *Patriot*. *Patriot* is a particularly low tech weapons system. If you look at the bits and pieces that make it up, it is pretty uninteresting; it is pretty boring. None of the technology that makes a *Patriot* into a *Patriot* or an *AMRAAM* missile, or a *Maverick* missile, or any other sort of weapon of that sort, is intrinsically very exciting. In fact, it is probably two generations, maybe three generations old. What makes it into the weapon is the ability to put all those bits and pieces together in a useful way. The current control regimes do not recognize that problem. To try and deny the use of computers has no real value in the market. To try to deny the shipment of pharmaceutical plants has no value in the market because a clever person in any one of 100 countries has the sophistication to make it into a weapon if the intention is there. If governments continue to want to control the way we have done it before, industry will absolutely help you define the parameters of control and the items to control. We would rather you look at a framework where you put a political overlay into place that recognizes that technology is freely and openly available and find a different solution to the problem that you are trying to solve, which is how to stop the offensive use of offensive and terrorist weapons. It is a much more difficult issue to address, and I do not have the solution to that.

3. Peggy Mason

Mr Woollen made a point about corruption in military procurement distorting the market. Of course, in some of the cases that he is referring to, this kind of activity is taking place in countries where there is, to put it mildly, very little transparency in the defence procurement process, and therefore little accountability, even broadly within government, let alone *vis-à-vis* the public.

In terms of promoting more transparency and in the context of emerging regional and subregional security dialogue, it has become apparent that some of the activity at the global level has proven to be a stimulus for regional and subregional dialogue in areas where there has not been such a tradition of dialogue. The emerging Asia-Pacific multilateral security dialogue forum is the case in point as is the UN within that overall development.

The UN arms register has led to a call by the Malaysian Defence Minister, as one example, for a regional register. However, it turned out that the level of dialogue had not proceeded to the point where one could imagine going that far yet. That process, it seems, has now come to an agreement reached last June among the 25 countries of the Asia-Pacific region to have a meeting of officials, although in their informal capacity. They began a discussion among all 25 countries of the region - in other words stopping before the subcontinent - on the basic issue of what does each country see as its defence needs and how does it go about meeting those needs. This is seen as a first step in a process of promoting a more open procurement process and ultimately leading to annual White Papers on defence.

Of course, a side benefit of this may well be less distortions in the market. But the primary benefit would be to lead to a more accountable process in the broadest sense.

4. Edward Woollen

Mr Anthony made a statement that if we allow for free and open competition, the losers will not let that happen because they know they are going to be losers. I do not subscribe to that. The world's weapons systems suppliers are all pretty good. The Europeans, the Russians, the Taiwanese, the Americans, the Brazilians are all pretty good. We all have about the same level of sophistication, skill, engineering, and manufacturing. We all are use to competing globally, in other than weapons markets, in a free and open competition. By the way, the Germans do a great job, the French do a great job, the Italians do a great job, and the Americans do a great job. We all win some and we all lose some. I do not automatically subscribe to a requirement for special government intervention as being useful for the end supplier. Another word for that is called protectionism or extra help.

Southeast Asia is a big buyer of equipment, and all of us would like to supply it. They are quite capable of buying and choosing properly between equipment. Most of the governments there are trying to do the best for their country and are trying to buy at the lowest cost for their taxpayer. It is not inappropriate at all to allow a hot competition in a Malaysia or an Indonesia or the Philippines, or wherever, among the five or six or ten sector suppliers for the particular product or the commodity up for tender. Leave it alone. Do not try to protect the industry. The industry knows how to adjust. We are all big people. Let the competition go forward. It is appropriate.

Now on the issue of corruption, the interesting thing is that those who try to bribe usually have to bribe. When you are known as a supplier who is a briber, everybody knows it, so all of the civil servants who do not make a lot of money know whom to ask for the money. The interesting thing is that they will also ask the ones that are not going to do it. There is a certain leveling of the pricing. If I price and bid competitively, very hard on pricing, and my competitor happens to also throw in a 15-20% bribe on top of his price, he is probably going to end up at the end of the day about 15-20% high on his procurement. It is then inappropriate for the supplier government to come in and try to offset that.

What we see is the Europeans, the Americans, and the Russians on the open market. We all price our capability at roughly the same price because we all operate from the same sort of engineering/manufacturing base. A $100 million procurement is roughly a $100 million procurement, within a fairly narrow range - maybe $90-110 million. What distorts this competition is if somebody comes in and throws a $20 million bribe on top. It happens frequently. Now it is $120 million on a conscious $100 million procurement. That contractor then runs to his government and says, "I am being unfairly competed against; you have got to help me." Not only is there a bribe on the table, but he then goes to the government and says, "You have got to help me because I am a high price bidder. Go intervene with the selection process." What you have now is a double distortion in the country. It is inappropriate behavior, and not necessary if we are truly trying to help the taxpayers of the world.

I would very much like to see an open regime, regional regimes, and also something called a "corrupt practices convention." I would love to see everybody sign up and say we will not subscribe to corrupt practices. I think what you will end up seeing is a much more orderly procurement process and the ability to buy the required weapons systems for a lot less money in the market place.

5. John Simpson

What are the technologies that are driving defence manufacture? How is that actually affecting the defence industry, and are these new technologies open to control? These questions are to some extent linked to another question, namely how is the new environment affecting defence procurement processes?

I am somewhat puzzled by certain of the presentations suggesting that, at the moment, technology is not driving defence manufacturing. If the comments on the older generations of computers being used in defence technology are anything to go by, what is driving defence technology are economic considerations. I am equally interested in the fact that this is an area where there is a clear differentiation within Third World suppliers. There clearly are some new Third World suppliers who have expertise in certain areas of defence technology, which gives them a competitive advantage over other suppliers who do not have that competitive advantage.

Finally, in these circumstances are there new technologies which are driving defence manufacturing? Are they technologies which are open to control, or, in fact, are there not any new technologies?

6. Guennadi G. Ianpolsky

There are some areas of technological development, mostly found in the missile technologies, lasers, and optical weapons systems, that should be subject to international community controls. We in Russia have become members of export control systems, and we are now in the process of establishing a system in our country that enables us to control the arms related technologies, both at the level of individual enterprises that produce military equipment and at the state level and under State control.

It is right that some degree of competition should be given to companies and enterprises, but in which areas and directions in connection with which weapon systems? This is the big question here.

7. Luis Bitencourt

Looking at the Brazilian case that is represented here, the Brazilian industries had some success during the 1980s in selling weapons, mainly to the Middle East countries. They were not able to offer some extraordinary high technological weapons. The reason they got that market was mainly due to good sales packages, to offer low or medium technological weapons, and because they could assure their customers that credit was available.

It was weapons directed to some of the very specific applications that were sold successfully. For instance, it included training airplanes and armored cars. Our initiatives in developing and selling a high technology main battle tank were not successful. The enterprise, so called ENGESA (Engenheiros Especializades S.A.) that developed the "OSÓRIO," the main battle tank went to bankruptcy. As you can see, they had more success at medium level technology than they had when trying to compete above the technological hi-tech barrier.

Why did Brazil's defence industries have some successes? It was because of this primary condition: the sales were not based on any ideological or political position, nor did the sales' contracts impose any constraints on the use of the equipment. Thus, we had an opportunity to sell equipment under the conditions that prevailed at that time. After the Persian Gulf War and the subsequent general constraints in the arms sales of that market, there is no doubt that the South American and Brazilian enterprises have lost a great part of its armaments market share, which was driven mainly by the Middle East.

Essentially, we have a technological barrier. For example, one enterprise, the AVIBRAS, who sell mainly the Astros - a system of rocket launchers - overcame the economic crises caused by declining sales of defence products mainly because they sell some civilian products connected with their existing defence technology. They overcame the crises and again started to sell some astrosystems, a medium technology system. We can see that to go beyond that technological level, they need to establish a joint venture, for which they are looking. The EMBRAER, an airplane factory that produces the *TUCANO*, is looking for that, too.

In fact, there is a technological barrier. After the demonstrated effect of the Persian Gulf War, it is becoming more and more difficult to sell older products. In addition, there are now a lot of high tech products on the market, with still more high tech products coming from the Warsaw Pact countries.

8. Edward Woollen

If I was Santa Claus or I could ask Santa Claus, I would ask him to bring me the technology that helped me the most. I will give it to you roughly in the order desired.

1. First, and most important, is computer-aided design, computer-aided manufacturing, that is called respectively CAD and CAM or CAD-to-CAM. The way you win in this business is through flexible manufacturing processes. It is in bits and pieces that in manufacturing processes wins and looses manufacturing competitions, so give me the best possible CAD and CAM. That is number one.

Number two would be efficient software design tools. Object-oriented software programming is far more critical to the total cost of the system than any of the bits and pieces that I buy on the open market. My number one technology desire is to possess manufacturing process technology, CAD-to-CAM specifically, and number two, efficient software development tools. Please do not try to restrict those. Those are critical.

Number three would be system integration to put the bits and pieces together and make them work. That is a unique art. That is the art of the military systems guy.

2. Then the bits and pieces. Number one on my list would be batteries - efficient batteries. Forget all the rest of that fancy stuff. Batteries are the biggest problem we have. Number two would be efficient power amplifiers, so I do not drain my battery too quickly. Number three would be lasers, but more importantly, tunable lasers. I need not just single frequency lasers, but tunable lasers. Please do not limit them because I also need them in the environmental business. Four, I need optical windows to go in front of those lasers. Number five would be frequency absorbing material. It is good for stealth aircraft, but also very good for telecommunication EMI reduction. Number six would be focal plane arrays, particularly high density like a 512 X 512 or larger focal plane arrays for high resolution, preferably multispectral. I would like to have at least two colors, preferably three. I would also like to have that in police work and also for environmental work. And lastly data deconverters. I want to see at least twelve bits of specific bits running at about four gigahertz because I will use that in electronic countermeasures. I will use that in radars, but I will also use it in civil telecoms. If you are going to talk about my favorite technologies, the top one - CAD, CAM, and the software environment tools, the process tools - are far more critical than the technology themselves.

All of those kinds of bits and pieces that I absolutely need are technology drivers for my defence industry, and every one of them is a technology driver in telecommunications, medical imaging, medical products, and so forth. If you limit industry on the defence side, you are also going to not let it be sold to hospitals on the other.

9. *Richard Grimmett*

I wish to address a broad fundamental question to Mr Ianpolsky of the Russian Federation, in particular, although the current panelists may also have perspectives to share on this matter as well. There is a question coming from the difficulties of defence industries at this time in maintaining their viability as national budgets are reduced and defence requirements change: is there a high probability in the future of a greater degree of supplier-buyer co-operation developing, leading to transfers of both weapons systems and technology as a way to maintain Russian production lines necessary for its national defence requirements, while also permitting establishment of production lines in a purchasing country?

To illustrate this question, in the case of Russia and China or in the case of Russia and India (which is a supplier-buyer relationship of a longer duration) questions of economic interest seem to dominate for both Russia and the respective weapons-purchasing country. Maintaining jobs is important for both parties. Agreement on defence technology transfers also seems to be central to creating defence-related jobs and production capabilities in several purchasing countries. Is this approach the wave of the future? Will state-to-state collaborative ventures be the principal way used to solve the basic problems created by reductions in national defence spending in arms supplying countries such as Russia, while serving as a way to assist purchasing countries in enhancing their own military production capabilities?

10. *Amit Bhaduri*

The basic mode for transfer of technology to countries which could not pay the royalty fees until the early 1980s was basically through private investment. It had its pluses and minuses in terms of balances of payments, and we do not have to go into the economics of it now. It suffered from one basic problem - the security of investment was tied to the geopolitics of the Cold War - which has fundamentally changed with disarmament and the end of the Cold War. There are many unemployed now, many of them highly or moderately skilled and employed formerly by the defence industry; 40 percent of the engineers and technologists formed the labour force in the former defence industry. This is a really a vast amount of skilled manpower waste. If this manpower could be relatively easily converted to be used in the long term capital goods production system, then it would contribute vastly to economic development everywhere. Someone like me who is not a technologist, can easily think of very large areas where support for skilled employment in the West, through public funding, would be perfectly compatible with some of the special technological requirements in poorer countries.

Unemployment, specifically of technical people, was kept in check because defence industries in opposing camps were in competition during the time of Star Wars (SDI). But with the coming down of the socialist bloc and the employment problem becoming more serious, there is a possibility, with some imagination and discussion in this area. We could kill two birds with the same stone.

11. Guennadi G. Ianpolsky

In a number of countries, based on the licenses provided by the Soviet Union, production of certain weapon systems was organized. But these were the easiest weapon systems to produce. Scientifically complicated and sophisticated technologies were not licensed to other countries. Today, our position on this issue has drastically changed. States would like to have at their disposal more sophisticated weapons. Therefore, some of the States make offers to Russia to buy licenses for the production of certain kinds of weapons and armaments systems. The controlled system now in existence in the Russian Federation enables it to reach such agreements and to sign conduits under the Presidential decree only with the consent of the President. That is why if such agreements should be reached, these will be based not only on economic but also on political considerations.

For our part, the industry finds ourselves in an extremely difficult situation. We determine our policies depending on, shall we say, the abilities of our partner States to participate in a particular project. Such licenses can be granted provided that they are subject to the state control system and provided that all the international, legal, and other requirements are met.

12. Luis Bitencourt

We have heard some very interesting approaches concerning export controls. I would like to hear some comments about the internal side of the establishment of export controls. Sometimes it is very difficult to reach agreement between the interests of the central government to establish the controls and the interests of the enterprise.

13. Kensuke Ebata

In the case of Japan, we are still in a very peculiar position in terms of government control. Actually, our government still has very effective control over industry regarding export control. This might be difficult being understood by foreign countries, but our Ministry of International Trade and Industry has a strong influence on government direction in order to get agreement from private industry. If our government actually has decided we needed not to export this kind of goods, statistically every company and industry should follow the government's direction. Sometimes they violate the laws, but basically it is not difficult in Japan to get into an agreement between government and private industry.

14. Edward Woollen

On intellectual property and technology transfer, first of all, the good news in the regime of infrastructure transportation, telecommunications, and so forth, is that most of the technology that is relevant is in the public domain. The problem is, and let's say the challenge, is more exploitation. The exploitation of technology generally costs 10-100-1000 times more than the development of the initial intellectual event.

The people who understand that best (and I am awestruck at how well they do it) and properly exploit technology, are the Japanese. In a perfectly legal, proper, and appropriate way, they carefully look at the technology available in the public domain. It is not just patents, but it is also in the public literature. In conferences, they take the time, energy, and effort to visit and have technical discussions with universities and companies. Then they go home. They are masters of exploitation. They know how to turn an idea into a useful and interesting product. For that, we have to be indebted to them for delivering to us American design. As you know, Americans designed the tape recorder, and they turned out the VCR. Americans designed the first video camera, and then we were incapable of exploiting it properly, so the Japanese properly and very correctly turned it into a marketable product.

Rather than being focused on the pure technology, I would propose, as you said, to the countries in the South that the place to make money is in turning the technology into a product. You will find there is more than enough technology available for those purposes.

15. Amit Bhaduri

It is true that in the public domain there are a lot of technologies which could be exploited by the countries in the South. But if you look at most of the dominant countries of the South, the most important technologies which affect the lives of the ordinary rural people are technologies which, for various reasons, do not exist in that form in the North. Take three very modern examples. If you take the entire agricultural sector which includes something like 60% of the people in all the countries of the South (and includes the poorest people), whether you have a free market or you do not have a free market, whether you have a liberal economic regime or you do not have a liberal economic regime, their living conditions are not easily going to be affected for years and years to come.

What would however easily make a difference is if productivity per person employed in agriculture in, let us say, South Asia, goes up from its present level. It is, you know, even by Asian standards, about one-third of agricultural productivity. The technology for the proper exploitation of water including water management, proper exploitation of hybrid seed, and the combination of the two, exists in some way, but to think of this technology and productivity as a package also requires a substantial amount of initial investment, as with the green revolution which for about ten years was entirely supported by public investment in the North, especially the USA. And no other technology has made a greater difference to conflict resolution and reduction of human suffering than the green revolution technology. In the recorded history of mankind, there is no other example of a faster growth in agricultural output than in the 10-15 year green revolution period, which helped countries like India, Pakistan, and others make the transition from being on the verge of famine to being self-sufficient in food. Just imagine if it had not happened.

If you look at the investment, if you look at the money that was spent to develop that technology, it was very little. But if you look at the sophistication which is needed in the beginning to put together the package - what amount of control of water would be needed, with which combination of seeds and fertilisers and the whole package of technology which is needed - I am not sure it could be developed simply from knowledge that exists in the public domain. It needed incentive, initial investment on the ground and determination at the political level of leadership.

It is still not achieved, for example, in Africa. For exactly the same reason: the initial impetus of the technological thrust which has to be made has not been made in Africa. I think it is true that public knowledge about the technology exists, but it has not been adapted to reality at the ground level. Contrast this with what Japan has been able to do very successfully, but it is mostly in the manufacturing industry. What I am talking about is a level of technology which is lower but which affects many, many more human lives. This is where public funding of research, and development (call it aid or whatever you like), could really be very useful for both North and South. This requires one very important thing. It requires getting away from the notion that technology and national pride are linked through military might. It is not an easy thing for a poor country nor is it for a rich country, but this is where the solution to the problem will have to begin.

16. *Kensuke Ebata*

It is true that we, Japan, learned much about higher technology from the United States. We have also experienced a similar situation because developing countries like South Korea introduced and learned much about advanced technology from our country. They are getting very advanced technology, like shipbuilding, automobiles, electronics, and so on. It is the nature of technology, like the flow of a river, that the high technology flows from the high point to lower points.

Unfortunately, today, most of our advanced countries are adopting protectionist policies to protect their own prosperity and knowledge base. I do not know if this trend is correct or not, but protectionism is becoming a big issue all over the world.

Part IV

Facilitation of Economic Growth/ Maximizing Regional Security and Stability

Chapter 15
The Impact of Technology Control Regimes

David Hobbs

This Chapter looks mainly at the supply side of technology control regimes and tries to draw out lessons from past experience which might be relevant to future efforts to introduce new forms of technology control regimes. At the outset, it must be stressed that the impacts of technology control regimes are enormously difficult to assess. Impacts vary from regime to regime and can be seen quite differently by the supplier and the recipient. In other words, assessments inevitably involve judgments about whether the wine glass is half full or half empty.

I - Co-operative and Adversarial Regimes...

There are, in effect, two types of technology control regimes. On the one hand, there are those which involve a mainly co-operative relationship between suppliers and recipients and, on the other hand, those which involve a basically adversarial relationship between suppliers and recipients. The nuclear Non-Proliferation Treaty is an example of a co-operative regime. In this, the suppliers agree to help recipients with the peaceful applications of technology and in return the recipients agree to avoid pursuing the technology's military applications.

COCOM in the Cold War represented an adversarial regime in which the COCOM nations sought to prevent certain other nations from acquiring military or militarily useful technology. There was, of course, no co-operation between COCOM's member nations and the targets of the COCOM regime.

II - ... And Their Impact

The following is a necessarily selective look at some specific impacts of past and present technology control regimes.

As regards the NPT, there is a great deal of literature about NPT's successes and failures which evokes the "wine glass" story. Most would give the non-proliferation regime a pass mark but probably not a good grade. It passes because over the past 25 years, the nuclear club has not grown by a lot and the NPT has made it harder for nations to acquire nuclear weapons.

But the NPT does not receive a good grade because it certainly has not been completely successful. As well as the obvious failures, there are also other suppliers or potential suppliers which have emerged who are outside the scope of NPT safeguards.

As regards the non-proliferation regime's economic impact, it has benefited all parties. Many nations feel that the benefits from participating have been insufficient but there have been benefits. If nations had had to develop nuclear power alone, it would have been technically extremely difficult and far more expensive than it was in co-operation with other nations.

Of course, the nuclear supplier nations have benefited as well. Without a co-operative regime, sales would have been far more problematic since there would have been much greater concern about potential abuses of the technologies and goods sold.

In sum, the non-proliferation regime which involves a *bargain* between the nuclear "haves" and the nuclear "have-nots" has broadly succeeded in its aim of slowing down the spread of *military* nuclear technology and has accelerated the spread of *civil* nuclear technology.

It is interesting now to look back briefly at COCOM.

COCOM was the informal organization used by the West to limit technology transfers to the East. It was an adversarial regime that arose in the Cold War. Its purpose was to harmonize the export controls on military, nuclear and dual-use technologies that COCOM's members applied on transfers to the East.

COCOM's military and nuclear controls were broadly unproblematic but COCOM's member were frequently at loggerheads over dual-use exports. The issue here was technology which could be sold for economic gain but presented the risk that it could be used for its military applications and not its civilian ones. Essentially, the United States had a more restrictive view of dual-use technologies and it also insisted on keeping track of its technology exports to its COCOM allies to ensure that American goods did not find their way to the East even indirectly when embodied in larger products.

Contrary to popular opinion at the time, these additional controls harmed the American economy and were not some cunning means of gaining economic advantage. Indeed, in 1985, the American National Academy of Sciences estimated that the United States was losing about $9.3 billion per year through its technology export controls and about two thirds of that was in lost sales to allies. Taking into account knock on effects in the economy, these controls were estimated to have caused a reduction in GNP of about $17 billion. Unfortunately, there was no systematic study of total losses to all the COCOM nations but anecdotal evidence suggested that losses were substantial.

In any event, there were many disputes between the COCOM nations and COCOM's restrictions undeniably caused economic losses to its members. And most disputes centred on whether potential dual-use exports would be diverted to military ends or not.

Another area of debate was the utility of controls in the face of suppliers outside the regime. Some of the controlled technologies were readily available in the Far East and some member nations resented the fact that they had to forgo sales, in effect, for no reason. If they did not export the goods, a non-COCOM third party supplier would.

As regards the effect on COCOM's targets, the Warsaw Pact nations probably were harmed economically by COCOM's restrictions but this is an academic point. The damage was limited because many dual-use commodities were available elsewhere and any harm done paled into insignificance compared with the damage done by the domestic economic policies prevailing there at the time.

III - Motives for Exporting

It is useful to explore briefly the motives for exporting and importing weapons and weapons related technologies.

Looking first at the weapons exporters, weapons production is expensive and exports help to amortize development costs, improve the national balance of payments by bringing in foreign currency and provide employment. So if exporters are to deny themselves sales they need a good reason for doing it. Looking at the potential suppliers of military technology now, it is clear that the nations with the strongest motives for exporting are those currently experiencing the greatest economic difficulties; the nations in Central and Eastern Europe.

During the Cold War, the Soviet Union and its allies were major arms exporters. Although many exports were, in effect, transfers to allies, revenue generating sales were also significant. The former Czechoslovakia, for instance, was in 1987 the seventh largest arms exporter in the world. Armaments represented about 3 per cent of the nation's industrial production and about 80 per cent of its armaments production was exported. One of the aims of Czechoslovakia's first democratically elected government was to curb its arms exports dramatically and it banned sales to many former customers such as Iran. Subsequently, however, a more flexible export regime was introduced in the Czech Republic and Slovakia has made it clear that it simply cannot afford to phase out arms production and exports at the rate envisaged before the break-up of Czechoslovakia.

Russian arms sales are also low compared with those of the former Soviet Union and probably now amount to about $4 billion per year. Russia estimates that United Nations arms embargoes have cost it $16 billion and there is a strong desire to see sales rise.

There is certainly a problem here. Arms are among the few commodities where Central and Eastern Europe are internationally competitive. And although the Western nations complain about their own economic problems, they are trivial compared with those in Central and Eastern Europe.

Care must be taken in dealing with this problem. Western arms exports are far more substantial with the United States alone accounting for 57 per cent of arms exports to the developing world in 1992 with sales of almost $24 billion. And last year, total American arms exports exceeded $34 billion. Also last year, the United Kingdom broke its arms export record with sales exceeding $9 billion.

It is hypocritical simply to ask Central and Eastern European nations to deny themselves revenue from arms exports when the West is predominantly the main world armaments supplier. Expecting Central and Eastern European nations to be satisfied with the warm glow of being responsible members of the international community is not enough. If the East is to exercise restraint, there must be incentives and examples for doing so.

The key problem for suppliers is that an armaments export control regime is more likely to resemble the adversarial COCOM rather than the cooperative NPT. It will therefore result in net economic losses and probably political friction among the suppliers. The benefits should be enhanced national security, improved security of friends and allies, or a general contribution to global stability. The regime's rationale must be to balance these political *advantages* against the regime's economic *disadvantages*. But not everyone will agree on how to strike that balance. Nations will each differ in their perceptions of the political and economic costs and benefits of a particular sale.

IV - Motives for Importing

Turning now to the demand side of the equation - the importers - every nation has the right to self defence and if a nation cannot meet its perceived legitimate defence needs domestically, it will naturally turn to suppliers abroad.

There can be no doubt, however, that one nation's self defence is another nation's threat. To cite just one example, Malaysia recently decided to purchase Russian Mig-29Rs in a deal worth $660 million. Malaysia also decided to purchase F/A-18s from the United States. News of these purchases has led the Philippines to speed up the planned up-grade of its air force while Thailand, Singapore and Indonesia are also looking at new arms purchases. In the words of McDonnell Douglas' chief financial officer, the Malaysian sale "opens up a number of opportunities for us in Southeast Asia".

It is tempting to argue that all these nations would have been better off if there had been restraints on the initial Malaysian purchases. But, in fact, the effects of arms purchases such as these are very difficult to assess. Sales often include attractive off-sets and co-production arrangements so the initial customer finds the purchase less burdensome and may itself benefit from future exports.

The economic effects of technology control regimes are equally difficult to assess.

It is interesting to recall the case last year when Russia wished to sell cryogenic rocket engines and the technology to produce them to India. The United States objected strongly to this sale and eventually persuaded Russia to forgo the sale of the production technology. India will be able to develop it domestically but it will take about ten years. If it does so, it will then be able to sell that technology abroad.

As regards conventional weapons, if an embargo is imposed, the *economic* effects might be minimal if that embargo is only imposed by some suppliers. If American F-15s are not available, then British Tornadoes might not be a bad alternative. If an embargo is more comprehensive and difficult to circumvent and the domestic procurement route is pursued, it will probably be more expensive in the short and medium terms, but the situation is less clear in the long term if that nation itself becomes a supplier.

Consider the impact on South Africa of United Nations sanctions. One effect was to stimulate the domestic armaments industry. South Africa is now a potential supplier of a broad range of military equipment.

There are many sources of supply so technology denial efforts by only *some* nations will not succeed in preventing other nations from acquiring weapons elsewhere or from producing them domestically. And the dynamics of the marketplace are such that purchasers can have long-term incentives for becoming short-term customers.

V - The Nature of Military Technology

Another factor which must be central to any form of technology control effort in the conventional arms field is the relationship between military and civilian technology.

It used to be taken for granted that military technology led civilian technology. Technological spin-offs were seen as a one-way street leading from the military sector to the civilian sector. Gradually, this situation has changed so that there is now a two-way street and it is difficult to decide which way most of the traffic goes.

The information technology revolution is largely responsible for this situation. Military technology increasingly relies on information technology. Electronics are at the heart of many, if not most, modern weapons. Precision guided munitions, combat aircraft, tanks, communications systems: virtually any military item depends upon electronics. The difference between a good tank and a bad one can simply be an electronic black box. But innovation in electronics is overwhelmingly led by the civilian sector. The military is more or less a customer, albeit an unusual one, for the electronics industry.

Although the relationship is less clear in other sectors, the overlap between military and civilian technology remains substantial. Civilian rockets are not ideal missiles but the technologies have much in common. Military reconnaissance satellites, particularly those being developed in Europe, owe much to civilian remote sensing programmes. And communications systems now being developed for commercial applications could easily be adapted for military use.

This evolving relationship between military and civilian technology is crucially important. As mentioned earlier, most of COCOM's problems centred on dual-use technology. Agreements on weapons and nuclear exports were straightforward but there were continual disagreements on technology that could be used for either military or civilian applications. In the future, this problem can only worsen as the dividing line between military and civilian technology becomes less clear or even imaginary in some areas.

Furthermore, technologies such as electronics and communications which are the basis of critical force multipliers in the military context are also crucial to economic development. Export restrictions put on these types of technologies for military reasons will all too easily be interpreted in the developing world as hypocritical impediments to economic growth.

It is already difficult to isolate technologies which are critical uniquely to the military. In the future, it will be even more difficult. In practical terms, this means that the problems COCOM had in drawing up embargo lists of dual-use technologies will be magnified in COCOM's replacement.

Trying to draw a line round those technologies which might be militarily useful will enclose a very large area which will increasingly include those technologies which are economically useful or even critical.

VI - Future Technology Control Regimes

The various themes addressed in this paper can be brought together in order to assemble the list of considerations which must feature in future efforts to promote restraint in the transfer of military technologies.

These considerations are relevant to the new, improved COCOM soon to be unveiled and intended to allow the former Cold War adversaries to co-ordinate their technology export controls. Perhaps further into the future, they could be relevant to a United Nations based regime.

Irrespective of the specific regime, there is an urgent need to reduce economic dependence on the armaments sector, particularly in Central and

Eastern Europe where export controls are less well developed and economic problems are most severe. Assistance is needed to reduce the economic pain of winding down armaments industries and building new civilian ones.

At the same time, the Western nations must become less dependent upon arms exports. The West too should be active in reducing the economic significance of its armaments industries and will have to make sacrifices. At present it preaches the need for export restraint but does not seem to be exercising much itself.

Dual-use technology will inevitably by a thorny issue. The list of prohibited technologies should be kept as small as possible by taking full account of "third-party" suppliers. It makes little sense to limit technologies which can be obtained readily elsewhere.

Even with that provision, if a regime embraces many suppliers so that the "third country supplier" problem is not too significant, the regime's members will still have to deal with a large and growing list of dual-use technologies. The solution to this problem is to concentrate not on export prohibitions but verification of end use. This concept was introduced in COCOM towards the end of the Cold War when nations such as Hungary said that they would accept inspections to verify end use.

Different regional or national "targets" of control regimes could have different degrees of verification imposed as a condition of sale depending upon the specific situation. And the selection of *targets* and the *degrees of verification*, should be based on *agreed criteria*. For example, the criteria for selecting export control targets could, in some cases, be linked to the criteria for providing development aid.

The United Nations Development Programme in 1991 stated that resources are being wasted on rising military expenditures, inefficient public enterprises, prestige projects, and extensive corruption. When nations such as Angola, Chad, Pakistan, Peru, Syria, Uganda and Zaire spend at least twice as much per year on arms as on health and education, development aid is hard to justify.

The United Nations Development Programme also produced an index of human rights, scoring nations on factors such as multi-party elections, press freedom, the rule of law, and ethnic rights. It suggested that this could be used to assess eligibility for aid.

These types of factors could also be used to assess eligibility to import arms. It would surely be possible to use factors such as military spending versus spending on health and education, respect for human rights, and adherence to multi-party elections as indicators of eligibility both for aid and for receiving arms sales or determining the degree of end-use verification required to permit transfers of certain dual-use technologies.

Why should the Norwegian tax payer provide aid to a nation which has a nuclear weapons programme, builds missile delivery systems and chooses to spend more on the military than on health when there are many other potential aid recipients. And why should such a nation have easy access to military or militarily-related technologies? If such formulae could be adopted, then a strong case could and should be made for making greater development funds available.

Another criteria for favourable treatment could be adherence to regional arms control agreements. The arms suppliers have a great deal of expertise in arms control. The CFE Treaty, for instance, reduces offensive systems and includes extensive verification provisions. This experience could be applied to produce similar regional equivalents and to help nations produce less threatening military postures. Participation in arms control negotiations could even be a condition of sale, as could participation in the NPT, the CWC and the UN Register of Conventional Arms.

Special sympathy should also be given to those nations which are directly threatened by "pariah" nations which accumulate conventional arms beyond the needs of self defence and which seem bent on acquiring weapons of mass destruction.

The essential point is that there are objective criteria which could be used to make determinations about exports of arms and militarily-related technology and the degree of verification needed on "end use". Precisely how these criteria would be applied would be, of course, a matter for political negotiation.

Most fundamentally, there must be broad dialogue among suppliers *and* recipients. With this type of dialogue it should be possible to bring together creatively the exploitation of dual-use technology, regional arms control efforts, development aid, and military exports. If so, it might be possible to formulate a control regime which is not wholly adversarial and which could be substantially co-operative.

VII - Conclusion

In conclusion, it is instructive to use an analogy. The proliferation of weapons and military technologies can be likened to a disease. As with any disease, there is a tendency to focus on the symptoms and weapons proliferation is no exception.

But it is critically important that weapons proliferation is recognized as a symptom and not a disease in itself. The disease is caused by factors such as regional rivalry, nationalism, ethnic hatred, religious animosity, greed, evil and any of the all too numerous sources of human conflict. It is made worse by the economic imperative to export arms.

Technology control regimes are not a cure for those ills. They are a means of relieving the symptoms. They buy time. The real challenge is to use that time to treat the disease itself. There is a need for a holistic approach which seeks to reduce the economic motivation to export arms, which builds regional arms control agreements, forges political settlements and promotes confidence-building measures.

In other words, the reasons why nations seek military technologies and why others export them must be addressed. If that is not done, then ultimately the disease will run its course.

Chapter 16
NPT, CWC, and BWC: How Effective are they Likely to be?

Section I: Evolution of Multilateralism, Definitions and Verification

Marcos Castrioto de Azambuja

Our time is perhaps the only one in modern history in which wide, profound and abrupt changes in the international scene have not been accompanied by a major effort to give shape to a new international order. Nothing like the Congress of Vienna, the Treaty of Versailles, or the Conference in San Francisco has occurred to give new directives and a new focus to a dramatically changed international environment.

We are using old tools, old structures and old models to cope with the new circumstances. We have, to some extent, succeeded in doing so, but it is apparent that we must, in the near future, undertake a far reaching revision of the form and substance of international relations.

It is against this background that this question has to be addressed: how likely to succeed are the BWC, the CWC and the NPT?

- I -

Let's take first the Biological Weapons Convention (BWC). It is a framework agreement without any verification procedures, compliance with which depends essentially on the good faith of the signatories. It is a largely declaratory document, extremely worthwhile as it is, but requiring a comprehensive review process to give it the desirable efficacy.

It covers an extremely wide array of possible agents and existing verification procedures that, as far as I can see, would pose almost unsurmountable problems.

The NPT is the archetypal non-proliferation treaty and has the inherent fragilities of this type of arrangement. In a way, non-proliferation regimes suffer from the basic flaw of establishing different rights and responsibilities for their signatories, and must always be seen as interim arrangements paving the way for truly universal regimes, negotiated with great transparency and aiming at the greatest possible credibility.

These comments should not be construed as expressing too critical a view of the NPT. We would be in far worse shape today had no such Treaty existed, and almost all countries have either adhered to it or sought alternative ways to indicate their unambiguous commitment to the vital goal of curbing the proliferation of weapons of mass destruction.

The Chemical Weapons Convention (CWC) is on the other hand a very good example of an instrument negotiated in truly democratic *fora* over a long period of time, and which is equipped with elaborate and reliable machinery to verify compliance. It represents, so to speak, another "generation" of international instruments, and it stands out as a model for future multilateral agreements in this field.

We must move away from "primitive multilateralism" to a fully developed multilateral approach, meaning the establishment of mechanisms fully responsive to the legitimate concerns and expectations of all actors, and which are seen to function in an equitable and transparent way.

Such supplier "clubs", and other informal arrangements that now exist, are perhaps the best solution that could be found under Cold War conditions. In a new era we can perhaps do better and give them greater legitimacy and more dependable machinery.

Summing it up. It is perhaps too soon to tell how effective these various international instruments have been or will be. Imperfect as they are, they are truly essential to world peace and security. More than finished products, they must be seen as dynamic structures capable of growth and of becoming more responsive to the expectations of the world community. We have been rather fortunate - we should not neglect "luck" as a relevant, although perhaps an irrational fact, in international relations - inasmuch as nuclear energy did not become the gateway to the future as was widely believed some thirty or forty years ago.

At the same time, the end of the Cold War eliminated a number of scenarios which could be used by certain threshold countries to justify the acquisition of a military nuclear capability. Chemical weapons, on the other hand, have always been, and remain, a very specific branch of chemical science and industry, and their production has not opened up the path to any new territories but has led only to the dangerous blind alley of the production and stockpiling of such weapons. One wonders how effective the NPT might have been in different historical and scientific circumstances and how effective the Chemical Weapons Convention might prove to be if both nuclear weapons and chemical weapons had been seen as the necessary keys to new and promised territories. The future functioning of the CWC machinery and the results of the 1995 NPT review conference will help to answer the question that I was addressed. Both regimes must remain stable and true to their long-term objectives, but must not rigidify into concepts or structures incapable of evolution or constructive change.

The natural development would be for the NPT to be followed by the negotiation of a complete nuclear test ban treaty, and - in the more distant future - to generate the momentum towards a world free from nuclear weapons. For the CWC, the next and urgent step is to accelerate the process of ratifications for itself, so that the machinery that is being set up on a temporary basis can become fully operational, hopefully in 1995.

- II -

There is also an area of major concern. It is the problem of defining, with any measure of objectivity, what dual-technologies are or could be. Very challenging conceptual and political difficulties ahead of us in this field can be anticipated over the coming years.

It is necessary for us to look into ways and means whereby sensitive technologies could be transferred to countries requiring them in "bona fide", while at the same time making sure that these technologies would not be diverted to uses which are seen to be dangerous, either in a subregional, a regional or a global context. We must explore possible avenues which could lead to a broad expansion of scientific and technological knowledge, while safeguarding against improper use by eventual recipients of such knowledge.

Another area of concern, and one which bears directly on the future effectiveness of the three instruments, is the question of verification in all its multiple aspects. Verification, as such, is a new territory in international relations and, both in the legal and scientific dimensions, much remains to be done to give to this new concept the necessary transparency and legitimacy. One basic question is to find out how much verification should be "treaty specific" or how much verification should exist as an abstract domain of rules and methods which could be made applicable to a wide number of current and future international instruments.

Perhaps the only way to overcome these difficulties and to build up effective regimes to curb the spread of, or to eliminate the very existence of, weapons of mass destruction is to seek co-operative rather than the adversarial modes of action. Universal instruments negotiated freely in a truly transparent way, and the setting up of a fair balance of duties and privileges among all signatories, will remain the best course to achieve just and lasting results.

Section II: Non-Proliferation Versus Eradication

Sirous Nasseri

There is a major difference between the CWC, BWC and the NPT. The objective of the CWC and BWC is to remove a whole class of weapons and to prohibit further production. The NPT, like the CTBT which is much talked about nowadays, aims at non-proliferation. This difference is significant in the sense that there is a division of positions between basically, I can say, developing and developed countries. Non-proliferation measures are usually protested against or, at least, not favoured by the developing world, whereas it is the direction taken up in most cases by the developed countries.

This has a direct relevance to the question of effectiveness, as it is reasonable to believe that an objective shared by all will be more effectively fulfilled than that which faces divided opinion. In this sense the CWC and the BWC should presumably be more effective than the NPT.

Then comes the question of verification, which is the essential point in determining or in predicting whether a treaty would be effective or not.

I - CWC

1. Mechanism

For the CWC, one can fairly suggest that after more than two decades of negotiations, a feasible, reliable, extensive and intrusive mechanism has been established. This is the first convention that provides for a verification system that covers almost an entire industry; an industry that is vast and produces chemicals that constitute the ingredients for many things that we use in our daily life. It also has the innovative mechanism of challenge inspection which is aimed at removing or, at least, minimizing substantially the possibility of violations. At the same time, it envisages sanctions towards countries that have not joined the convention, and therefore have not committed themselves to its objectives.

The preparatory work is now under way at The Hague. As the Chairman of the OPCW, I have had the opportunity to have an overall view as to how things are moving:

- the infrastructure is developing rapidly: the organization has already part of the personnel that is needed, and is functioning smoothly;
- Good progress has also been made in a number of areas where elaborations or other forms of preparation were needed before the Convention comes into force.

2. Problem Areas

There are still a number of major areas in which a substantial amount of work remains to be done. These, incidentally, relate to the areas where, during the negotiations, ambiguities remained or agreements were not deep and comprehensive.

A fundamental problem lies in the definition of "chemical weapon". Because of its importance, I will explain this a little further.

In the early stages of negotiations, a definition was formulated for CW which included first the chemicals, second the weaponry and third the delivery systems. During further elaborations the complexity of the issues surrounding chemicals overwhelmed completely the other two parts. Only at the very last stage of negotiations - almost two months before the final conclusion - was this realized; of course, then it was too late to engage in real discussions, as it would have risked the postponement of arrival at a final agreement for the Convention.

The ambiguity that has ensued may eventually have a decisive impact on the actual implementation of the Convention.

The challenge inspection may be adversely affected by this, as abuse can become prevalent. On the basis of the text of the Convention and, with the definition as it stands, any country may challenge another member in order to acquire intelligence information. Any type of airplane, tank, artillery, even hand grenades, may become subject to challenge. There is no easy solution to this. But at least one hopes that the PREPCOM can try to find ways to manage this problem to some extent. The PREPCOM has decided to take this matter up.

The enormity of the work during the first phase is another major problem. It has been estimated that some 100,000 facilities would have to come under some sort of inspection and this even excludes the so-called capable facilities. For the time being, the organization has anticipated starting its work with 250 inspectors, as even the training of this number and provision of the necessary equipment is very hard to do.

It is expected that the inspections will primarily focus on chemical weapons, *i.e.*, what is contained in schedule 1 of the CWC. The organization may be forced to accept that part of the verification of destruction of CW will be done by the countries themselves. At later stages inspection will be extended to schedule 2 chemicals which constitute the precursors for CW, and, then to schedule 3 which includes many of the chemicals that are produced in large quantities and have dual-use character.

Inspection manuals are also yet to be prepared and there are many details which have been left in this regard to the PREPCOM to deal with... and... as the saying goes..., the devil is in the details...

Other issues such as inspection site and requested or alternative perimeters, confidentiality, conclusiveness of the report remain to be dealt with and agreements arrived at.

In addition, the issue of destruction versus conversion remains unsettled, though the Convention has clear provisions for this.

II - BWC

As far as the BWC is concerned, the discussions to develop a verification system are only at the preliminary stage. The States Parties to the process have established a series of meetings of scientists and experts called VEREX. The major problem there is in the fact that the BWC deals with substances used in pharmaceutical activities including not only all forms of medicines and medications, but also the important area of vaccines and serum production. Therefore, devising regimes that may be intrusive enough to provide a reasonable level of reliability in challenging violations and, at the same time, permissive in the pharmaceutical field, is a complicated task. It has been realized already, therefore, that the model of the CWC cannot be directly copied here.

Some progress has been made, nonetheless, in trying to formulate a package of various single potential verification measures, and some combinations thereof, to yield perhaps a reasonable method of verification.

It is suggested that a special conference be convened in order to examine and consider the results of the VEREX.

III - NPT

1. Problems

For the NPT the problems are abundant.
Major issues are yet to be discussed before the 1995 conference:

• First, what is to be done with countries that have remained outside the NPT and are on the verge of becoming Nuclear Weapon States (NWS).

In current negotiations on CTBT some ideas have been emerging which may be of use to the NPT Review Conference. For instance, it has been proposed that CTBT will not enter into force until and unless all NWS's, including all those who are on the threshold, join and ratify the Treaty. It has also been suggested that the emergence of any new NWS will be tantamount to an end to negotiations and, hence, the nullification of the Treaty.

The *raison d'être* of the NPT was to prohibit the possibility of another Nuclear Weapon State. It is, however, common knowledge that, ever since its inception in 1968, a number of countries have become nuclear. Applying the above ideas to the NPT may prove to be instrumental for its survival.

• Second, the other major issue is to have a time-bound framework for Nuclear Disarmament and to set a target date - a reasonably estimated one - for elimination of all nuclear weapons. I have stated at the CD that, with the demise of the Cold War, we no longer need a START Treaty, but a STOP Treaty: STRATEGIC AND NUCLEAR ARMS OUT OF OUR PLANET. Significant also is the issue of Negative Security Assurances. The best idea there may be to extend the commitments of the NWS's in the Tlatelolco Treaty to all NPT members.

These are some of the questions which surround the possibility of an extension of the NPT.

2. Assessment

One could say that CWC has a good chance of being effective; BWC is still too young to make a judgement about; the NPT has been effective only in the case of countries that have joined and accepted the safeguards voluntarily, except for one or two who have followed the path of proliferation. For the NPT to become more effective, one could envisage the improvement of the safeguards, but more important is to renew incentives for the NNWS's and insure the "have nots" against the "haves" through dealing promptly with nuclear disarmament, with the NSA, with the threshold States and with the CTBT.

3. Question of Peaceful Use

Essential to all of these is the guarantee for peaceful use and, I mean, a real guarantee.

In the chemical field the Australia Group, established in 1985, has developed a list containing 54 chemicals, 20 of which are not even included in the CWC. With CWC coming into force, the export regime set forth by the Australia Group should be abandoned; at least, that is what has been agreed.

The early indications are otherwise: at the OPCW, Australia has proposed a model legislation which includes export control on chemicals beyond what is prescribed by the CWC. Clearly, the intention is to justify, and legalize though legislature, continuation of the Australia Group.

Moreover, at the last UN General Assembly, the West refused inclusion of a phrase from the Convention into the UNGA resolution, which relates to technological co-operation for peaceful use.

These are alarming. The worst that the CWC can see is a renewed clash over this essential issue. Not just its effectiveness, but the whole of the Convention may then be at stake.

The Australia Group also restricts, for the time being, export of 65 biological agents. The Group, during VEREX, refused to make a commitment to remove restrictions even after an effective verification system has been established. If this position remains firm, we may not see an effective BWC with a reliable verification mechanism at all.

For the NPT, the situation is much worse. Here the Treaty ensures peaceful use (Article IV). It was even understood that material and technology for peaceful use would be provided to NPT members at lower prices (FANFANI PROPOSAL). Most NNWS NPT members have been cold-shouldered instead, by restrictions of the London Club: hence the reluctance to extend the NPT - even a limited extension.

The fate, and not just effectiveness, of the CWC, BWC and the NPT lies in a change of policy and attitude, indeed a change of heart, on peaceful use.

Section III: Functioning of the Three Global Multilateral Regimes

Richard Starr

1. The acquisition of *weapons of mass destruction* (WMD), particularly in association with missile delivery systems, forms by far the most destabilising factor in any regional security equation with great potential for negative impact on economic confidence and progress. The threat of acquisition therefore warrants major and sustained efforts to control and to prevent the spread of these weapons, and to give effect to our aspirations for eventual disarmament in this area.

Efforts to control or eliminate WMD may impinge on legitimate security and economic concerns. Compliance cannot be verified without some degree of intrusion, including access to defence establishments, and while attempts to acquire these weapons continue there will also be a requirement for the export licensing (as distinct from the banning) of trade in the most relevant sensitive goods and services.

It must be emphasized, however, that the more effective these global multilateral conventions are in achieving their arms control and disarmament objectives, the more improved will be the circumstances promoting legitimate trade in the related goods and information. A basic purpose of international nuclear verification and control is to support peaceful nuclear trade and co-operation. Likewise CW and strengthened BW conventions will assist trade in sensitive chemical and biological items.

2. The *Nuclear Non-Proliferation Treaty* has a record of achievements, and recent challenges have resulted in revived interest in, and support for, strengthening the effectiveness of the NPT verification role played by IAEA safeguards.

The main flaw in the previous operation of IAEA controls, as highlighted by the experience with Iraq, was that it was limited in its ability to detect clandestine nuclear-weapons-related activities at undeclared installations. These by definition were quite separate from those declared to the IAEA and inspected by it.

Important work has been undertaken in Vienna since the Gulf War to strengthen and increase the transparency of IAEA safeguards, in particular through the reaffirmation of the Agency's right to conduct special inspections. The provision to the Agency of design information on nuclear facilities, and the establishment of a more comprehensive reporting system are other important steps.

For the verification provisions of the Treaty to work, the Agency must have access to a free flow of information, as well as access to possible undeclared sites. The importance of this cannot be overstated, as has been demonstrated all too clearly by the situation in Iraq and by the current difficulties in verifying the DPRK's nuclear program. Information as well as access underpins the capabilities of all arms control regimes.

Effective nuclear and nuclear dual-use export controls complement NPT verification activities. The 1990 NPT Review Conference agreed that fullscope safeguards should be a condition of significant new nuclear supply to non-Nuclear Weapons States, and the fullscope safeguards supply policy of the Nuclear Suppliers Group reinforces the basic safeguards standard already accepted by all non-Nuclear Weapon States Party to the NPT.

The NPT addresses nuclear disarmament under Article VI, and some of the most positive and significant developments have been on this side. Nuclear confrontation has ended and the major nuclear arsenals are being substantially reduced by bilateral agreement; after a consensus resolution of support in the General Assembly, negotiations here in Geneva are now underway on a Test Ban Treaty; and we are also looking forward to an early start to negotiations on a Cut-Off treaty.

3. In comparison to the NPT, the *Chemical Weapons Convention* is untested, but it has strong potential. The provisions represent evolutionary

thinking in arms control, particularly on verification. Negotiation of an effective CWC presented the international community with unique problems: how to eliminate production of a weapon of mass destruction which could be so readily manufactured throughout the world's sprawling chemical industry, and how to stop chemical weapons acquisition without damaging legitimate, universal access to chemicals.

The solution was the development of a general monitoring mechanism for the industry with added, and vital provisions for what, in effect, are inspections of any site on demand. The wide acceptance of intrusive verification as standard and essential is the revolutionary element in the global multilateral field. It holds the key to cost effective monitoring of all the WMD regimes including a CTBT. Moreover, it is through the acceptance of this mechanism that constraints and regulations in the economic and commercial field can be held at quite manageable levels.

Nevertheless effective restraint on the spread of weapons of mass destruction still requires buttressing by export licensing measures. Thus in the case of the CWC we believe there is a clear legal and moral obligation under the Convention for States Parties to satisfy themselves that relevant (and I would stress, only the relevant) chemicals they export, will not assist in making chemical weapons. This position holds whether those chemicals are included in the Convention's schedules or not.

It is my understanding that certain chemicals not listed in the CWC schedules - for example hydrogen fluoride and fluorine salts - are necessary in the manufacture of a range of chemical weapons. These include nerve agents found by UNSCOM in Iraq, and of a type used by Iraq in the Iran-Iraq War. It would clearly contravene the letter and spirit of the CWC to export such chemicals if this served to assist such a CW program.

The Australian Government is convinced that the operation of a licensing system for such exports is in active support of the aims of the CWC, including those reflected in Article XI and the companion reference in the Preamble. We believe export licensing permits our exporters to operate with greater confidence, free of concern that chemical exports may be diverted to activities prohibited by the CWC. If we failed to offer our exporters such a systematic procedure for securing reassurance, this might create uncertainty about the final use of an export, and hence inhibit legitimate trade.

There is a further important aspect to this approach. All of us, governments and industry, look to the increasing effectiveness of the CWC after its entry into force to lessen the necessary scope for such action. We recognize parallel obligations to facilitate legitimate trade. The Australian Government has formally adopted the policy that it will review its export licensing arrangements for the benefit of States Parties in good standing under the CWC.

4. Time does not permit proper coverage of the *BWC*, but our attitude is very clear. This largely declaratory instrument of the early seventies must be modernized. It has, usefully, served to set something of a norm against BW acquisition, but recent history shows good intentions are not good enough.

5. What is greatly encouraging in considering the *future effectiveness of the three WMD regimes*, however, is the remarkable evolution in political attitudes that is permitting, in fact demanding effectiveness. The world has accepted the passing of an era when sovereign States could be expected merely to commit themselves to the extent of declarations of good intent. Useful though declaratory measures can be as a preliminary step, confidence can only come from the demonstrable monitoring of compliance and, as regards WMD, effective measures against proliferation and towards the prospect of eventual disarmament.

There is widespread acceptance that the nuclear non-proliferation regime based on the NPT and the IAEA safeguards system, imperfect though it may be in the view of many, is vital as a barrier to the destabilising spread of nuclear weapons. In endorsing by consensus the most recent global disarmament treaty, the CWC, UN members accepted the need for narrowly targeted, but still unprecedented intrusive verification to enable the monitoring of the world wide industry and capability in chemical production. This same spirit has driven positive reconsideration of the patently inadequate BWC. Parties to the Treaty are motivated by a realization that we must find a way of monitoring compliance under the BWC before it is too late.

In looking ahead, the most important variable in the question of these conventions' effectiveness, and hence their positive impact on security and economic circumstances, is the degree of political will shown by the international community. The modern approach to arms control negotiations is producing conventions with substantive and effective verification mechanisms. The issue is whether they will be properly used and firmly supported. If they are, we will see the evolution of attitudes fostering the emergence of a normative force sufficient to outlaw these weapons. Responsibility lies with all countries to take steps multilaterally and nationally. In this process, a clear understanding by all of the broad aims, the means by which they are achieved and the costs and greater benefits of the process, is crucial for gaining wide international support. This Conference serves that crucial objective.

Chapter 17
What are the Obstacles to Regional Arms Limitation Agreements?

Section I: Disparities and the Peace Process in the Middle East

Aharon Klieman

1. It is fair to say that the Middle East region has entered a different and, in many ways, exciting era. From an historical perspective, perhaps three ostensibly positive developments highlight this transition, and bear directly on arms control prospects. From the standpoint of the region as a whole, for the first time essentially since 1798 and Napoleon's invasion of Egypt, its inhabitants do not face any direct, overt or immediate threat of encroachment and domination from an extra-regional great power, acting as an agent of either the balance of power or imperialism. Thus we are free to concentrate energies on internal and regional development, if only we should choose to do so.

The second encouraging event, in my view, was the 1991 precedent set during the Kuwait crisis for a collective approach to security in countering aggression. Success was owed to the efforts of an international coalition acting, however, under special controlled conditions. One key component in this case study of effective international crisis management surely was the extraordinary realignment among the regional States themselves, that temporarily cut across differences of leadership personality, regime-type, economic stratification and ideological orientation, but which nonetheless confirmed the ability even of Middle Eastern antagonists to behave prudently in assuring the minimum of regional stability.

Third, and most recent, to be sure, are signs of forward movement in the more specific Arab-Israel peace process. Although originating earlier with the 1977 Sadat initiative and 1979 bilateral Israel-Egypt treaty, the negotiating format was dramatically altered and improved by the 13 September 1993 Oslo-framework accord that, for the first time, directly encompasses the Palestinian dimension of the conflict.

2. Previously, when confronted with the difficult decisions, tradeoffs and concessions which regional security and the wages of peace require, Middle Easterners habitually would have responded: "let's double-cross that bridge when we come to it"! Of late, by contrast, there is an honest "good-faith" effort at actually crossing those bridges, by directly confronting the many issues involved in any comprehensive Arab-Israel peace formula - including, most particularly, collective, region-wide, as well as individual State security.

Consequently, there are grounds for guarded optimism, if only the three positive precedents registered since the start of this decade can be kept in force: a strategy of regional development, of acting in concert and in persevering toward the goal of conflict termination. However, taking my assignment literally, I have been invited most explicitly to consider the *obstacles* to regional arms limitation agreements, rather than the incentives.

It is thus in keeping with the traditional nature of the region to confound conventional assumptions that even these three central achievements - while perhaps not in the category of unmitigated obstacles - nevertheless do caution arms control enthusiasts against any rush to judgment in declaring a "new Middle East order", governed by fresh thinking and improved norms of political behaviour which embrace whole-hearted commitment to halting the regional arms race.

I - Disparities

If asked to select a single impediment - one that also provides a useful and economic organizing concept for my remarks - it would be condensed into the theme of "disparities".

1. Starting with the general security environment, disparity expresses itself firstly in something as basic as defining *the* "Middle East." At the very outset of any (and every) discussion such as ours relating to regional problems, analysts will differ sharply, insisting either in conceiving of this elusive geopolitical, economic and cultural region narrowly and exclusively (the "Arab world", the "Arab Middle East"), or else in far more inclusive terms, pushing outward and stretching from Morocco in the Maghrib, west to Turkey in the north, Iran and Pakistan in the east, and Sudan in the south. The political and diplomatic implication is that the more inclusive our working definition, the greater becomes the difficulty in achieving any kind

of negotiating consensus, let alone unanimity, as in the clarion call for a demilitarized or nuclear-free Middle East.

2. Secondly, within the region, however defined, great disparities exist among whatever combination of Member States are viewed as comprising the region, as regards their individual threat perceptions and power capabilities, as well as in their political intentions. There is a wide spectrum ranging from genuine security dilemmas (especially when strategic surprise remains a distinct possibility) all the way to aggressive designs and aspirations to regional hegemony. To make our point we need merely add to this the exceptionally large number of sub-sets of regional disputes, of interstate ("dyadic") rivalries, claims and pretensions, and of multiple contingencies. Nor are these security concerns alleviated by the mounting suspicion that, rather than being a "defining moment" and the critical precedent established for joint security, the Kuwait case may come to be recalled as the exception proving the general rule of individual State solutions to their enduring security dilemma.

It is here that concern must also be voiced that the opportunity afforded by the end of the Cold War to put our own Middle East house in order may be squandered, with Saddam Hussein's unilateral military initiative providing an intimation of things to come, as local actors come to feel less constrained by Super-Power or great power considerations in unilaterally pursuing national agendas and separate objectives inside the region. Moreover, there is good cause for concern that Middle East politics in the next 2-5 years may experience a new cycle of instability due to leadership succession or possibly even regime changes, as well as to a fresh round of accelerated rearmament. It must be stressed with full candour that the ascendance of anti-American, anti-European, anti-modernist and anti-Israel elements from within the region, marked by their attaining power in any one of the pivotal Arab and Islamic countries, will only exacerbate the existing perceived sense of insecurity. It is the latter which, for the present, constitutes the sole common denominator uniting regional members - and not the shared dream of economic development, prosperity and integrated markets.

3. Moving from the general security environment to the specific cause of arms moderation, this issue, too, is hampered by disparities once again: the overall theme of these remarks.

On the demand side, there are those weapons customers in the region enjoying established supplier relationships (Turkey, Egypt, Israel, Saudi Arabia); ease of access; purchasing power; and some degree of indigenous arms-manufacturing capability - as opposed to those countries deficient in any or all of the categories.

The same theme of disparity is also mirrored on the supplier side of the equation. A disparity, if you will, between word and deed, whereby lofty and inspiring calls for curbs and for control regimes by leading international actors (who also happen to double as the front-ranking weapons proliferators worldwide and to the Middle East) coexist uneasily with their intensifying national weapons sales marketing drive in the post-Gulf war period. It is, frankly, more than slightly ingenuous to find the loss of momentum in the 1991 sequence of US, Big 5 and G-7 conventional arms initiatives, attributed in the literature on the international and Middle East arms trade, for instance, to China's obstructionism, without underscoring the major economic, industrial, corporate and commercial incentives driving the primary exporters to sustain their sales promotions to the Middle East.

II - Peace Process and Arms Control

1. Finally, a word about the Madrid and Oslo peace processes from the standpoint of arms control. Before there was any peace process to speak of, and so long as it remained an impractical goal, the inclination among Middle East peace activists, whether academics, statesmen or arms control experts, quite legitimately, was to settle for advocating limited confidence-building measures as part of an incremental approach ("the building-blocks to peace", "pre-negotiation", "negotiating about negotiations", creating the proper climate, etc.) CBMs, in short, served both as a substitute and as a precondition for eventual peacemaking. CBMs in general, and arms limitation proposals in particular, in the past were held hostage to Arab-Israeli hostility, whereas now they are still dependent, but on the peace process itself.

It means that while it is well and good to have the bilateral political talks proceed in parallel with the multilateral Working Group on Arms Control and Regional Security, any genuine progress on the latter front apparently must await agreement at the political negotiating level. And within a settlement, moreover, which must be comprehensive, conducted through a process that is proving slow-paced, painstakingly detailed and complicated, and hence protracted. Witness the months of procedural wrangling over micro-issues like the geographic confines of Jericho, for example. Given this bargaining pattern, the concern is that security issues, such as prompt, immediate arms restraint measures, may be put on hold. Especially when the final example of disparity is mirrored in the divergent security concerns, priorities, and solutions now on the arms negotiating table.

2. The Arab position cites Israel's qualitative edge, and insists therefore upon first addressing the nuclear end of the scale. Israeli thinking, conversely, is preoccupied with Arab quantitative superiority; hence Jerusalem's insistence that the conventional arms problem receive priority attention.

In a speculative vein, given the extreme and contradictory premises serving as the respective sides' opening arms bargaining positions, just possibly there is some merit in proposing to square the difference. Rather than focus initially and exclusively on *either* the conventional *or* the strategic, nuclear and non-conventional level - assured non-starters diplomatically - might there not be some practical as well as conceptual merit in starting serious arms limitation negotiations by focusing on the middle rung of the arms ladder, namely the category of most immediate security concern: biological and chemical weapons, missiles and delivery systems?

In concluding, it is but another of the many historical and political ironies posed by the Middle East that a peace process which ought to be inspiring, in the short term at least, represents as much a part of the immediate problem for any arms control breakthrough, as it does the ultimate solution.

Section II: CSCE Confidence-Building Process and Other Regions

Rakesh Sood

1. The end of the Cold War marks a watershed in the 20th century. A transformation of the political landscape has taken place in recent years. Strategic thinkers and political leaders are still trying to develop new concepts and adapt existing institutions to cope with the challenges posed by these changes.

Among the Western countries there is often a debate as to who was responsible for winning the Cold War. The arms control community is convinced that the victory has been theirs. Similarly, the export control community and the architects of COCOM would be equally confident that they had the right strategy. Among the arms control community there would be some who would give credit to the bilateral arms control negotiators, while others would attribute greater importance to the proponents of CBMs in Europe. It is unlikely that these debates can be resolved. Whether regional arms control in the European context was the key factor may be debatable, but it is certainly true that the CSCE process, aimed at improving confidence and enhancing security in Europe, did play a role in easing the tensions of the Cold War.

2. Given the coincidence of the evolution of the CSCE process and the end of Cold War, there is perhaps a natural and understandable desire on the part of its authors and negotiators to try and fit other regions characterized by a hostile relationship into the same mould. This is, however, a risky exercise. The concept of regional arms limitation has to be placed in its proper context, namely the framework of regional confidence-building. The CSCE experience is clear evidence that negotiations on arms limitation became possible only after many years of patient and arduous negotiations on confidence-building measures.

The Helsinki Final Act, signed in 1975, focused primarily on the principles governing the conduct of relations between States. These principles:

- inviolability of frontiers,
- territorial integrity of States,
- non-use of force,
- non-intervention in internal affairs, etc.,

are not different from the provisions of the UN Charter. Yet, reiteration in the regional context is often perceived as politically more significant than in the global context. The Helsinki Final Act only provided for limited transparency, based more on voluntary actions. The only mandatory aspect was that both sides would provide advance notification on military exercises above a certain threshold. It took eleven more years of negotiations before the Stockholm Document was signed in 1986, which provided for the presence of observers at military exercises and inspection of military activities. From becoming a voluntary political act, transparency was being gradually backed up by mandatory obligation. However, an arms limitation agreement was still further down the road. It took four more years when the Vienna Document was concluded in 1990, increasing the verification requirements and also setting limits on conventional military forces. However, it is important to underline that, between 1986 and 1990, the European political landscape underwent a transformation, and this political development was primarily responsible for bringing about an early agreement on the Vienna Document and later in 1992, on the CFE.

What were the CBMs that found utility and acceptance in the CSCE? Broadly, these fall into three categories:

- communication-related CBMs dealing with conflict prevention, hot links, etc.;
- transparency-related CBMs dealing with pre-notification of military activities, inspections and presence of observers; and
- restraint-related CBMs relating to ceilings or establishment of non-deployment zones, etc.

In Europe, where the CSCE exercise focused in large measure on arms control, the evolution from voluntary transparency to mandatory transparency to arms limitation was gradual and assisted by political developments. In other parts of the world, the notion of security is somewhat different. The political factors and the contextual factors are different. The security concerns of countries in other regions are not limited to only the military field but also have a non-military dimension. This creates the need for an expanded notion of CBMs rather than the narrower arms limitation focus.

3. There are basic differences in the realities on the ground that have characterized the CSCE process and other regional CBM exercises. In Europe, nuclear deterrence was in operation. Secondly, there was a rough parity in conventional forces, notwithstanding the qualitative dimension of the military hardware. Thirdly, CBMs were addressed from one alliance to another, across a common perceived dividing line running through Europe. The bi-polar nature of the political order reinforced this line. Finally, the

ideological conflict augmented the confrontation. None of these factors characterize the situation on the ground in the Middle Eastern, Asian and Pacific regions. Nuclear deterrence is not operational. Bipolarity does not exist and there is no single underlying ideological conflict. There is no commonly perceived dividing line and each country has more than one neighbour. This makes the notion of parity unrealistic. Achievement of mutually-balanced and enhanced security through CBMs can therefore not be realized through arms control measures, but more broadly-based interactions.

4. Nevertheless, there are certain lessons that can be drawn from the CSCE exercise. These relate, not to the actual agreements of the CSCE, but to the political dynamics of the negotiations. Firstly, the evolution of regional CBMs is a long-drawn-out exercise. Major achievements often follow political breakthroughs, as in the case of Europe. Secondly, while the goals may be ambitious, progress will only be incremental. While political developments make initiation of the negotiations possible, even incremental achievements reinforce the positive political momentum. In Europe, it must be recalled that the MBFR talks were stalled for more than ten years, reflecting that arms limitation could hardly form the first strand of regional security and that the process had to begin with a more modest exercise in confidence-building. Thirdly, the road to arms limitation starts with conflict avoidance and moves through transparency, in different stages, initially voluntary and subsequently mandatory. In the European context, conflict avoidance was characterized by trying to prevent the possibility of a large-scale surprise conventional attack. In other regions, conflict avoidance may assume different forms, such as the hot line, etc.

Transparency is a difficult exercise among States that have different political structures. Nevertheless, it is a prerequisite because reduction of secrecy among adversaries regarding their military activity lies at the origin of attempts for confidence-building. Finally, development of institutional mechanisms, both for negotiations and for implementation, are important in their own right. To an extent, these provide a buffer from the political swings of the bilateral relations, bringing a sense of predictability to the CBM exercise. The existence of an institutional mechanism just prior to a political breakthrough, can have a radical impact on reviving the CBM process among adversaries.

5. The expanded notion of CBMs has been implicitly accepted in some of the recent initiatives in the Asian and Pacific regions. The ASEAN Regional Forum which came into being in 1993 reflects a group of countries that do not fall within a defined geographical zone, *i.e.*, it includes ASEAN States, dialogue partners and other countries, too. This indicates that the regional security calculation can often be based on equations other than those characterizing the regional economic calculation, or the geographical definitions of a region. The logic of the composition of the ASEAN Forum is a reflection of the political dynamics. Similarly, another CBM initiative in the region has been launched by President Nazarbaev of Kazakhstan. Addressing the UNGA in 1992, President Nazarbaev called for the establishment of a Conference on Interaction and Confidence-Building in Asia.

Two expert group meetings have taken place with a view to preparing for a Ministerial conference. At the second expert group meeting, representatives from DPRK, ROK, Japan, China, India, Pakistan, Iran, Israel, Russia and Australia were among the 25 countries present, either as participants or as observers. The agenda of the meeting reflects a focus on security enhancement that covers confidence-building and co-operation in the scientific, environmental, economic and humanitarian fields. Both these initiatives are in early stages, but clearly the political leadership behind these initiatives has implicitly acknowledged the broad-based nature of regional confidence-building that is essential in areas marked by diversity and plurality.

6. In conclusion, there are no obstacles to regional arms limitation agreements, provided these are placed within the context of regional confidence-building, an exercise whose momentum is governed by the specificity of the political dynamics in the region. The example of the CSCE is useful and, at the same time, reveals the difference in the situation on the ground characterizing Europe in the 70s and the other regions in present times. The initiatives in the Middle East, as well as in the Asian and Pacific regions, are new and it will be premature to pass any judgments. However, these have had a promising start, reflecting a responsiveness to the characteristics of the region. The Middle East peace process with its bilateral and multilateral tracks is quite different from the ASEAN Regional Forum or the CICA initiative. Eventually, the arms limitation criteria will not be the sole criteria because confidence-building will encompass a broader scope.

Chapter 18
Discussion

1. *Serguei Batsanov*

Perhaps we are now coming to the heart of the problem. My impression at the beginning was that perhaps we were more on a technical side of whether this specific restriction in export control or licensing would help achieve non-proliferation goals. I am very grateful to David Hobbs for giving a rather comprehensive presentation and for advocating the co-operative development of these regimes; I think this is what should be our goal in these different cases.

Mr Hobbs' presentation, however, raises another question. How many regimes should we eventually have? It appears to me that the tendency until now has been to develop specific regimes for specific purposes, and that technique is predominantly a technical approach. To what extent the world would be prepared to move towards an integrated arms control regime is an open question, but I would hope that some further thought will be given to that problem, which I accept is a very difficult one.

In my view, the Chemical Weapons Convention probably offers a lot of potential benefits as an effective nonproliferation instrument. It is not only about nonproliferation, but it also exerts a nonproliferation affect even though the Convention is not yet in force. A lot has to be done to implement the agreement, of course, but, hopefully, its nonproliferation mechanism, in addition to its other mechanisms, will continue to produce much-desired results.

I would like to conclude my observation by stressing the need in many countries to accelerate the work by bringing into force the Chemical Weapons Convention. In addition to problems to which Ambassador Nasseri referred, and indeed, these are problems that have been raised by several countries at meetings in the Hague and in New York, there are a number of problems that each country has to work on: to identify the facilities that should be declared, to talk to the industry, and to prepare and enact implementation legislation. There appears to be an enormous amount of work that needs to be done, as we have heard from different countries.

2. David Markov

What is the cost of these particular treaties, and specifically the CWC treaty, on the participants, particularly, in regard to the comment on the cost to the governments to comply, update, and maintain the required lists and also to conduct the inspections themselves? Secondly, I would like to hear what the cost is projected to be for the businesses that have to comply with these inspections and maintain documentation with their government? Have any discussions been held on how to reduce costs to host governments and businesses involved?

3. Rakesh Sood

There is a need to change methods of implementing technology export controls from an adversarial mode to a co-operative mode. At the same time, some of the recommendations for using various indices based on human rights and quality of life in the UNDP reports, using military budgets, arms imports and exports as a criteria for permitting technology transfers do not lead in this direction. There appears to be a contradiction because using such criteria does not appear to be a co-operative approach to technology transfer. It still appears to me to remain an adversarial approach.

The second point is about the ISRO-Glavkosmos issue on cryogenic engine technology transfer. There is no ballistic missile today that uses a cryogenic engine. Enough has been written about it, and everyone is aware that using cryogenic fuels, such as liquid hydrogen or liquid oxygen, requires a large amount of preparation time in terms of fuelling. Somebody once joked that if you put a cryo engine on a Minuteman, it will become a "Week Man". It is very clear that what we are talking about here is technology denial. The Russian Government invoked the *force majeure* clause just before President Yeltsin went to attend the Tokyo G-7 Summit. There may be some linkages there. The discussion with US show that concerns relate not to the transfer of the engines themselves, but to the transfer of technology. That is the nub of the problem.

How this issue is resolved eventually, whether India develops it indigenously, or whatever, remains to be seen. We are essentially talking about civilian technology denial. It is important to look at this particular example in this context rather than in terms of transfer of a military system or the transfer of technology for a military system.

The third point is whether these arms control regimes are properly used and properly supported. Some claim that if these are, we will see the evolution of attitudes fostering the emergence of a normative force sufficient to outlaw these weapons. I would like to ask, as we complete 25 years of the NPT, given the fact that it is so widely universal and that there are just three significant countries still outside the treaty, has that normative force evolved in the context of nuclear weapons? If it had evolved, the normative force should have succeeded in outlawing these weapons through development of a "non-use" norm. This has not happened. Current doctrines of Nuclear Weapon States still predicate the use of their nuclear arsenal. If the normative force had evolved, then we would be engaged in negotiations on a Nuclear Weapons Convention much like the negotiations on a Chemical Weapons Convection, which concluded successfully in 1992.

4. David Hobbs

It is certainly true that what I was suggesting was a mixture of some incentives and disincentives, carrots and sticks. All the discussion of incentives and disincentives could take place in a co-operative framework. There are all sorts of factors which can be brought to bear. Some suppliers will not like the fact that they cannot sell; some of the potential recipients would not like the fact that they may not be able to buy. I see it as being a mixture of things, not a contrast: it is not one or the other. You have incentives, you have disincentives, all taking place within a dialogue. It is the dialogue which is the most important thing.

Regarding the point made about missile delivery vehicles and space launchers, I agree entirely. People tend to think that a satellite launcher and a missile are the same thing. They are not. Of course, you could use a space launcher as a weapons delivery system, but you would not want to. I am not really an expert on that particular issue, but I agree that sales of cryogenic engines are not ones to get too worked up about in a proliferation context, even though the technologies and associated technologies are relevant in many areas.

5. Marcos Castrioto de Azambuja

The nature of the incentive, positive or negative, does not make the relationship adversarial. What makes it co-operative is the manner in which incentives or disincentives were agreed on. What is important is not the nature, positive or negative, of whatever stimuli or contrary stimuli you want to apply, but whether these sets of rules were agreed upon in a consensus or in a negotiating mode.

Addressing the question of cost, the absolute true answer is that no one really knows. I do not think we have a reliable assessment. For many years there was an idea that disarmament measures would generate savings, which in turn would be used to fuel and promote development. Then we adopted a rather neutral view: that arms control would not generate anything, that there was to be no dividend. Now we are coming to the other end of the spectrum: that arms control measures are a very expensive thing. I am always a bit concerned, not that we are not getting any dividends, but that disarmament measures would appear to be so cumbersome and expensive that ultimately they might become less attractive to developed and developing countries alike.

6. Sirous Nasseri

I, too, see that the important thing, as to whether or not incentives or disincentives are co-operative or adversarial in nature, is how they have been arrived at. Indeed, we spent years and years in negotiation to define and to be as clear as possible as to what incentives or disincentives should be in relation to a certain class of weapons. For instance, take what we did in the case of the Chemical Weapons Convention. The common understanding was eventually rather clear as to what was included in an article of the Convention, Article 11, that made provisions for the removal of export controls as long as the removal is not incompatible with CWC obligations.

But, if that was to mean that certain regimes may remain in order to simply continue to monitor, as though monitoring is anything different than verification - verification is the more evolved version of monitoring - that is indeed what has been the subject of negotiations for years and years. If we were to have a regime that is internationally accepted and then separate regimes that are provided for and presented by certain countries, then what

Discussion

is the use of the international regime at all? We could have just gone ahead and lived with the regimes that have been provided by certain countries. It is very significant eventually that we come to an understanding between the developing countries and the developed world.

Where do we draw the line on being sure that there is compliance? I think that also comes from negotiations, and if you want to draw our own line further again we are making the wrong conclusions. We are allowing our own perceptions, our own interpretations, to turn into policy. There has been one example in the case of IAEA. One country, my own, has accepted verification of the most intrusive nature, something similar to challenge inspection in CWC on an informal basis. The team was allowed to look anywhere where information has been received that there maybe a possibility of some sort of violation. They went and they came back and said they had the opportunity to go wherever they wished. They had the information from all the countries that had some views about this available to them and they found nothing. Then, you see, even someone in the position of Mr Hans Blix will have to be very cautious to say: but Iran is a very vast country. What does that mean? The IAEA should one day be able to examine every inch of each country's territory to come up with a conclusive statement in order to allow for peaceful use? That is the type of problem that we have. Everything remains interpretative where complaints are issued.

7. Richard Starr

1. Let me make an observation. In negotiating the CWC we did so in close consultation with industry, not just Australian industry, but various industry associations around the world. Most countries which were involved in these negotiations also consulted with their particular industrial associations. I remember visiting Brasilia, and the Brazilian government was extremely careful to make its responses on the CWC contingent on consultation with industry.

The CWC convention was concluded with the full endorsement of international industry - full, and even enthusiastic endorsement when eventually they understood the scope, the nature of the obligations, and after they had made their own assessment of costs. That was when they had reached an understanding that without a chemical weapons convention to provide a certainty, an assurity, a predictability of trade, the costs to trade in chemicals eventually would be far more severe than any administrative charges that they faced under the convention. Chemical industry faces a whole range of administrative charges, environmental and others, and they are able to fit these together fairly efficiently.

2. With regard to the role of global regimes on weapons of mass destruction, we are very firmly of the view that the global multilateral regime must be made to work. It must be made to work on a co-operative basis; it is only through effective global multilateral regimes that you can get control of this problem. The responsibilities of nations under that regime may vary with the perceptions of various countries. We have taken a certain attitude towards our national obligations. There are other countries with similar views, and we consult, but this is not a formal legal regime. This is a means by which countries with like-minded objectives seek to ensure that this particular weapon of mass destruction, or that one, is not allowed to proliferate. The surety that comes with the establishment of effective regimes will allow those measures on trade to be wound back. It is only though the effective implementation of global regimes that we can reduce these measures. In fact, these measures are not that heavy. The burden is not great. We are talking really of quite small systems designed to deal with only the most relevant items.

3. There is no doubt that if the NPT is not extended for a very long period, and we would certainly prefer indefinite extension, the world system on the nuclear side will be thrown into a great deal of confusion. Trade and economic developments that are underpinned by nuclear trade will be thrown into doubt. We, for example, have pinned all of our uranium contracts to the continuation of safeguards under the NPT IAEA system. Where would we be? I am sure that other countries are in the same state.

The uncertainties regarding the acquisition of nuclear weapons was illustrated only too vividly by the experience in Iraq and now the DPRK. The world has little alternative, but to endorse what is an instrument that certainly could be improved upon, but nevertheless, is a vital instrument and by far the best thing that we have. There have been a range of measures, a range of advances, on both sides of the ledger under the NPT. There have been very substantial measures, measures which two or three years ago none of us really would have seen as possible. Certainly we did not think that we would be here negotiating a CTBT.

8. Peggy Mason

Mr Sood gave some examples of how this is developing in the ASEAN forum and of how it is focusing on confidence-building and security enhancement.

One can distinguish three levels of activity in the Asia-Pacific region. The region-wide activity includes the dialogue which Rakesh Sood talked about, but there are also issue-specific working groups which focus on particular issues such as the Spratley Islands (where only the countries that are most directly effected are involved and a few facilitators like Canada which pays for that particular exercise). The third level is that of sub-regional dialogues which focus on sub-regional interests (an example would be ASEAN itself, and also all the proposals for North Pacific dialogue). But there are remaining obstacles. What are the obstacles to the sub-continent getting into this game that you so accurately described?

9. Rakesh Sood

If we look at the ASEAN Regional Forum exercise, it is not just the ASEAN countries. It started out with the ASEAN and then expanded because the ASEAN countries themselves felt the need to involve other countries as partners in the security dialogue. Clearly, a kind of security environment was evolving without being given a geographical name. Similarly, in Kazakhstan, President Nazerbaev's initiative, there is a grouping of countries that is not geographically confined. At the second Expert Group meeting in August 1993 in Almaty, both Koreas were present; Japan was present; the US was not present; Israel, Iran, India and Pakistan were present; a lot of Central Asian countries were present, and so was China. If you look at this kind of a grouping, it is a fairly interesting grouping in terms of looking at regional security concerns.

The point I am trying to make here was a situation where both India and Pakistan were present. You are aware that India is engaged in a bilateral dialogue with both Pakistan and China. When our Prime Minister visited China last year an agreement on peace and tranquillity along the line of

Actual Control was signed. This is a fairly elaborate agreement. The recent Foreign Secretary level talks with Pakistan, held earlier this year, were the 7th round during the last three years. Subsequently, a number of non-papers on confidence-building measures, etc., have been formally proposed by India. That is the bilateral exercise. The participation of both countries in regional initiatives is another dimension of confidence-building. And the global negotiations whether it is in the CD, on negotiations like the Test Ban etc., in the General Assembly is yet another strand in the web of building greater confidence.

Concluding Remarks

1. Sverre Lodgaard

I shall interpret the task assigned to me very liberally: the following remarks are only some personal reflections of one of the most difficult dimensions of security considerations - both conceptually and politically - in the aftermath of the Cold War.

1. While the volume of arms trade has decreased significantly in recent years, some factors have made it more difficult to control and restrict the flow of arms.

First, the market favours the buyer. It is no longer segmented: everybody is trying to sell to everybody, so for a typical buyer there are more sellers at hand. Furthermore, because of the overcapacities in a number of supplier States, more sophisticated technologies are offered for sale at depressed prices.

Second, the transfer mechanisms have become more diverse, largely because of sales to a variety of non-traditional clients. Typically, these are sales to the rapidly growing number of warring factions that have emerged in recent years, delivered directly or through various sorts of intermediaries.

Third, some of the modern, sophisticated gadgets are by their very nature more difficult to track. The emphasis is increasingly on enabling technologies rather than ready-made systems. Among the low-technology gadgets, many items are difficult to monitor simply because they are small: nearly all the wars that are being waged today are internal wars consuming large amounts of small arms and ammunition. While measures are being taken to create greater openness in the transfer of major arms, we are still faced with an illicit, non-transparent sector the magnitude of which is hard to estimate.

2. When trying to come to grips with very complex and difficult problems, single recipes seldom suffice. Multi-pronged approaches are needed.

In addition to the much-discussed supplier regimes, recipient understandings to restrain the acquisition of arms must also be encouraged. Such understandings should be developed on a regional basis. Furthermore, there is a growing need for supplier-recipient agreements on the rules to govern international transactions. A broader consensus is particularly important as regards dual-use technologies.

At the end of the 1970s, some consideration was given to the elaboration of consensus rules in the nuclear field. The Cold War of the 1980s brought those attempts to a halt. Now, time seems ripe for more comprehensive endeavours to develop mutually acceptable market rules across the board. At this conference, arguments and hints in this direction have been heard from representatives of many different constituencies. The need to alleviate brewing mistrust and conflict may be greatest and most urgent in the chemical field, in the context of the CWC and the Australia Group.

3. On the supplier side, elimination of overcapacities in arms production is a major, ongoing task. The planned withdrawal of forces from Germany, and the implementation of the CFE, will be accomplished in the near future. Big surplus stocks of arms will remain for a longer time still. Restructuring, diversification and adjustment of arms production facilities is another time-consuming process. In order better to cope with the consequences of large reductions in domestic military demands, many supplier States now tend to promote arms sales at the expense of export restraint. Today, there are some 10-12 multilateral arms control agreements of significance. They provide an important element of predictability in a rapidly changing and sometimes chaotic world. In order to enhance their efficacy and durability, further efforts must be made to eliminate the perceived discriminatory features of some of them. Such changes are mainly for supplier States to implement.

In Europe, there is a CSBM obliging all CSCE parties to present annual forecasts of planned arms acquisitions. For the time being, prior notification of intended exports and imports at the global level - between 180 States - is beyond reach. The P-5 talks conducted in the propitious circumstances immediately after the Gulf War demonstrated the difficulty of agreeing on prior notification. This exercise has not been continued.

Other suggested supplier restraints include exchange of information about cases that are deemed critical; sharing of intelligence; ceilings on certain types of weapons in a region; and agreement not to introduce new arms technologies into specified areas.

4. On the recipient side, there is great scope and need for similar measures on a regional basis. For instance, in the Middle East some kind of platform should be made - however modest - for joint deliberations on arms acquisitions. Such deliberations may start in pragmatic fashion, between two, three ... five countries. They could take the form of CSBMs integral to broader peace accords. Alternatively, annual forecasts of planned arms acquisitions might be agreed as a regional extension of the UN arms register, *i.e.* as a partial measure in its own right, not predicated on any major political rearrangement.

In Europe, second-generation CSBMs were developed more or less in conjunction with the concept of non-offensive defence. A non-offensive defence is a military system which is structured, equipped and exercised to fight in a defensive mode, and which is therefore most cost-effective when operating in that mode. The CFE agreement, which was influenced by the rapidly growing interest in the concept at the time, has a distinctly non-offensive profile. Non-offensive defence is an interesting proposition for other regions as well. For instance, an accord between Israel and Syria trading territory for peace would probably imply some kind of non-offensive defence arrangement, bolstered by CSBMs.

A defensive reorientation of arms exports, selectively prohibiting arms that are likely to be destabilizing while allowing sales to bolster predominantly defensive systems, would alleviate some of the negative repercussions of arms trade. To some extent, such a reorientation would meet the military concerns of importing States without undermining regional stability, and some of the objections of arms producers would be mitigated. It remains to define what is "destabilizing" and "excessive": however, it would seem that a viable definition can best be sought in the context of non-offensive defence.

5. Naturally, disarmament has been most substantial where the Cold War had its major impact: in Europe. At the same time, regional variations have become greater than ever before. While disarmament prevails in Europe, large arms purchases are made in the Middle East - as is usual after major wars there - and in East Asia vital economies are sustaining growing military budgets. The corollary is that regional approaches to security and disarmament have to be strengthened: the challenge is now to turn this observation into practical reality.

New ideas must be encouraged, *inter alia* to come around the much heeded supposition that little can be done unless all parties in the region agree. Attempts to do so encounter the well-known collective action dilemma for public goods: it is unlikely that collective action will come about unless all, or almost all, get on-board. However, in some cases the benefits may outweigh the costs even if all relevant parties do not participate from the beginning. The trick is then to move beyond traditionalism into an unprejudiced assessment of advantages and drawbacks.

The new multilateral arrangement now being established on the heels of COCOM, dealing with sensitive dual-use goods and conventional weapons, shall reportedly not impede normal trade. However, there are reasons to watch out for the erection of new barriers: in particular, initiatives to turn parts of the old COCOM lists 90 degrees - direction South - should be critically examined. In the field of weapons of mass destruction, similar claims have been made for the Australia Group, the MTCR, the Nuclear Suppliers Group and the Zangger Committee. Based on the idea of supplies in return for unambiguous non-proliferation commitments, these are important achievements. At the same time, they are imperfect arrangements that should be seen as interim measures. Today, there are many snags involved. Generally, this is the time to promote co-operation and avoid confrontation.

More and more, defence-related transfers involve dual-use technologies. Increasingly, these technologies are first developed in civilian sectors and then, eventually, made available for military purposes. Hence the significance of reaching agreement on a set of rules for technology transfers that better reconciles the objectives of development and security.

As usual, there has to be a certain reciprocity in rights and obligations. Recipients can do more to make their activities more transparent, and offer better possibilities to check compliance with end-use statements. Co-operation between recipients and suppliers in restricting illicit trade through non-transparent channels should also be encouraged. In supplier-recipient relations, incentives and disincentives should increasingly be shaped in a consensus spirit and in a negotiating mode.

6. Where States have no significant national interest, they prefer to deal with conflicts from a distance - e.g. through sanctions, flight exclusion zones and arms embargoes. If they nevertheless get involved on the spot, the threshold of pain in terms of material costs and human lives tend to be very

low. As a result, such operations become delicate: indeed, to be involved in war without risking the lives of one's own soldiers is an intriguing proposition. This speaks to the limitations and vulnerabilities of collective security actions.

Security management in a world characterized by the unpredictable interplay between integration and fragmentation can be no coherent, consistent and universal phenomenon. As long as the international community cannot guarantee the security of States and peoples - through the UN or regional organizations - weapons will be acquired for self-defence. In a long-term perspective, measures to enhance collective security are therefore measures to limit the flow of arms as well. So are stronger incentives and greater willingness to comply with international norms and obligations. Ultimately, conflict resolution is the most convincing way of stopping arms and technology transfers.

7. One of the most fascinating subjects in the social and political sciences is how decision-makers reduce the complexity of reality in order to come to grips with it. This is a reductionism that has many variations. One of them is to pick at one part or other of a much greater totality, such as a specific arms deal: this is sometimes what parliamentarians do - at the risk of treating the parts without due concern for the dynamics of the whole. It is much more difficult to develop broader perspectives and holistic views on such a complex subject as arms and technology transfers. This, too, is an exercise in reductionism, but of a different kind. To help facilitate a broader supplier-recipient consensus on market rules across the entire range of arms and defence-related technologies, the material presented at this conference should now be processed and further developed into complementary perspectives on the majority, if not the totality, of the issues we have been dealing with these days.

2. *Robert L. Pfaltzgraff, Jr.*

It is abundantly apparent, especially as reflected in our discussions of this Research Report, that to discuss the security and economic considerations of arms and technology transfers, is to address a phenomenon of enormous complexity that is both multifaceted and in the process of change before our very eyes. To a large extent, we are in the position of the proverbial blind person and the elephant. We grasp and describe parts of the animal's anatomy without a clear understanding of its totality. It seems easier to deal with the phenomenon within its reductionist elements than to set forth in all of its dimensions what it is and how the component parts relate to one another in dynamic and systemic fashion.

Nevertheless, it seems to me that we have made considerable progress both in aggregating and disaggregating the various parts of the phenomenon encompassed by the major themes of this conference. Throughout our proceedings we have addressed various unifying themes and more or less agreed on their basic elements. Let me provide a brief summary:

- **Transparency** - The *sine qua non* for controlling transfers is the greatest possible transparency to provide information, as well as timely warning, about what is being transferred or likely to be transferred. We need to extend transparency to a host of arenas, building on what has been achieved in the UN Register of Conventional Arms and providing for greater transparency both at the global and regional levels. We will need to achieve a greater complementarity among existing and potential regimes for controlling arms transfers. We will also have to give greater attention to the problem of defining the operational meaning of transparency. What are the additional categories of armaments that should be included? How do we reconcile differing meanings of transparency based on diverse security needs in volatile regions such as the Middle East?

- **The definition of the term "armaments"** - and the distinction between conventional (or non-apocalyptic) weapons and weapons of mass destruction (apocalyptic) weapons. Here we considered categories to be blurred in the sense that, especially in protracted wars as in the former Yugoslavia, hundreds of thousands of casualties result from the use of relatively basic weapons whereas, for the coalition allies at least, casualties were minimal in the Gulf War, in which highly sophisticated weapons were used in a conflict of short duration. If we can properly define weapons of mass destruction, our preference is to ban them - especially biological and chemical weapons - while we are limited to controlling conventional systems because they are far more numerous and more widely available. Our problem of defining what is meant by armaments is complicated by the advent of a host of modern technology systems. While the trade in basic conventional weapons has been stable in recent years, we are in the midst of a sharp increase in nuclear weapons programs and countries based to some extent on lessons learned in the Gulf War. Furthermore, the meaning of armaments has been broadened by such developments as the unprecedented importance of information technologies essential to the integration of battle management. The emphasis, likely to be increased in the years ahead, on a large number of **more** lethal systems, perhaps as counters to existing advanced technologies, further complicates our ability to bound the phenomenon with which we are dealing in arms transfers.

- **The dual-use question** - another pervasive theme of this conference was shown repeatedly throughout our discussions to be complex. If, as was suggested, civilian technologies are advancing at a more rapid pace than military technologies, a focus on military technologies addresses only part of the transfer problem, and not necessarily the part that will be most important in defining **future** dual-use possibilities. This problem is further complicated by the fact that dual use technologies can be used - in fact are indispensable - in the development of weapons of mass destruction - nuclear, biological, and chemical weapons notably. We were reminded that efforts to control dual-use technology are not new. What **is** new is the unprecedented dynamism of technology both in its capacity to produce innovation and in its propensity to spread geographically from its point of origin and at the same time to be available for civilian and military applications. Somehow we will need to draw a more clear-cut distinction in arms control regimes such as MTCR between the civilian and military dimensions. In the discussion of limitations on dual-use technology, we face the need to find answers to such basic conceptual questions as how to avoid discrimination against countries seeking access to such technologies for the "legitimate needs" of civilian applications; or even in the military sector for strictly defensive as opposed to offensive purposes. Closely related is the question of the meaning of terms such as a "margin of security" to which countries are entitled, especially in the Middle East.

- **The relationship between conventional systems and weapons of mass destruction** - this was yet another issue area of great concern during the conference. It was addressed not only in relation to lethality consequences, as already noted, but also in a discussion of the need for our various arms control regimes to deal in as comprehensive a way as possible with such armaments. States that are already heavily armed conventionally may also acquire weapons of mass destruction, while others may seek WMD as a more affordable alternative to conventional systems, especially in situations, as in the case of Israel or Pakistan, where WMD may be seen as strategic equalizers and as weapons of last resort against numerically superior conventional forces. Without reaching definitive conclusions, we discussed the intriguing question of the future of nuclear weapons, asking whether its present post-Gulf War, post-Cold War position provides an incentive for greater nuclear disarmament by the United States, or whether instead we face the prospect, from the standpoint of regional actors, that we will see an enhanced incentive to confront outside powers such as the United States with regionally based nuclear capabilities, with their political, military, and psychological consequences.

In our discussions it was suggested that the present situation is perhaps best characterized by ambivalence. We have States such as Iraq and North Korea which have attempted to acquire weapons of mass destruction. Other States, such as Brazil, Argentina, and South Africa, have approached and then retreated from the nuclear threshold. Overall, arms acquisition appeared to be a higher priority for many States in the 1980s than in the 1990s, although the conflict map of the world as we move toward the year 2000 gives no clear basis for concluding that there will not once again be an upward trends on a global basis. All kinds of equipment and technologies, including the most up-to-date systems, are available on an unprecedented scale. Furthermore, the controls that we have in place - notably in the NPT, but in other agreements and regimes as well - have not prevented States determined to circumvent them from doing so, as in the case of Iraq, whose program was under tight international control. In the final analysis, we were left with a large number of unanswered, and perhaps unanswerable, questions arising from the very nature of the issues with which we were dealing. Such questions include, but are not confined to, the following:

- If technology is widely available and if all, or nearly all, technologies are dual use, how do we prevent the acquisition of offensive weapons or terrorist weapons, especially where terrorists are not necessarily State actors?
- What are the primary factors driving the transfer of technologies and armaments? Are they primarily economic? Political? Is defence manufacturing being driven primarily by technology? By economic considerations? By politics, or by what combination of these factors?
- In light of our discussions, is a transaction-by-transaction approach to technology transfer and its control ineffective and perhaps counterproductive?
- To what extent should our policies take more fully into account types of government, levels of development, and nature of the national security policy of supplier and recipient States? What do we do about verification and assuring compliance - especially in the NPT and its 1995 review and renewal - and what are the limits of co-operative action?
- What are the implications of noncompliance for the Treaty or regime, and what do we do in the case of noncompliance?

In the final analysis, we are confronted with a phenomenon that is part of a broader framework for nonproliferation and counterproliferation as well as a security environment whose overall structure in the years to come will shape both the problems facing us and the options that will be available in addressing them.

UNIDIR Publications

The publications produced by UNIDIR are intended for publication and wide dissemination through free distribution to diplomatic missions, as well as research institutes, experts, academics and sales through the United Nations Sales Section and other outlets.

Under an arrangement concluded with the Dartmouth Publishing Company (UK), selected UNIDIR *Research Reports* are published by Dartmouth and are distributed through their sales network (books indicated by •; see also at the end of the list *How to Obtain UNIDIR Publications*).

Research Reports / Rapports de recherche

La guerre des satellites: enjeux pour la communauté internationale, par Pierre Lellouche (éd.) (IFRI), 1987, 42p., publication des Nations Unies, numéro de vente: GV.F.87.0.1.

* Also available in English: *Satellite Warfare: A Challenge for the International Community*, by Pierre Lellouche (ed.) (IFRI), 1987, 39p., United Nations publication, Sales No. GV.E.87.0.1.

The International Non-Proliferation Régime 1987, by David A.V. Fischer, 1987, 81p., United Nations publication, Sales No. GV.E.87.0.2.

La question de la vérification dans les négociations sur le désarmement aux Nations Unies, par Ellis Morris, 1987, 230p., publication des Nations Unies, numéro de vente: GV.F.87.0.4.

* Also available in English: *The Verification Issue in United Nations Disarmament Negotiations*, by Ellis Morris, 1987, 230p., United Nations publication, Sales No. GV.E.87.0.4.

Confidence-Building Measures in Africa, by Augustine P. Mahiga and Fidelis Nji, 1987, 16p., United Nations publication, Sales No. GV.E.87.0.5.

Disarmament: Problems Related to Outer Space, UNIDIR, 1987, 190p., United Nations publication, Sales No. GV.E.87.0.7.

* Existe également en français: *Désarmement: problèmes relatifs à l'espace extra-atmosphérique*, UNIDIR, 1987, 200p., publication des Nations Unies, numéro de vente: GV.F.87.0.7.

· *Interrelationship of Bilateral and Multilateral Disarmament Negotiations / Les relations entre les négociations bilatérales et multilatérales sur le désarmement*, Proceedings of the Baku Conference, 2-4 June 1987 / Actes de la Conférence de Bakou, 2-4 juin 1987, 1988, 258p., United Nations publication, Sales No. GV.E/F.88.0.1, publication des Nations Unies, numéro de vente: GV.E/F.88.0.1.

Disarmament Research: Agenda for the 1990's / La recherche sur le désarmement: programme pour les années 90, Proceedings of the Sochi Conference, 22-24 March 1988 / Actes de la Conférence de Sotchi, 22-24 mars 1988, Geneva, 1988, 165p., United Nations publication, Sales No. GV.E./F.88.0.3, publication des Nations Unies: GV.E./F.88.0.3.

Conventional Disarmament in Europe, by André Brie (IIB), Andrzej Karkoszka (PISM), Manfred Müller (IIB), Helga Schirmeister (IIB), 1988, 66p., United Nations publication, Sales No. GV.E.88.0.6.

* Existe également en français: *Le désarmement classique en Europe*, par André Brie (IIB), Andrzej Karkoszka (PISM), Manfred Müller (IIB), Helga Schirmeister (IIB), 1989, 90p., publication des Nations Unies, numéro de vente: GV.E.89.0.6.

• *Arms Transfers and Dependence*, by Christian Catrina, 1988, 409p., published for UNIDIR by Taylor & Francis (New York, London).

Les forces classiques en Europe et la maîtrise des armements, par Pierre Lellouche et Jérôme Paolini (éd.) (IFRI), 1989, 88p., publication des Nations Unies, numéro de vente: GV.F.89.0.6.

* Also available in English: *Conventional Forces and Arms Limitation in Europe*, by Pierre Lellouche and Jérôme Paolini (eds) (IFRI), 1989, 88p., United Nations publication: GV.E.89.0.6.

• *National Security Concepts of States: New Zealand*, by Kennedy Graham, 1989, 180p., published for UNIDIR by Taylor & Francis (New York, London).

• *Problems and Perspectives of Conventional Disarmament in Europe*, Proceedings of the Geneva Conference 23-25 January 1989, 1989, 140p., published for UNIDIR by Taylor & Francis (New York, London).

* Existe également en français: *Désarmement classique en Europe: problèmes et perspectives*, 1990, 226p., publié pour l'UNIDIR par Masson (Paris).

The Projected Chemical Weapons Convention: A Guide to the Negotiations in the Conference on Disarmament, by Thomas Bernauer, 1990, 328p., United Nations publication, Sales No. GV.E.90.0.3.

Verification: The Soviet Stance, its Past, Present and Future, by Mikhail Kokeev and Andrei Androsov, 1990, 131p., United Nations publication, Sales No. GV.E.90.0.6.

* Existe également en français: *Vérification: la position soviétique - Passé, présent et avenir*, 1990, 145p., publication des Nations Unies, numéro de vente: GV.F.90.0.6.

UNIDIR Repertory of Disarmament Research: 1990, by Chantal de Jonge Oudraat and Péricles Gasparini Alves (eds), 1990, 402p., United Nations publication, Sales No. GV.E.90.0.10.
• *Nonoffensive Defense: A Global Perspective*, 1990, 194p., published for UNIDIR by Taylor & Francis (New York, London).
Aerial Reconnaissance for Verification of Arms Limitation Agreements - An Introduction, by Allan V. Banner, Keith W. Hall and Andrew J. Young, D.C.L., 1990, 166p., United Nations publication, Sales No. GV.E.90.0.11.
Africa, Disarmament and Security / Afrique, désarmement et sécurité, Proceedings of the Conference of African Research Institutes, 24-25 March 1990 / Actes de la Conférence des Instituts de recherche africains, 24-25 mars 1990, United Nations publication, Sales No. GV.E/F.91.0.1, publication des Nations Unies, numéro de vente: GV.E/F.91.0.1.
• *Peaceful and Non-Peaceful Uses of Space: Problems of Definition for the Prevention of an Arms Race*, by Bhupendra Jasani (ed.), 1991, 179p., published for UNIDIR by Taylor & Francis (New York, London).
In Pursuit of a Nuclear Test Ban Treaty: A Guide to the Debate in the Conference on Disarmament, by Thomas Schmalberger, 1991, 132p., United Nations publication, Sales No. GV.E.91.0.4.
Confidence-Building Measures and International Security: The Political and Military Aspect - A Soviet Approach, by Igor Scherbak, 1991, 179p., United Nations publication, Sales No. GV.E.91.0.7.
• *Verification of Current Disarmament and Arms Limitation Agreements: Ways, Means and Practices*, by Serge Sur (ed.), 1991, 396p., published for UNIDIR by Dartmouth (Aldershot).
* Existe également en français: *La vérification des accords sur le désarmement et la limitation des armements: moyens, méthodes et pratiques*, 1991, 406p., publication des Nations Unies, numéro de vente: GV.F.91.0.9.
The United Nations, Disarmament and Security: Evolution and Prospects, by Jayantha Dhanapala (ed.), 1991, 156p., United Nations publication, Sales No. GV.E.91.0.13.
• *Disarmament Agreements and Negotiations: The Economic Dimension*, by Serge Sur (ed.), 1991, 228p., published for UNIDIR by Dartmouth (Aldershot).
* Existe également en français: *Dimensions économiques des négociations et accords sur le désarmement*, par Serge Sur (éd.), 1991, 211p., publication des Nations Unies, numéro de vente: GV.F.91.0.18.
Prevention of an Arms Race in Outer Space: A Guide to the Discussions in the Conference on Disarmament, by Péricles Gasparini Alves, 1991, 221p., United Nations publication, Sales No. GV.E.91.0.17.

Nuclear Issues on the Agenda of the Conference on Disarmament, by Thomas Bernauer, 1991, 108p., United Nations publication, Sales No. GV.E.91.0.16.

• *Economic Adjustment after the Cold War: Strategies for Conversion*, by Michael Renner, 1991, 262p., published for UNIDIR by Dartmouth (Aldershot).

Verification of Disarmament or Limitation of Armaments: Instruments, Negotiations, Proposals, by Serge Sur (ed.), 1992, 267p., United Nations publication, Sales No. GV.E.92.0.10.

* Existe également en français: *Vérification du désarmement ou de la limitation des armements: instruments, négociations, propositions*, par Serge Sur (éd.), 1994, 246p., publication des Nations Unies, numéro de vente: GV.F.92.0.10.

National Security Concepts of States: Argentina, by Julio C. Carasales, 1992, 131p., United Nations publication, Sales No. GV.E.92.0.9.

* Existe également en français: *Conceptions et politiques de la République argentine en matière de sécurité*, par Julio C. Carasales, 1992, 136p., publication des Nations Unies, numéro de vente: GV.F.92.0.9.

National Security Concepts of States: Sri Lanka, by Vernon L. B. Mendis, 1992, 205p., United Nations publication, Sales No. GV.E.92.0.12.

• *Military Industrialization and Economic Development. Theory and Historical Case Studies*, by Raimo Väyrynen, 1992, 121p., published for UNIDIR by Dartmouth (Aldershot).

European Security in the 1990s: Problems of South-East Europe, Proceedings of the Rhodes (Greece) Conference, 6-7 September 1991, by Chantal de Jonge Oudraat (ed.) / *La sécurité européenne dans les années 90: Problèmes de l'Europe du Sud-Est*, Actes de la Conférence de Rhodes (Grèce), 6-7 septembre 1991, sous la direction de Chantal de Jonge Oudraat, 1992, 219p., United Nations publication, Sales No. GV.E/F.92.0.14, publication des Nations Unies, numéro de vente: GV.E/F.92.0.14.

Disarmament and Limitation of Armaments: Unilateral Measures and Policies, Proceedings of the Paris Conference, 24 January 1992, by Serge Sur (ed.), 1992, 94p., United Nations publication, Sales No. GV.E.92.0.23

* Existe également en français: *Désarmement et limitation des armements: mesures et attitudes unilatérales*, Actes de la Conférence de Paris, 24 janvier 1992, sous la direction de Serge Sur, 1992, 103p., publication des Nations Unies, numéro de vente: GV.F.92.0.23.

Conference of Research Institutes in Asia and the Pacific, Proceedings of the Beijing (China) Conference, 23-25 March 1992, 1992, United Nations publication, Sales No. GV.E.92.0.29.

Maritime Security: The Building of Confidence, by Jozef Goldblat (ed.), 1992, 163p., United Nations publication, Sales No. GV.E.92.0.31.

- *Towards 1995: The Prospects for Ending the Proliferation of Nuclear Weapons*, by David Fischer, 1992, 292p., published for UNIDIR by Dartmouth (Aldershot).

From Versailles to Baghdad: Post-War Armament Control of Defeated States, by Fred Tanner (ed.), 1992, 264p., United Nations publication, Sales No. GV.E.92.0.26.

- *Security of Third World Countries*, by Jasjit Singh and Thomas Bernauer (eds), 1993, 168p., published for UNIDIR by Dartmouth (Aldershot).
- *Regional Approaches to Disarmament, Security and Stability*, by Jayantha Dhanapala (ed.), 1993, 282p., published for UNIDIR by Dartmouth (Aldershot).

Economic Aspects of Disarmament: Disarmament as an Investment Process, by Keith Hartley, 1993, 91p., United Nations publication, Sales No. GV.E.93.0.3.

* Existe également en français: *Aspects économiques du désarmement: le désarmement en tant qu'investissement*, par Keith Hartley, 1993, 104p., publication des Nations Unies, numéro de vente: GV.F.93.0.3.

- *Nonmilitary Aspects of Security - A Systems Approach*, by Dietrich Fischer, 1993, 222p., published for UNIDIR by Dartmouth (Aldershot).

Conference of Latin American and Caribbean Research Institutes, Proceedings of the São Paulo Conference, 2-3 December 1991, by Péricles Gasparini Alves (ed.), 1993, 202p., United Nations publication, Sales No. GV.E.93.0.8.

- *The Chemistry of Regime Formation: Explaining International Cooperation for a Comprehensive Ban on Chemical Weapons*, by Thomas Bernauer, 1993, 480p., published for UNIDIR by Dartmouth (Aldershot).
- *Civil Space Systems: Implications for International Security*, by Stephen Doyle, 1994, 271p., published for UNIDIR by Dartmouth (Aldershot).

Nuclear Deterrence: Problems and Perspectives in the 1990's, by Serge Sur (ed.), 1993, 173p., United Nations publication, Sales No. GV.E.93.0.16.

Conference of Research Institutes in the Middle East, Proceedings of the Cairo Conference, 18-19 April 1993, by Chantal de Jonge Oudraat (ed.), 1994, 132p., United Nations publication, Sales No. GV.E.94.0.13.

- *Disarmament and Arms Limitation Obligations: Problems of Compliance and Enforcement*, by Serge Sur (ed.), 1994, 296p., published for UNIDIR by Dartmouth (Aldershot)

* Existe également en français: *Obligations en matière de désarmement: problèmes de respect et mesures d'imposition*, sous la direction de Serge Sur, 1994, publication des Nations Unies (à paraître)

European Security in the 1990s: Challenges and Perspectives, by Victor-Yves Ghebali and Brigitte Sauerwein, Avant Propos by Serge Sur, 1995, 230p., United Nations publication, Sales No. GV.E.94.0.28.

Arms and Technology Transfers: Security and Economic Considerations Among Importing and Exporting States, Proceedings of the Geneva (Switzerland) Conference, 14-15 February 1994, by Sverre Lodgaard and Robert L. Pfaltzgraff (eds), 1995, 287p., United Nations publication, Sales No. GV.E.95.0.10.

Nuclear Policies in Northeast Asia, Proceedings of the Seoul (South Korea) Conference, 25-27 May 1994, by Andrew Mack (ed.), 1995, 263p., United Nations publication, Sales No. GV.E.95.0.8.

• ***Building·Confidence in Outer Space Activities: CSBMs and Earth-to-Space Monitoring***, by Péricles Gasparini Alves (ed.), 1995, 357p., published for UNIDIR by Dartmouth (Aldershot) **(forthcoming)**

Research Papers / Travaux de recherche

No. 1 - *Une approche juridique de la vérification en matière de désarmement ou de limitation des armements*, par Serge Sur, septembre 1988, 70p., publication des Nations Unies, numéro de vente: GV.F.88.0.5.
* Also available in English: *A Legal Approach to Verification in Disarmament or Arms Limitation*, 1988, 72p., United Nations publication, Sales No. GV.E.88.0.5.

No. 2 - *Problèmes de vérification du Traité de Washington du 8 décembre 1987 sur l'élimination des missiles à portée intermédiaire*, par Serge Sur, octobre 1988, 64p., publication des Nations Unies, numéro de vente: GV.F.88.0.7.
* Also available in English: *Verification Problems of the Washington Treaty on the Elimination of Intermediate-Range Missiles*, by Serge Sur, October 1988, 62p., United Nations publication, Sales No. GV.E.88.0.7.

No. 3 - *Mesures de confiance de la CSCE: documents et commentaires*, par Victor-Yves Ghebali, mars 1989, 112p., publication des Nations Unies, numéro de vente: GV.F.89.0.5.
* Also available in English: *Confidence-Building Measures within the CSCE Process: Paragraph-by-Paragraph Analysis of the Helsinki and Stockholm Régimes*, by Victor-Yves Ghebali, March 1989, 110p., United Nations publication, Sales No. GV.E.89.0.5.

No. 4 - *The Prevention of the Geographical Proliferation of Nuclear Weapons: Nuclear-Free Zones and Zones of Peace in the Southern Hemisphere*, by Edmundo Fujita, April 1989, 52p., United Nations publication, Sales No. GV.E. 89.0.8.

* Existe également en français: *La prévention de la prolifération géographique des armes nucléaires: zones exemptes d'armes nucléaires et zones de paix dans l'hémisphère Sud*, par Edmundo Fujita, avril 1989, 61p., publication des Nations Unies, numéro de vente: GV.F.89.0.8.

No. 5 - *The Future Chemical Weapons Convention and its Organization: The Executive Council*, by Thomas Bernauer, May 1989, 34p., United Nations publication, Sales No. GV.E.89.0.7.

* Existe également en français: *La future convention sur les armes chimiques et son organisation: le Conseil exécutif*, par Thomas Bernauer, mai 1989, 42p., publication des Nations Unies, numéro de vente: GV.F.89.0.7.

No. 6 - *Bibliographical Survey of Secondary Literature on Military Expenditures*, November 1989, 39p. United Nations publication, Sales No. GV.E.89.0.14.

No. 7 - *Science and Technology: Between Civilian and Military Research and Development - Armaments and development at variance*, by Marek Thee, November 1990, 23p., United Nations publication, Sales No. GV.E.90.0.14.

No. 8 - *Esquisse pour un nouveau paysage européen*, par Eric Remacle, octobre 1990, 178p., publication des Nations Unies, numéro de vente: GV.F.91.0.2.

No. 9 - *The Third Review of the Biological Weapons Convention: Issues and Proposals*, by Jozef Goldblat and Thomas Bernauer, April 1991, 78p., United Nations publication, Sales No. GV.E.91.0.5.

No. 10 - *Disarmament, Environment, and Development and their Relevance to the Least Developed Countries*, by Arthur H. Westing, October 1991, 108p., United Nations publication, Sales No. GV.E.91.0.19.

No. 11 - *The Implications of IAEA Inspections under Security Council Resolution 687*, by Eric Chauvistré, February 1992, 72p., United Nations publication, Sales No. GV.E.92.0.6.

No. 12 - *La Résolution 687 (3 avril 1991) du Conseil de sécurité dans l'affaire du Golfe: problèmes de rétablissement et de garantie de la paix*, par Serge Sur, 1992, 65p., publication des Nations Unies, numéro de vente: GV.F.92.0.8.

* Also available in English: *Security Council Resolution 687 of 3 April 1991 in the Gulf Affair: Problems of Restoring and Safeguarding Peace*, by Serge Sur, 1992, 65p., United Nations publication, Sales No. GV.E.92.0.8.

No. 13 - *The Non-Proliferation Treaty: How to Remove the Residual Threats*, by Jozef Goldblat, 1992, 36p., United Nations publication, Sales No. GV.E.92.0.25.

* Existe également en français: *Le Traité sur la non-prolifération: comment parer les menaces*, par Jozef Goldblat, 1993, 40p., publication des Nations Unies, numéro de vente: GV.F.92.0.25.

No. 14 - *Ukraine's Non-Nuclear Option*, by Victor Batiouk, 1992, 34p., United Nations publication, Sales No. GV.E.92.0.28.

No. 15 - *Access to Outer Space Technologies: Implications for International Security*, by Péricles Gasparini Alves, 1992, 160p., United Nations publication, Sales No. GV.E.92.0.30.

No. 16 - *Regional Security and Confidence-Building Processes: The Case of Southern Africa in the 1990s*, by Solomon M. Nkiwane, 1993, United Nations publication, Sales No. GV.E.93.0.6.

No. 17 - *Technical Problems in the Verification of a Ban on Space Weapons*, by Stanislav Rodionov, 1993, 104p., United Nations publication, Sales No. GV.E.93.0.12.

No. 18 - *Index to the Chemical Weapons Convention*, by A. Walter Dorn, 1993, 59p., United Nations publication, Sales No. GV.E.93.0.13.

No. 19 - *Migration and Population Change in Europe*, by John Salt, 1993, 86p., United Nations publication, Sales No. GV.E.93.0.14.

No. 20 - *La sécurité européenne dans les années 90, défis et perspectives. La dimension écologique*, par Jean-Daniel Clavel, 1993, 40p., publication des Nations Unies, numéro de vente: GV.F.93.0.15.

No. 21 - *Les minorités nationales et le défi de la sécurité en Europe*, par Dominique Rosenberg, 1993, 45p., publication des Nations Unies, numéro de vente: GV.F.93.0.21.

No. 22 - *Crisis in the Balkans*, by Ali L. Karaosmanoglu, 1993, 22p., United Nations publication, Sales No. GV.E.93.0.22.

No. 23 - *La transition vers l'économie de marché des pays "ex de l'Est"*, par Louis Pilandon, 1994, 90p., publication des Nations Unies, numéro de vente: GV.F.94.0.3.

No. 24 - *Le désarmement et la conversion de l'industrie militaire en Russie*, par Sonia Ben Ouagrham, 1993, 110p., publication des Nations Unies, numéro de vente: GV.F.94.0.4.

No. 25 - *Development of Russian National Security Policies: Military Reform*, by Andrei Raevsky, 1994, 48p., United Nations publication, Sales No. GV.E.94.0.5.

No. 26 - *National Security and Defence Policy of the Lithuanian State*, by Gintaras Tamulaitis, 1994, 66p., United Nations publication, Sales No. GV.E.94.0.11.

No. 27 - *Le défi de la sécurité régionale en Afrique après la guerre froide: vers la diplomatie préventive et la sécurité collective*, par Anatole N. Ayissi, 1994, 138p., publication des Nations Unies, numéro de vente: GV.F.94.0.17.

No. 28 - *Russian Approaches to Peacekeeping Operations*, by A. Raevsky and I.N. Vorob'ev, 1994, 182p., United Nations publication, Sales No. GV.E.94.0.18.

No. 29 - *Une approche coopérative de la non-prolifération nucléaire: l'exemple de l'Argentine et du Brésil*, par Thierry Riga, 1994, 100p., publication des Nations Unies, numéro de vente: GV.F.94.0.22.

No. 30 - *The CTBT and Beyond*, by Herbert F. York, 1994, 21p., United Nations publication, Sales No. GV.E.94.0.27.

No. 31 - *Halting the Production of Fissile Material for Nuclear Weapons*, by Thérèse Delpech, Lewis A. Dunn, David Fischer and Rakesh Sood, 1994, 70p., United Nations publication, Sales No. GV.E.94.0.29.

No. 32 - *Verification of a Comprehensive Test Ban Treaty from Space - A Preliminary Study*, by Bhupendra Jasani, 1994, 58p., United Nations publication, Sales No. GV.E.94.0.30.

No. 33 - *Nuclear Disarmament and Non-Proliferation in Northeast Asia*, by Yong-Sup Han, 1995, 83p., United Nations publication, Sales No. GV.E.95.0.3.

No. 34 - *Small Arms and Intra-State Conflicts*, by Swadesh Rana, 1995, 52p., United Nations publication, Sales No. GV.E.95.0.7.

No. 35 - *The Missing Link? Nuclear Proliferation and the International Mobility of Russian Nuclear Experts*, by Dorothy S. Zinberg, 1995, United Nations publication (**forthcoming**)

No. 36 - *Guardian Soldier: On the Future Role and Use of Armed Forces*, by Gustav Däniker, 1995, United Nations publication (**forthcoming**)

No. 37 - *National Threat Perceptions in the Middle East*, 1995, United Nations publication (**forthcoming**)

UNIDIR Newsletter / Lettre de l'UNIDIR
(quarterly / trimestrielle)

Vol. 1, No. 1, March/Mars 1988, *Disarmament-Development/Désarmement-Développement*, 16p.

No. 2, June/Juin 1988, *Research in Africa/La recherche en Afrique*, 28p.

No. 3, September/Septembre 1988, *Conventional Armaments Limitation and CBMs in Europe/Limitation des armements classiques et mesures de confiance en Europe*, 32p.

No. 4, December/Décembre 1988, *Research in Asia and the Pacific/La recherche en Asie et dans le Pacifique*, 40p.

Vol. 2, No. 1, March/Mars 1989, *Chemical Weapons: Research Projects and Publications/Armes chimiques: projets de recherche et publications*, 24p.

No. 2, June/Juin 1989, *Research in Latin America and the Caribbean/La recherche en Amérique latine et dans les Caraïbes*, 32p.

No. 3, September/Septembre 1989, *Outer Space/L'espace extra-atmosphérique*, 32p.

No. 4, December/Décembre 1989, *Research in Eastern Europe/La recherche en Europe de l'Est*, 48p.

Vol. 3, No. 1, March/Mars 1990, *Verification of Disarmament Agreements/La vérification des accords sur le désarmement*, 48p.

No. 2, June/Juin 1990, *Research in North America/La recherche en Amérique du Nord*, 72p.

No. 3, September/Septembre 1990, *Nuclear Non-Proliferation/La non-prolifération nucléaire*, 43p.

No. 4, December/Décembre 1990, *Research in Western and Northern Europe (I)/ La recherche en Europe de l'Ouest et en Europe du Nord (I)*, 72p.

Vol. 4, No. 1, March/Mars 1991, *Research in Western and Northern Europe (II)/La recherche en Europe de l'Ouest et en Europe du Nord (II)*, 72p.

No. 2, June/Juin 1991, *Biological Weapons/Armes biologiques*, 40p.

No. 3, September/Septembre 1991, *Naval and Maritime Issues/Questions navales et maritimes*, 54p.

No. 4, December/Décembre 1991, *Bilateral (US-USSR) Agreements and Negotiations/Accords et négociations bilatéraux (EU-URSS)*, 52p.

Vol. 5, No. 1, April/Avril 1992, *Conference on Disarmament/La Conférence du désarmement*, 63p.

No. 18, June/Juin 1992, *Disarmament - Environment - Security/Désarmement - Environnement - Sécurité*, 52p.

No. 19, September/Septembre 1992, *Economic Aspects of Disarmament/Aspects économiques du désarmement*, 66p.

No. 20, December/Décembre 1992, *The Chemical Weapons Convention/La Convention sur les armes chimiques*, 100p.

Vol. 6, No. 21, March/Mars 1993, *Research in the Middle East/La recherche au Moyen et Proche Orient*, 70p.

No. 22-23, June-September/Juin-septembre 1993, *START and Nuclear Disarmament: Problems of Implementation/START et le désarmement nucléaire: problèmes d'exécution*, 101p.

No. 24, December/Décembre 1993, *Peace-Keeping, Peace-Making and Peace Enforcement/Maintien, construction et imposition de la paix*, 88p.

Vol. 7, No. 25, March-April/Mars-avril 1994, *Research in Eastern Europe and in the Newly Independent States/Recherche en Europe de l'Est et dans les nouveaux Etats indépendants*, 70p.

No. 26/27, June-September/Juin-septembre 1994, *Non-Proliferation/Non-prolifération*, 91p.

Vol. 8, No. 28/29, December 1994-May 1995/Décembre 1994-mai 1995, *Land Mines and the CCW Review Conference/Les mines terrestres et la Conférence d'examen de la Convention sur certaines armes classiques*

How to Obtain UNIDIR Publications

1. *UNIDIR publications followed by a United Nations Sales Number (GV.E... or GV.F...) can be obtained from UNIDIR or from bookstores and distributors throughout the world. Consult your bookstore or write to United Nations, Sales Section, Palais des Nations, CH-1211 Geneva 10, Switzerland, Phone (41.22) 917.26.12, Fax (41.22) 740.09.31, or United Nations, Sales Section, UN Headquarters, New York, New York 10017, USA. The UNIDIR Newsletter is available at a voluntary subscription price of US $ 25 a year.*
2. *UNIDIR publications published by Dartmouth can be obtained through Dartmouth Publishing Company Limited, Gower House, Croft Road, Aldershot, Hampshire, GU11 3HR, England, Phone (0252) 33.15.51, Fax (0252) 34.44.05.*
3. *UNIDIR publications published by Taylor and Francis can be obtained through Taylor and Francis Ltd, Rankine Road, Basingstoke, Hants RG24 8PR, England, Phone (0256) 84.03.66, Fax (0256) 47.94.38.*